Familiar Faces

Familiar Faces

Photography, Memory and Argentina's Disappeared

Edited by
Piotr Cieplak

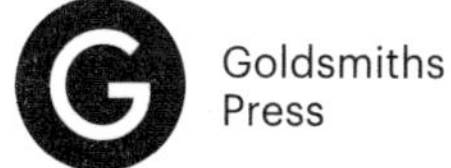

Goldsmiths
Press

Copyright © 2024 Goldsmiths Press
First published in 2024 by Goldsmiths Press
Goldsmiths, University of London, New Cross
London SE14 6NW

Printed and bound by Short Run Press Limited, UK
Distribution by the MIT Press
Cambridge, Massachusetts, USA and London, England

A CIP record for this book is available from the British Library

ISBN 978-1-913380-76-2 (pbk)
ISBN 978-1-913380-75-5 (ebk)

www.gold.ac.uk/goldsmiths-press

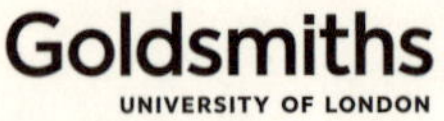

Contents

Acknowledgements

A lot of the research and writing for this book took place during lockdowns caused by the Covid19 pandemic. I would like to thank the contributors for their brilliant work under such challenging and uncertain circumstances. This gratitude extends not only to completing the chapters for this collection but also to a decade of nourishing conversations about photography, memory and politics in Argentina, and the seemingly boundless generosity during my research fieldtrips. Many thanks also to Jorge Salvetti for his meticulous translation and attention to detail.

I would like to thank the following photographers and artists for allowing us to reproduce their work in *Familiar Faces*: Hugo Aveta, Eduardo Di Baia, Daniel García, Eduardo Gil, Pablo Lasansky, Adriana Lestido, Eduardo Longoni, Mario Manusia, Lucila Quieto, Inés Ulanovsky, Dani Yako, Helen Zout and Silvio Zuccheri. Special thanks to Gabriel Orge for the wonderful cover image and to Ana Iliovich for allowing the use of her family photographs. I would like to express my gratitude to the Memoria Abierta Archive and the National Memory Archive in Buenos Aires, and the Provincial Memory Archive in Córdoba (especially María Eleonora Cristina and Pablo Becerra) for providing images from their unique collections. Thanks to Los Ríos Editorial for permitting the reproduction of the cover of *El Silencio: Postales de la Perla*.

I am very grateful to the British Academy for its continuous support of my work. This book is an output of the "Intimate moments, public acts: photographs of the disappeared and memory politics in Argentina" project (SRG20\200164). I would also like to thank the research team in the School of Media, Arts and Humanities at the University of Sussex, and especially Sarah Maltby and Ben Highmore for their help with the funding application. Special thanks also to Jordana Blejmar, Chris Brown, Ben Burbridge, Elizabeth Edwards, Zoe Norridge and Emma Wilson for their intellectual guidance.

I am thankful to Susan Kelly, Sarah Kember, Ellen Parnavelas and Angela Thompson at Goldsmiths Press for taking on the book and for their excellent work on it.

Matthew Flacks and Chris Brown have provided unwavering support during the writing and editing of *Familiar Faces*, like they do with all my projects. I am so grateful for that. Thanks also to Beata Cieplak for providing the peace, quiet and beautiful surroundings that made the editing and writing so much more pleasurable.

Lastly, my sincere thanks to Rodrigo, Martín, Nat, Cora and Ana for making Buenos Aires feel like home, and to Mariana, María, Ludmila, Carlos, Seba, Ana and Gabriel for doing the same in Córdoba.

Glossary[1]

CoNaDeP (Comisión Nacional sobre la Desaparición de Personas) [National Commission on the Disappearance of Persons]: a commission established in 1983 by the democratically elected president Raúl Alfonsín to investigate the disappearances and murders carried out under the dictatorship. CoNaDeP delivered its report *Nunca Más* [*Never Again*] in 1984.

Death Flights: a form of extrajudicial killing employed by the most recent Argentine dictatorship. Following a period of torture and imprisonment, prisoners (often drugged) were put on planes or helicopters and thrown into the Atlantic Ocean or La Plata River. Most of the bodies were never recovered.

ERP (Ejército Revolucionario del Pueblo) [The People's Revolutionary Army]: a militant guerrilla organisation active in Argentina in the 1970s and the armed wing of The Workers' Revolutionary Party [Partido Revolucionario de los Trabajadores]. ERP was perceived as the enemy by successive governments and subject to repression since the beginning of the 1970s, which reached its peak during the dictatorship.

Escrache: a form of direct action adopted by the members of H.I.J.O.S. in Argentina (see **H.I.J.O.S.**). The practice, which emerged in the mid-1990s, involves gathering around the homes of known repressors, torturers and agents of the dictatorship and publicly exposing their deeds to their neighbours and communities. The early escraches were a response to the controversial pardon laws introduced by president Carlos Menem.

ESMA (La Escuela Superior de Mecánica de la Armada) [The Higher School of Mechanics of the Navy]: the site of one of Argentina's best-known, emblematic and most notorious clandestine detention, torture and extermination centres. It is estimated that around 5,000 people were held in ESMA during the dictatorship and only 150 survived. Situated in

---

[1] The terms and acronyms in this glossary are not an exhaustive index of the terminology associated with the most recent Argentine dictatorship and its enduring legacies. Rather, these are the terms and acronyms repeatedly referred to by the authors in this collection and are provided here for ease of reference and avoidance of repetition. Other, specific, terms appear as footnotes in individual chapters.

Buenos Aires, on seventeen hectares of land, the former ESMA, or ex-ESMA as it is commonly referred to, is a vast complex of streets and buildings. In 2004, the site was designated as a Space for Memory and Human Rights ex-ESMA [Espacio Memoria y Derechos Humanos ex-ESMA] and is now home to a memorial museum, as well as the headquarters of national institutions – e.g. the National Memory Archive, the Secretariat for Human Rights and the Argentine Forensic Anthropology Team – and non-governmental human rights organisations – e.g. the Grandmothers of Plaza de Mayo.[2]

Ford Falcon: a car model manufactured in Argentina between 1962 and 1991. Symbolically, the car – especially the green Ford Falcon – is associated with the repressive activities of the dictatorship. The model was often used by paramilitary groups, including the notorious Argentine Anti-Communist Alliance, known as the Triple A or AAA, to conduct armed raids, kidnappings and murders.

H.I.J.O.S. (Hijos por la Identidad y la Justicia Contra el Olvido y el Silencio) [Sons and Daughters for Identity and Justice Against Forgetting and Silence]: established in 1995, H.I.J.O.S. is an association representing the offspring of the disappeared, with many local chapters across the country.

Montoneros: a left-wing Peronist organisation in Argentina, targeted by the civic-military dictatorship in the 1970s and 1980s.

Never Again [*Nunca Más*]: a report compiled and published by CoNaDeP in 1984. As well as containing the depositions of the survivors of detention, disappearance and other forms of dictatorial violence, the report documented 8,961 individual deaths and disappearances. It also identified numerous clandestine detention, torture and extermination centres and some mass graves with the remains of the disappeared. *Never Again* shed light on the mechanics and extent of the dictatorship's crimes. It became a bestseller in Argentina and has been in print since its original publication.

The "Round" of the Mothers of Plaza de Mayo: a weekly march/protest of the Mothers around the May Pyramid on Plaza de Mayo in Buenos Aires.

[2]More information about the Space for Memory and Human Rights ex-ESMA is available at www.espaciomemoria.ar.

The "Round" has been taking place since 1977 on Thursday afternoons. The ritual has been replicated in other Argentine cities.

Whitewashing (from the Spanish blanquear): in the dictatorial jargon, the act of moving an illegally detained prisoner into the official system, usually by transferring them from a clandestine detention centre to a regular jail. This often implied better chances of survival, since not only was it possible for others to know that the prisoner was still alive, but also where he or she was being kept.

1

Intimate Moments, Public Acts: Argentina's Long Relationship with the Photographs of the Disappeared

Piotr Cieplak

Encounter 1: April 2022[1]

On a bracing Thursday morning, the employees of the Provincial Memory Archive [El Archivo Provincial de la Memoria] (APM) in Córdoba, Argentina's second-largest city, leave their desks and come out into Pasaje Santa Catalina, the pedestrianised street that separates the APM from the city's grand 16th century cathedral. One by one, bundles of folded vinyl squares attached to pieces of sturdy twine are placed in neat piles every ten or so meters along the narrow, cobbled lane. Life continues around – and is seemingly oblivious to – this activity. People rush to work. A school trip is getting ready to tour the inside of the cathedral, the stern instructions of the guide about the etiquette of the visit not quite able to capture the full attention of the teenagers. Soon, the operation gathers steam. Ladders are brought out and the lifeless bundles unravelled, lifted, stretched along the width of the Pasaje and attached to hooks drilled into the walls on both sides (with enough give to sag slightly, garland-like, in the middle). There is a sense of routine to the ritual. Whatever the APM's employees are doing, they've done it before. They check that the numbers that label each pile of vinyl squares correspond with the numbers written next to the hooks affixed to the walls. It matters which one goes where. The whole thing takes half an hour, maybe forty minutes.

And the result? A conspicuous presence. The photos of the faces of Córdoba's disappeared during Argentina's most recent dictatorship, at once hardy and vulnerable, flap in the autumnal wind, in the middle of the city, each accompanied by a name and the date of the kidnapping and subsequent disappearance.[2] They hang two or three feet above the heads of the passers-by. On the whole, they keep themselves to themselves. Many people don't pay much attention; they walk by as they normally would. But some pause, look at the faces, read the captions. Even some of the teenagers, about to enter the cathedral, point to individual faces and offer a comment. All without reverence, done matter-of-factly. There is no particular veneration here, no pathos.

And yet, there is a sense of an interaction, a two-way dynamic. A sense of the past and the present not so much in conversation with each other but rather greeting each other with a subtle nod, the non-committal yet habitual gesture of two acquaintances. This reciprocity, this sense of agency in otherwise lifeless photographs of the disappeared in Argentina, has been conceptualised and spoken about over decades. When recalling seeing the images during demonstrations, the photographer Inés Ulanovsky, an interview with whom appears in Chapter 5, notes that she "had the sensation that [the disappeared] weren't dead. That they observed everything from their own photos. That *they* looked at *us*" (Ulanovsky 2006, back cover; emphasis added).

The faces displayed in Pasaje Santa Catalina are familiar to many of Córdoba's inhabitants. They are installed in this space on most Thursdays. Ludmila da Silva Catela, the APM's founding director, states that the ritual "repeats the act of remembering our dead again and again. It's a ritual both of inscription and remembrance" that harks back to the early days of the resistance to the dictatorship by "showing the faces of the disappeared, of identifying them, of situating them once again in the place of humanity" (Cieplak 2020, 11). This action of situating the past in a human present also forms a connecting thread throughout this book. *Familiar Faces* is best understood as a series of encounters with photographs, but also with their diverse political, memorial and affective uses and functions. Through specific case studies, the collection is envisaged as an interdisciplinary exploration of the prominence and role of photography in Argentina, and of its unique malleability when it comes to creating meaning related to the legacy of the dictatorship. At the heart of *Familiar Faces* is an exploration of the tensions that surround photographs – family snaps and ID portraits of the disappeared, but also other images that emerge alongside them,

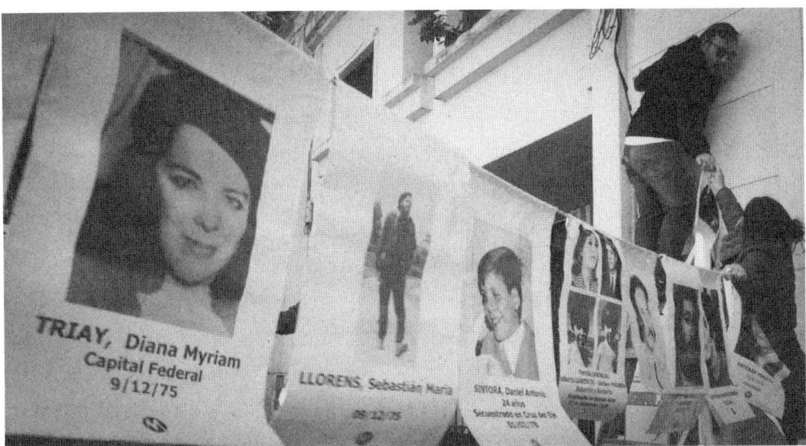

Figure 1.1 Images of the disappeared being prepared for display in Pasaje Santa Catalina, Córdoba.
Source: Piotr Cieplak.

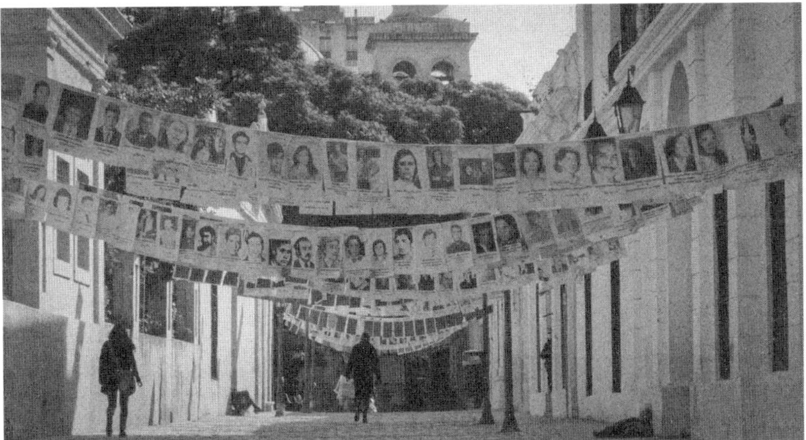

Figure 1.2 Images of the disappeared displayed in Pasaje Santa Catalina, Córdoba.
Source: Piotr Cieplak.

including those produced by the dictatorial state itself. These tensions are between history and memory; the private and the public; the real and the imagined; the personal and the political; index and icon; document and artefact; record and affect.

A Coup like no Other?

Twentieth century Argentina was no stranger to military-led takeovers. The coup d'état of 24 March 1976, which overthrew María Estela Martínez de Perón's troubled but democratically elected government and installed a tripartite military junta in power, followed nine "civilian-backed" military overthrows since 1930 (Feitlowitz 2011, 5).[3] The new regime was not especially enduring – democracy was restored in 1983 – but proved particularly deadly and perverse.[4] Thirty thousand people were disappeared and/or killed by what has become known as seven years of state terrorism.[5] Just like coups, political violence had been present in Argentina before 1976. However, Emilio Crenzel notes that "the systematic practice of forced disappearance" enacted by the dictatorship posed a radical, historical change in the country's political landscape, on at least two counts. Firstly, "the disappearances demonstrated the development of an obvious determination on the part of the state to exterminate its opponents." And, secondly, they "introduced a new characteristic to politically motivated murder – its clandestine practice" (Crenzel 2008, 174–175).[6]

Alongside deregulating the economy, suspending democratic institutions and political parties, limiting civil right and liberties, and seizing control of the press, The National Reorganisation Process [El Proceso de Reorganización Nacional], as the juntas were known, waged war on the perceived enemies of the state. The construction of this enemy initially centred on trade union activists but quickly expanded to other forms of "subversion." Amongst those targeted were the members of the Peronist organisation Montoneros and the Workers' Revolutionary Party – The People's Revolutionary Army [Partido Revolucionario de los Trabajadores – Ejército Revolucionario del Pueblo] (ERP).[7] Eventually, however, the terror and persecution spread to the wider population and organisational belonging gave way to much more arbitrary criteria for being subject to state terrorism.

The tactics employed in the "war against subversion" – in the alleged defence of "Christian and family values" – were brutal. Kidnappings in broad daylight. The illegal detention of suspects. Looting and appropriation of property. Systematic torture. Rape and sexual violence. It is estimated that a network of around 500 clandestine detention centres (CDCs) existed in the country. That's where, mostly, people disappeared to. That's where they were tortured and killed.[8] Crenzel notes that the clandestine nature of these places, often housed in sites that were part of the military infrastructure, "promoted the denial of the captives' existence and gave their captors ample freedom to physically eliminate them." He goes on to add that disappearances enabled the regime and its supporters:

to take torture to extreme levels and to carry out the elimination of thousands of secret captives, unhindered by legal or political obstacles. In this way, no traces were left; the bodies of the abducted became invisible to the public, their captivity and murder could be denied and no one was held accountable.

(2008, 175)

The official veil of silence that surrounded the disappearances also extended to the eventual final fate of many of the detainees. Those killed were often buried in anonymous, unmarked graves, further extending their disappearance and the inability of their loved ones to know what happened and, indeed, to mourn. For decades now, the world-famous Argentine Forensic Anthropology Team has been doing painstaking work to identify secret burial sites and, subsequently, the bodies found in them. Another perverse way of disposing of the disappeared involved the so-called Death Flights. Inmates were drugged, barely conscious, loaded onto planes and thrown into the sea or La Plata River.

The majority of the disappeared were young people (da Silva Catela 2001, 152). The impact of the illegal, forced disappearances and extrajudicial killings was, however, multigenerational. It affected not only the existing family members, who, initially, had no idea what happened to their loved ones, but also future generations. Many female detainees who had small children or were pregnant at the time of the kidnapping, or who became pregnant while in captivity, had their offspring taken away from them. The children were then, again unlawfully and with no information provided to their biological families, given up for illegal "adoption" (often to people associated with or favoured by the regime). It is estimated that as many as 500 children were appropriated in this way, with the majority – now in their forties and fifties – still unaware of their true identity.[9]

The defeat in the Falklands/Malvinas, the worsening economic situation in the country and growing international condemnation led the junta to surrender power in 1983, followed by democratic elections.

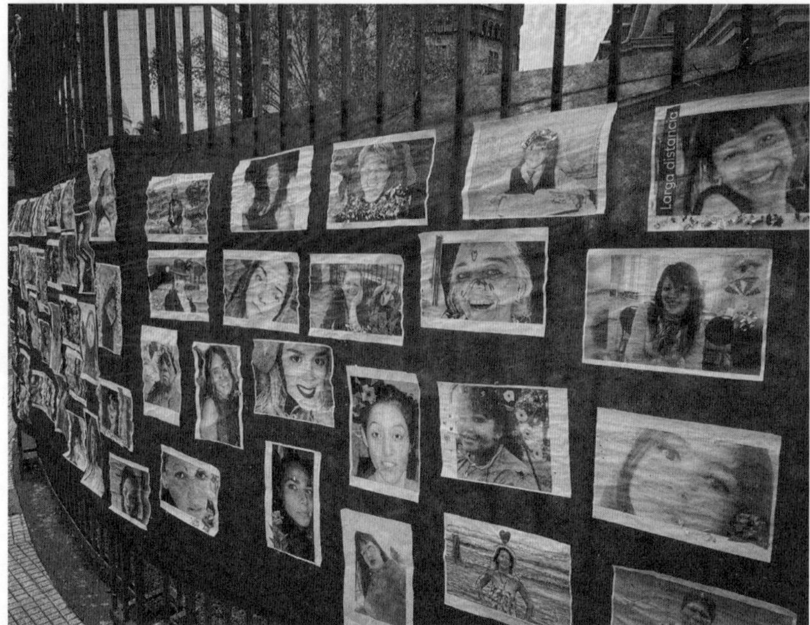

Figure 1.3 Printed photographs of the victims of gender-based violence in Plaza de Mayo, Buenos Aires.
Source: Piotr Cieplak.

The relatively long run-up to the transition allowed the regime to destroy many of its records in an attempt to eliminate the traces of its criminal activity. Then, the fraught justice-seeking process began. Some of its key moments have been dramatised on film, further building collective memory, such as the Trial of the Juntas in 1985, recently portrayed in an Oscar-nominated film *Argentina 1985* (Mitre 2022). But there have also been many setbacks in the form of pardons and legislation designed to limit the accountability of the perpetrators.

Encounter 2: June 2022

On a wintry Buenos Aires afternoon, the temporary fence erected around the May Pyramid, the capital's oldest monument, is covered in photos. Some of the faces are accompanied by the names that belong to them. The images appear less permanent, more fleeting than their counterparts in Córdoba's Pasaje Santa Catalina. No sturdy vinyl that can stand up to rain, no reinforced twine that can withstand the persistence of wind. Instead, the photos, all of them of women, have been printed on A4 pieces of paper, in black-and-white. Unlike the images safely stored in the APM and brought outside on most Thursdays, the photos surrounding the May Pyramid seem more open to visible, conspicuous interventions. Many are adorned with pieces of red string, others with ribbons. The women's black-and-white faces often explode with unexpected, Warholian colours – hair painted green or yellow; bright red lips breaking out from the surrounding greyscale. There are other materials present: garlands, splotches of glitter, sunrays drawn in colourful crayon. These, too, are photos of disappeared, and often murdered, Argentines. Not during the dictatorship, but now, recently. They are part of the campaign Not One Woman Less [Ni Una Menos], which tries to address Argentina's catastrophic rates of misogynist, gender-based violence against women.

On the face of it, these images have nothing or little to do with those disappeared during the dictatorship. And yet, when one looks closely, the connections abound. It is in this particular location, in Plaza de Mayo in Buenos Aires, in the capital's heart and right in front of the Pink House, also known as the Government House, that the Mothers of Plaza de Mayo have been doing their weekly, Thursday afternoon round for over forty years, demanding, first, the return of their disappeared children, and, later, justice for and recognition of the crimes committed by the state. Even though the Mothers, many of whom have now died, are not there on this particular June afternoon, their presence is felt. The wide, circular pavement surrounding the May Pyramid, the original round, is adorned with white stencils of handkerchiefs – the Mothers' most recognisable symbol.[10]

Then, there is the formal resonance that comes with the use of photographs – and in particular photographs that focus in such a familiar way and so squarely on the face, on the individual identity of the person depicted. This resonance doesn't reside solely in the photographs but also in what is done *to* them. Ludmila da Silva Catela's (2001) long-term ethnographic work on the uses of family photos has shown that interventions such as adorning images with paper flowers are a common practice amongst the relatives of the disappeared. In Chapter 4, when analysing the work of the artist Lucila Quieto, Natalia Fortuny writes about the DIY practice of collage and the use of crayon and other materials to disconcert the solidity and "frozenness in time" of the images of the disappeared, especially in artistic endeavours undertaken by their offspring. In Chapter 3, María Eleonora Cristina also speaks of a time when the photographs became subject to "interventions" such as "enlargement, projections, use in collages and audio-visual projects, addition of colour and flowers." She sees it as part of the development of "new languages of remembrance and, to a certain extent, desacralization" (Cristina in this volume, p. 74).

Looking beyond the formal connections and resonances, the presence of these images in this particular, symbolically charged space speaks of a political extension that occurred in Argentina after the dictatorship and which makes it particularly pertinent to analyse the way in which the photos of the disappeared have been and continue to be used. I mean here the adoption by the Mothers, but also their allies and supporters, of other social justice causes (Jelin 2021), including those related to the LGBTQI+ community and the right to legal, safe and free abortion, and, indeed, their pivotal role in the feminist movement in Argentina (Longoni 2020).

Making Things Visible: Against Disappearance

In one way or another, all the contributions to this collection wrestle with the complexity of disappearance: actual, conceptual, ontological, political, affective, photographic. Just as it was at the centre of the dictatorial regime's clandestine policy of extermination, so the erasure it implied was at the heart of the opposition to what was happening in the country, as well as the decades-long Argentine struggle for justice, recognition and memory. It was the disappearances, accompanied by the lack of information about their victims and, often, outright denial of their existence, that precipitated the initial acts of resistance to the junta's actions (Longoni 2010a; Jelin 2021; and Gamarnik in this volume). But from very early on, these acts of resistance had a companion, which continues to be faithfully present to this day: photography.

Cora Gamarnik charts the ways in which the Mothers of Plaza de Mayo, donning white handkerchiefs on their heads and protesting with the photographs of their disappeared children, themselves eventually became the iconic image associated with the dictatorship and its legacy.[11] She writes that "almost from the very beginning of their search, the Mothers and other relatives of the disappeared carried with them the photographs of their children, husbands, grandchildren" (Gamarnik in this volume, p. 44). The practice "inaugurated a prolific genealogy for the public use of photography in the struggle of the human rights movement against the official denial of the killings" (Longoni 2010a, 6). As to the functions of these images, Longoni notes their role in reaffirming "the existence of a biography that predated these subjects' kidnapping, an existence that was categorically negated by the regime" and the process of individualisation of the victims by evidencing that "the disappeared had names, faces, identities, as well as families who were looking for them and reclaiming their appearance" (2010a, 6). Perhaps most enduringly, the public use of private images in this context would eventually allow the petitioners and, later, activists to "claim the political as personal" (Arnold-de Simine 2018, 190).

But the beginnings were largely driven by pragmatic need rather than ideological or political convictions. Speaking about the types of photographs initially chosen to help in the Mothers' search, Ulanovsky observes that "these photos were what people turned to in order to address a specific emergency." They "were sought out in a desperate attempt to make absence visible" (Ulanovsky in this volume, p. 131). Da Silva Catela notes that the early uses of photographs tended to rely on "small black-and-white ID photographs [that] were not intended 'to make history.'" Images that once belonged to "identity documents or membership cards for clubs, libraries, unions, political parties or universities" were transformed into "a tool with which to report missing people" (Cieplak 2020, 11). These early attempts at using photographs as a form of denunciation marked the beginning of their journey from the private to the public sphere (Longoni 2010a, 6). A journey that continues to this day, some forty years later.

As time went by, the uses – and the kinds of images resorted to – developed and diversified. But at the beginning, choices were often limited. For instance, the availability of photographs varied from family to family and was constrained by the fact that the objects of the regime's repression were often clandestine militants who purposefully avoided having their photographs taken so as not to imperil their own and their comrades' political militancy.[12] In addition to official identity documents, another source of images was the family album. On the face of it, it might have not mattered to the Mothers and other relatives of the disappeared where the image of the child or brother or sister they were looking for came from. But Longoni points out that the presence of the two categories of photographs – those from the family album and those from official documents – is significant in how the images can be read as a whole. The family photographs – showing holidays, family occasions, the birth of a child[13] – signalled, on the one hand, "the family ties that linked victims to those who demanded their reappearance" and, on the other, "a domestic order, before it was shattered by the violence of the state" (Longoni 2010a, 7). Citing Nelly Richard, Longoni makes the point that:

the latent tension between the past carelessness of the face that remains unaware of the imminent drama at the moment when the photograph was taken, and the present time from which we look tragically at the picture of someone who has subsequently become a victim of history, generates the desperate *punctum*.
(Richard 2000, 168, cit. in Longoni 2010a, 7; original emphasis)

This "desperate *punctum*" of the family images was to become even more prominent as years went by. In Chapter 4, for instance, Fortuny analyses the engagement of some of the children of the disappeared with the family album and, especially, with the gaps created in it by disappearance.[14] In Chapter 7, on the other hand, Mariana Tello Weiss demonstrates how a common family portrait can connote a multitude of initially invisibilised meanings, especially when it comes to photographic representation of the survivors of CDCs.

In the case of the other group of photographs, those that originated as part of official documentation, it has been argued that they have the potential to "isolate the missing person's identity" and, at the same time, "blur his or her personal ties and [place] him or her in an impersonal register" (Longoni 2010a, 7). Unlike a family album photograph, a passport photo already has inscribed in it the ideas of classification, categorisation, counting and aesthetic normativity. However, like with much else, there is space for subversion here. Longoni writes that when used in public, especially under the circumstances in which the Mothers were using them, such photographs can have "the unexpected effect of interpolating the very state that ordered the disappearances, for it was the same state that had earlier fulfilled an identifying function, registering those individuals whose disappearance was later arranged and whose existence was now denied." She goes on to add that "[t]he fact that the relatives used those photographs as evidence served to reveal and dramatise the paradoxical overlap between the state's control machinery and the state's machinery for the extermination and disappearance of its subjects, between identification and destruction, control and denial" (Longoni 2010a, 7).

While the photographs primarily pertained to the disappeared, it is also worth noting the function they fulfilled for those who searched for their loved ones, demanded information and refused to be silenced – often at a tremendous cost to themselves. Firstly, in the early days of their search efforts, "during a still spontaneous and decentralised stage," the photographs allowed the Mothers to recognise each other (Longoni 2010a, 6). Arguably, this marked the beginning of an enduring relationship between the Mothers and, later, other relatives of the disappeared and members of human rights organisations, and symbolism and iconicity. White handkerchiefs, silhouettes, imprints of hands and, more fleetingly, masks would also be employed as symbols – emphasising internal group cohesion and identity, as well as providing outward messaging about the Mothers' cause (Longoni 2010a and da Silva Catela in this volume). Secondly, the initial practice of "attaching the images to their [the Mother's] own bodies, hanging photos around their necks, or carrying them as placards or banners" served as a visual and symbolic reiteration of kinship (Gamarnik in this volume, p. 45).[15] It denoted "the strength of the family tie that linked the missing with the one wearing his or her portrait" (Longoni 2010a, 6). And family was important in more than one way in this context. The dictatorial regime and the moralistic, "Christian values" it purported to promote cast family ties as the bedrock of Argentine society.[16] If that was the case, how could mothers be challenged for merely wanting to find their children?

The dual function of these photographs as, on the one hand, pictures of particular, specific individuals attached to specific, particular people who search for them, and, on the other, as symbolic, collective signs, inscribes itself into the tensions that surround them. Tensions between the private and the public; between the collective and the individual. What was asked of the photographs, and what continues to be asked of them, is to be at once indexical, metonymic and iconic. With time, the strain of the expectations, and the sometimes-conflicting visions about the most effective ways of opposing the dictatorship and then bringing it to justice, also affected how different groups related to the photographs of the disappeared, especially in the public sphere. Longoni sees the production of the first banner of photos to be carried in protests as the beginning of the process of "*collectivisation* of the resources for exhibiting the photographs" (2010a, 6; original emphasis). This process would eventually map onto "the tension between different positions among the Mothers," which can be defined as "the difference between a *private mourning* and a *collectivised motherhood*" (2010a, 16; original emphasis). As Gamarnik charts in Chapter 2, a split occurred within the Mothers in 1986 into: the Mothers of Plaza de Mayo – Founding Line; and the Association of the Mothers of Plaza de Mayo. The latter group "decided that they would stop individualising the photographs of the disappeared" and "proposed that each Mother carry any placard, not necessarily one with the photograph of her own child," demanding the return of all 30,000 (Gamarnik in this volume, p. 46). The Founding Line Mothers continued to carry photographs of their own children. "Since then, the two groups continue to exist – and march weekly at Plaza de Mayo – separately" (Jelin 2021, 142). The politics of memory, demands for justice and resistance in Argentina would be subject to further complexities, lively discourse and sometimes conflicting priorities of different stakeholders (Maguire 2017, Jelin 2021). But even though their uses and functions diversified and multiplied, da Silva Catela points out that "the photos of the disappeared" continue to be "one of the most commonly used ways to remember them" (2001, 137).

Encounter 3: December 2022

The Grandmothers of Plaza de Mayo – an organisation dedicated to the search, identification and restitution of children either kidnapped or born in captivity during the dictatorship and appropriated by the state – are getting ready to begin a press conference in their headquarters, the Identity House [La Casa por la Identidad]. It is a relatively rare celebration. The gathering has been called to announce the successful identification and restitution of Grandchild 131.[17] It is led by the Grandmothers' long-serving president, Estela Carlotto. Argentina's Secretary for Human Rights, Horacio Pietragalla Corti, is also present.

Before turning to politics, Pietragalla Corti came to public prominence for being Grandchild 75, identified by the Grandmothers in 2003.

A notable absence at the gathering is that of the found grandson himself, who has asked for time to get to know the surviving members of his biological family before being publicly named.[18] But Carlotto assures us when the conference begins that "he was very excited when we showed him the photograph of his father, because he looks just like him" (Centenera 2022). And it is the photo of Grandchild 131's parents that represents the affected family at the event. It's placed right next to Carlotto, facing the cameras. The image is faded and of its time, seventies-saturated sepia dominated by oranges and browns, unusual compared to the other mostly black-and-white photographs of the disappeared. It features not a singular face but two people, a man and a woman – Grandchild 131's real parents – surrounded by others and looking ahead, their attention fixed on something out of the frame. The man is wearing a smart jacket and the woman an elegant brown dress. It looks like they might be getting married. The presence of the photograph at the press conference feels both conspicuous and matter-of-fact. Matter-of-fact, because photographs of the disappeared have played such a prominent part in the Grandmothers' search over decades, accompanied by other ways of ensuring someone's identity, including genetic testing. Conspicuous, because these images, even after so many years, remain such a strongly symbolic, and yet specific, marker of disappearance.

Memory, Justice and Politics

These encounters with photographs in 2022 are just three of many. While crucial in the first years of the resistance to the dictatorship, the images of the disappeared have continued to be publicly and privately present and important long after the hope of finding the victims alive had faded. While never relinquishing their indexical connection to the people they show, the images also gained the "status of signs" which "refer unequivocally to the disappeared" (Longoni 2010a, 5). As time passed and as the nature of the struggle evolved, so did the uses of photographs.[19] They became not only a ubiquitous presence at marches and demonstrations but also in memory sites (often reclaimed spaces of former CDCs), court hearings, newspapers,[20] films and television programmes,[21] artistic – including photographic – practice, and in many other contexts. However, and perhaps most importantly, while the photographs of the disappeared made this transition from the private to the public, it did not mean that they lost their original function. They remain personal objects used to remember and mourn individual people.

Da Silva Catela has conducted a long-term study of the domestic uses of and interactions with the photographs of the disappeared (2001). She writes that in the homes of the families affected by disappearance, the photos of the victims often "occupy a central place [...] demarcating a ritual space" (2001, 137). She also describes the practices and rituals that surround or centre on the images (da Silva Catela in this volume) and the fact that "many people 'talk' with their dead, in front of the photo, out loud or internally, communicate their news, ask for advice, greet them, place flowers" (2001, 137). Interestingly, da Silva Catela points out that the importance of these photographs does not rely solely on the likeness of the subject that they offer but also on their materiality and, specifically, on the fact that they are sometimes perceived as objects that somehow belonged to or had a physical connection with the disappeared (2001, 139). What this important research shows most of all, however, is the fact that the transition from the private to the public is not synonymous with the photos of the disappeared somehow losing their intimate value. Rather than merely changing, their functions multiply.

When the power of the dictatorship and the imposed censorship waned, the photographs of the disappeared, formerly amongst the very few groups of images able to break through the veil of silence cast over visual communication in Argentina, were joined by other types of images. These include, but are not limited to, numerous fiction and documentary films and TV programmes on the subject,[22] photographs of the bodies found in mass graves,[23] groups of images taken in the CDCs and smuggled out, such as the collection preserved by Víctor Basterra from the notorious ESMA, and, albeit much later, images taken by the dictatorial apparatus itself.[24]

Arguably the first group of "other" photographs appeared as early as 1984, in the *Nunca Más* [*Never Again*] report published by CoNaDeP, the commission established at the behest of the democratically elected president

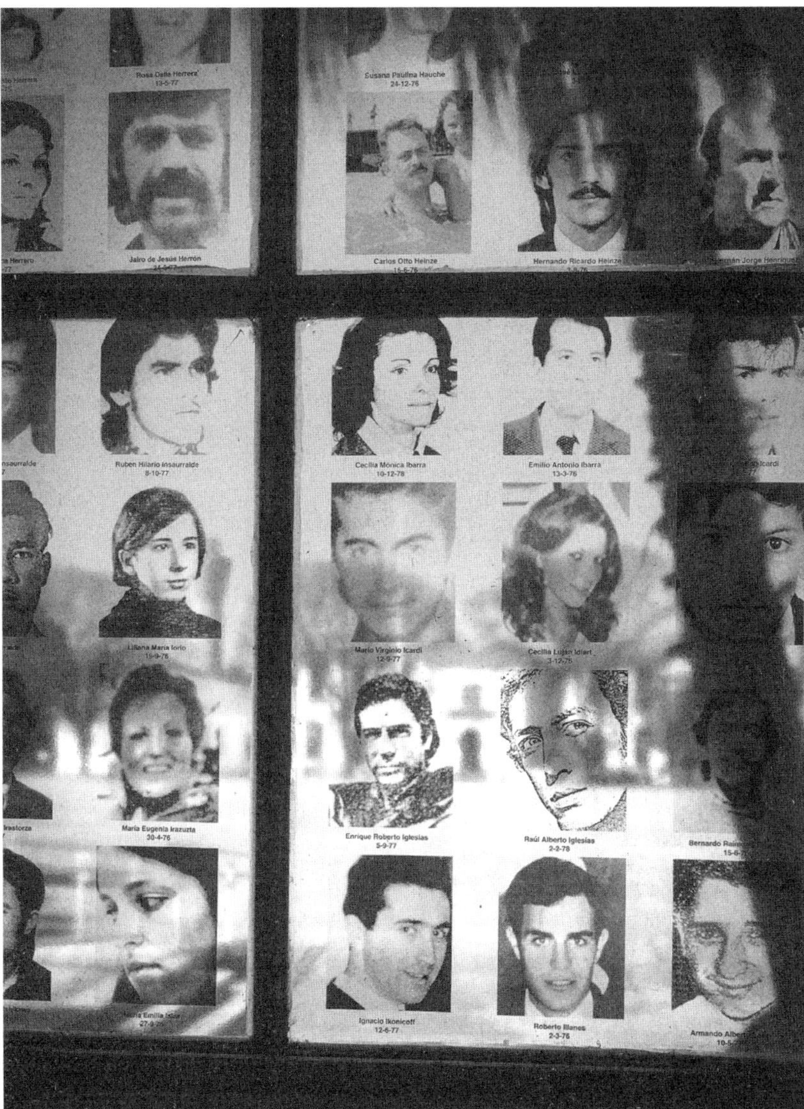

Figure 1.4 Photographs printed on the windows of the Officers' Casino in the former ESMA in Buenos Aires.

Source: Piotr Cieplak.

Raúl Alfonsín.[25] The widely read report contained photographs which did not correspond with the "portraits of the disappeared" which had been "brought to the public space by the human rights movement" (Feld 2010a, 3). The twenty-seven images included in *Nunca Más* (out of 2,020 taken during the investigation) were all of an "official nature" (Crenzel 2009, 293). Amongst other things, the published images show "members of the Commission touring, together with survivors, the buildings where clandestine detention centres operated" (Feld 2010a, 4). Even though the relatives of the disappeared submitted their photographs to CoNaDeP, as did Basterra, these images did not make it into the report. Crenzel writes that this decision "reveals that the Commission wanted to present its work within a framework of neutrality and impartiality" (2009, 293). However, the choice also marks an important landmark in the ongoing tensions still present in the Argentine memorial landscape, human rights movement and ongoing struggle for justice and remembrance: the tension between memory and history; the personal and the collective; politics and (often feared and criticised) affect.

Argentina has, arguably, one of the most vibrant and diverse political memory landscapes and human rights movements in the world. Over decades, the latter has been "responsible for the main political initiatives" when it comes to making "the state acknowledge its responsibilities for the recent past and seeking out institutional procedures to address dictatorship's legacy" (Jelin 2021, 44). Writing about the wider region's long relationship with memory activism and its predominant role within contemporary politics, Jelin also notes that it partly stems from the fact that "the page on the recent dictatorial past was not turned at the time of political transition" and that, instead, "this past retained a central place in political scenarios over the course of the decades that followed" (2021, 39).

But Jelin also observes that "memory is not, in fact, the past itself but the way in which people make sense of past experiences in the act of remembering, forgetting, and silencing, endlessly updating the past in connection to the present and to the desired future." Consequently, in Argentina, "it is impossible to find *one* memory" (2021, 15; original emphasis). Instead, the landscape is defined by "an active political struggle about the meaning of what went on and also about the meaning of memory itself." Jelin and Kaufman do not see the "'memory' camp" as "a unified and homogenous front." Rather, it is a space where struggles "emerge from the confrontation among different actors within it: struggles over appropriate means and forms of commemoration, about the content of what should be remembered publicly, and also about the legitimacy of different actors" (Jelin and Kaufman 2002, 41).

The human rights movement's diversity, longevity and evolution, as well as its involvement in current politics, mean that the differences of opinion and the changing nature of the struggle sometimes play out in public. Over the years, differing views and ways of continuing the fight included, for instance, topics such as participation in, and indeed the very occurrence of, the identification of found remains of the disappeared (Jelin 2021, 114) or the acceptance of financial reparations from the state by the relatives of the victims (Jelin 2021, 133). More generally, the relationship between Argentine human rights organisations and the state, or, more accurately, the government of the day, has been a complex and divisive situation, which underscores the fact that the movement operates not only in relation to the past but very much in the present. As Jelin observes, "political and cultural frameworks – and climates – are constantly changing" (2021, 21). Despite various, and mostly imperfect, earlier initiatives,[26] it was under the left-wing administration of the Kirchners that a lasting "rapprochement" occurred between the state and human rights organisations, which led to the former "largely adopt[ing] the movement's agenda" (Jelin 2021, 86–87).[27] It was in this period that many symbolic acts of recognition occurred. The anniversary of the 1976 coup – 24 March – became a national holiday. Many former CDCs were reclaimed from the military and turned into memory sites and museums, amongst them the symbolically charged ESMA in Buenos Aires.[28] Judicial trials against the perpetrators of dictatorial violence resumed. The work of the Grandmothers of Plaza de Mayo in identifying appropriated children gained public prominence. Jelin claims that in that period

The number of government initiatives and the administration's commitment to the visibility of issues related to the country's past [...] combined with [...] financial support [...] bring[s] up an almost classic quandary in the study of social movements. When a movement's actions result in the incorporation of its demands and agenda [...] the movement often loses autonomy and strength. This is because social movements stand united when they have a strong, unified adversary.

(2021, 137–138)

However, even if one were to agree with the latter part of Jelin's assessment, the human rights movement did not have to wait too long for the re-emergence of an "adversary," with the election in 2015 of the right-leaning Mauricio Macri to the presidency, whose attitude towards historical justice, statements about highly charged issues such as the debate about the number of the disappeared, and the general equating of the human rights movement with his political opponents on the left, caused a significant amount of "consternation" (Jelin 2021, 87), not least amongst those whose originally grassroot, oppositional structures had been by then subsumed into, and often funded by, the state.[29]

When it comes to the evolving nature of Argentina's memorial landscape, the emergence of one group was particularly notable: the children of the disappeared. Their presence and demands, as expressed in artistic and activist endeavours, had and continue to have an "intrinsic political core" (Maguire 2017, 3). Much excellent work has been done on the complexities of the position and cultural and political output of the children of the disappeared.[30] But I would like to briefly focus on two particular practices that involve photographs. H.I.J.O.S., the association of Sons and Daughters for Identity and Justice Against Forgetting and Silence [Hijos por la Identidad y la Justicia Contra el Olvido y el Silencio], was created in 1995 and one of its emblematic tactics, escrache, soon became known around the country.[31] Escrache is a form of direct action that involves a spontaneous campaign in the place where a known dictatorial repressor lives, designed to out the culprit and inform their neighbours about what they had done. The photos of the disappeared were often brought to escraches but so were the photos of the perpetrators. Claudia Feld writes that these gatherings "reversed the use of photography associated with disappearance" in that "instead of focusing its action on the exhibition of photos of the disappeared, H.I.J.O.S. proposed to show photos of the repressors who had not been punished or brought to trial" (2010a, 5).

The sons and daughters of the disappeared also became prominent in the already vibrant world of artistic responses to the dictatorship, especially when it came to photography. Artists such as Lucila Quieto (whose work is discussed in Chapter 4) and Inés Ulanovsky (Chapter 5) joined other photographers working on topics related to disappearance, either from the perspective of siblings, such as Marcelo Brodsky and Gustavo

Germano, or from the perspective of the direct experience of the dictator-ship, such as Helen Zout and Paula Luttinger.[32] Much of this work focused on re-contextualising, indeed sometimes even creating from scratch, fam-ily photographs marked, or made impossible, by disappearance. In this sense, numerous initiatives in this field focused on a very particular kind of world-building. According to Fortuny, who has conducted studies and analyses of Argentine photographic output related to the dictatorship (2014, 2021a), the two bodies of photographic material – private images used by the relatives of the disappeared and photos taken by professional press photographers during and after the dictatorship – should be con-sidered alongside a third: "the works of artists who, since the return of democracy to the present day, have built a repertoire of images that dis-turbingly investigate and make visible the relationship with the traumatic past through photographic essays" (2014, 11). Fortuny traces a correlation between the proliferation of this kind of photographic work and "hottest memory moments," such as the end of the 1990s (2014, 12). At the same time, she asks why it is that photography as a medium remains so particu-larly "fertile" when it comes to addressing Argentina's dictatorial past. One possible answer is that it is because "the photographic image combines its status as a trace of the real – of residue of what has been – with a use that is not strictly documentary, that is to say, with an ample metaphorical possibility" (Fortuny 2014, 12). Fortuny elaborates on this tension between document and construct, between a trace and an aesthetic construction in Chapter 4.[33]

Familiar Faces[34]

This truncated account of some of the memorial, activist and justice pro-cesses surrounding the relationship between photography and the legacy of the Argentine dictatorship is selective and partial but hopes to set the chapters that follow in some context. This book sits on the shoulders of the excellent research of many Argentine and international scholars. This includes the work with specific focus on different aspects of the photo-graphic image by Ludmila da Silva Catela (2001 and 2009), Emilio Crenzel (2009), Ana Longoni (2010a), Claudia Feld (2010a, 2010b and 2015), Augustina Triquell (2012), Natalia Fortuny (2014 and 2021a), Natalia

Magrin (2015) and Cora Gamarnik (2020 and 2021), and is joined by other in-depth studies, connected more generally to the memorial/political discourse, conducted by Pilar Calveiro (2001), Marguerite Feitlowitz (2011), Vikki Bell (2014), Jordana Blejmar (2016), Geoffrey Maguire (2017) and Elizabeth Jelin (2021).

In *The Art of Post-Dictatorship: Ethics and Aesthetics in Transitional Argentina* (2014), Bell grapples with the complex definition of "art" and its response to the experience(s) of the dictatorship that go beyond the often repeated concerns about authorship and ownership and, instead, address the multiple subjectivities and different senses of belonging that, in turn, result in the "questions of justice related to the last dictatorship [being] approached within a broad spectrum of engagements" (2014, 4). Dictatorship-related photography in Argentina – private, institutional, professional, artistic, and everything in between – is perfectly placed to examine the nooks and crannies of this spectrum. *Familiar Faces* shares Bell's call for the discovery and analysis of alternative epistemological models in aesthetic expression in post-dictatorial Argentina.

Familiar Faces also comes almost a decade after the publication (in Spanish) of *Instantáneas de la memoria. Fotografía y dictadura en Argentina y América Latina* [*Snapshots of Memory: Photography and Dictatorship in Argentina and Latin America*], edited by Jordana Blejmar, Natalia Fortuny and Luis Ignacio García (2014). As well as sharing some authors, *Familiar Faces* and *Instantáneas de la memoria* also share a commitment to interdisciplinarity and multiplicity of perspectives. This allows for the tracing of the developments in the field and, indeed, in the preoccupations of individual authors, and further evidences the enduring importance of photography in the Argentine memorial landscape, as well as the need for continuous study and engagement.

Another collection I would like to mention as a significant influence on *Familiar Faces* is Claudia Feld and Jessica Stites Mor's seminal *El Pasado que miramos: Memoria e imagen ante la historia reciente* [*The Past We Look At: Memory and Image in the Face of Recent History*] (2009). Even though more general in scope, and encompassing TV and film images as well as photography, *El Pasado que miramos* zooms in on the temporal convergence between memory and image in their simultaneous preoccupation with the past and the present (Feld and Stites Mor 2009, 25).

More specifically, the collection highlights the link between the eviden-tial claim of the documentary image as a trace of the real and the fact that the Argentine dictatorship so diligently tried to eliminate the traces of its crimes – from the bodies of the disappeared to the destruction of evidence in the run-up to the transition to democracy (Feld and Stites Mor 2009, 26–27). Many contributions to *Familiar Faces* share this preoccupation, which, although still rooted in the concept of disappearance, clandestin-ity and (in)visibility, is reframed here to think about not only how images can and do represent violence, but also how the nature of the violence that produced them dictates their uses.

Given the diversity of the chapters in *Familiar Faces*, as well as of the ecosystem of the scholarly and artistic work that surrounds it, it is per-haps most useful to introduce the contributions by mentioning the edito-rial, conceptual aspirations for the collection. The book is part of a wider academic project, supported by the British Academy, entitled "Intimate moments, public acts: photographs of the disappeared and memory poli-tics in Argentina." It is also an inevitably imperfect attempt at finding alter-native, less extractive ways of working in the Global South, by amplifying and creating international platforms for local voices. In this, the collec-tion can be seen as an English-language introduction to the wealth and breadth of Argentine scholarship on the topic, and to the vibrant dialogue between the voices of researchers and practitioners that informs much of Argentine memory-making.

Jelin (2021, 98) joins others in noting that, while extremely rich, a lot of the work about memorial and justice processes in Argentina tends to be Buenos Aires-centric. But dictatorial violence swept the entire country, and different places experienced it in specific ways and at specific times. Similarly, the memorial and justice initiatives often display local inflec-tions and gesture to local priorities. While the Argentine capital is amply represented in *Familiar Faces*, it was also an aspiration of the collection to engage with other contexts, including those from Córdoba, Bell Ville, La Plata and the north of the country (especially Jujuy).

While, on the whole, *Familiar Faces* investigates the evolution and longevity of disappearance-related photographs' centrality in Argentina, its particular focus is on how the experience of the violence and its aftermath by the images' diverse custodians (across generations and backgrounds) shapes how the photographs are used. The simultaneous uniqueness of each of these images and their collective ubiquity, not to mention the multiple tensions that define their operation in Argentine society, also cast light on some of the questions about the nature of the photographic medium itself. Specifically, the tension between index and context. Roland Barthes' *noeme*, "that-has-been" (2000, 96), André Bazin's claim that "the photograph as such and the object [being photographed] itself share a common being, after the fashion of a fingerprint" (1967, 15), and Susan Sontag's early proposition to see a photograph as alike to "a footprint or a death mask" (1978, 154) are in direct conversation here with the critics who emphasise the contextual over the ontological in how photography gains meaning (Berger 1972; Sekula 1982; and Tagg 1988). In other words, these images pose a very specific and complex challenge to the binary question of whether "photography [is] to be identified with (its own) nature or with the culture that surrounds it?" (Batchen 1997, 17).

What further complicates and enriches discussions within *Familiar Faces* is the presence of the familial gaze. When writing about family photography, especially in the context of violence, Marianne Hirsch points out that

it is precisely the indexical nature of the photo, its status as relic, or trace, or fetish – its 'direct' connection with the material presence of the photographed person – that at once intensifies its status as harbinger of death and, at the same time and concomitantly, its capacity to signify life.[35]

(1997, 20)

And yet, as can be seen from some of the processes described earlier and on the following pages of this book, this "fetish," while undoubtedly indexical, is, in the Argentine case, also very much physical. This creates another tension to consider. As Elizabeth Edwards and Janice Hart propose, "the concern with the indexical has [...] dominated writing on photographs." They add that it "privileges the idea that somehow photographs maintain a level of material transparency and that what is important about them is the content itself" (2004, 6–7). They go on to say that photography's "material and presentational forms" are "central to the function of the photograph as a socially salient object" (3).

Perhaps the most useful way of thinking through the images analysed in this book is Tina M. Campt's concept of "haptic images," defined as "objects whose effects are structured by a tripartite sense of touch – an indexical touch, a physical touch, and an affective touch" (2012, 43). This seems particularly apt in the Argentine context and the multitude of "enunciatory functions" photographs related to disappearance are asked to perform. For here, too, it is necessary to "think of [a photograph] as a highly affective object with and onto which we invest and project complex psychic and emotional, social and material, cultural and historical meanings and attachments" (2012, 34). This allows the authors of the chapters in *Familiar Faces* to propose alternative epistemologies that surround the photographs of the disappeared that go well beyond the index-context binary (Campt 2017).

In Chapter 2, "Constructing the Image of the Mothers of Plaza de Mayo Through Press Photography," Cora Gamarnik presents the interconnected histories of the Mothers and a group of photojournalists, Argentine and international, who took considerable risks in order to document and represent the Mothers' struggle. Gamarnik offers a detailed account and analysis of the early uses of photography by the women, before proposing that some of the press photographers operating in the country at the time created what amounted to a "safety net" for the Mothers facing the wrath of the dictatorial regime. Basing her research on the analysis of iconic photographs, as well as first-hand accounts from, and interviews with, the Mothers and the photographers alike, Gamarnik demonstrates the strong symbiotic elements of this co-existence and, through this, she sketches how, from very early on, photography in Argentina played a crucial part in challenging the regime's policy of double concealment – that "of the disappeared and that of their relatives looking for them" (p. 44). What also emerges as crucially important in Gamarnik's chapter is the evolution of the Mothers; from a loose grouping bound by personal loss and a sense of helplessness to women, forged in battle against the state apparatus of repression and censorship, keenly aware of the need for a media strategy that would allow "their claims to be heard and transcend national borders" (p. 38). Photographs, alongside TV interviews given to the international media, became the main executors of this strategy and had a tremendous impact on both the Mothers' cause and Argentine press photography.

In Chapter 3, "Ways of Looking: Violence, Archive and the Register of 'Extremists,'" María Eleonora Cristina, the director of the APM and the ex-D2 memory site in Córdoba, and a long-term member of H.I.J.O.S., also examines the role of photographs related to disappearance as communication devices. However, she does so specifically in relation to the difficult task of narrating and mediating Argentina's reclaimed CDCs. Cristina sees the images as " 'bridges of meaning' between the brutal past and the present," whose use in the "liminal" spaces of memory sites and in archives has changed significantly over time and "became less fixed" (p. 73).

Crucially, Cristina also expands the corpus of images analysed in *Familiar Faces* to include those produced by the repressive apparatus of the state. Given that the dictatorship went to great lengths to destroy materials documenting its crimes (Jelin 2021, 191 and 237), there often exists an assumption that "there are no photographs of the systematic programme of disappearing people," while, in fact, such images "do exist" and "in some cases, have been publicly available from soon after the dictatorial regime collapsed" (Longoni in this volume, p. 190). The APM is the custodian of the infamous Register of "Extremists" – a collection of police booking photographs and the accompanying ledger explaining how they and the detained were contextualised by Córdoba's Provincial Police. Guided by first-hand experience of working with the collection, Cristina explores the complex processes that are involved in its handling, from the highly emotive restitution of the images to the people who appear in them or to surviving relatives, to the curatorial discussions behind using the images in a 2012 public exhibition entitled *Moments of Truth: Photographs of the Register of Extremists from D2*. She offers sobering warnings against fetishising records created by a terrorist state. And, at the same time, she urges us to recognise the unique potential of archives that began their existence as tools of oppression to become complex, imperfect and valuable sources, and, eventually, memory and commemoration aides.

In Chapter 4, "Political Landscapes and Photographic Artefacts in Post-Dictatorship Argentina," Natalia Fortuny turns to artistic photographic practice and the ways in which it has been shaped by the ontologically complex concept of disappearance, with its "triple condition: the absence of a body, the lack of a moment of mourning and the impossibility of a burial" (p. 95). In particular, she explores how Argentine photographers have worked *around* the visual lack of their main referent through their insistence "on (re)presenting that which is no longer alive but whose death cannot be evidenced" and what this tells us about the age-old tension in how we perceive photography as a medium: the tension between a record and a representational construct (p. 95). Fortuny proposes the framework of three different kinds of landscape to examine this: the natural landscape (focusing on Helen Zout's portraiture and Gabriel Orge's use of projection), the urban landscape (focusing on Gerardo Dell'Oro's work of reconstruction) and the familial landscape (focusing on Lucila Quieto's collage and assemblage techniques).

In Chapter 5, "Waiting for the Light," the photographer Inés Ulanovsky situates the photographs of the disappeared in the domestic setting, but from a practitioner's perspective. In her seminal collection, *Fotos tuyas* [*Your Photos*] (2006), Ulanovsky documented the unique relationships between the surviving photographs of the disappeared and their custodians, usually family members.[36] What emerges here is the importance of materiality and touch, which are often the expressions of the painful desire for an impossible dialogue with the dead. A visual exploration, in other words, of the "contemplative moment in which the relatives look at these photos" (p. 125). While discussing her aesthetic approach to the project, Ulanovsky also touches on her childhood experiences of exile in Mexico, and the role the photographs of the disappeared played there. As a practitioner active at the time, Ulanovsky also speaks of a particular moment in 2000 and 2001 when the focus of much of the artistic output related to the dictatorship shifted to the photos of the disappeared, and how, "at this juncture," they "moved categories" and "entered a more artistic field" (p. 130).

In Chapter 6, "Photography and Disappearance in Argentina: Sacredness and Rituals in the Face of Death," Ludmila da Silva Catela continues the exploration of the theme of the tensions between the operation of the images of the disappeared in the domestic and public sphere. Building on her extensive and long-term fieldwork in La Plata, Jujuy and Córdoba, she tests the evidential claim of the photographic image against its ritual function as part of mourning practices in Argentina. Through this analysis, da Silva Catela addresses complex issues of the circulation, appropriation, sacralisation but also banalisation of the images. The deceptively simple question – what do people do with photographs? – returns multifaceted answers not only about remembering but also about forgetting and, as da Silva Catela argues, the images' simultaneous centrality and marginality in the mourning process. Taking an anthropological approach, she also places photographs of the disappeared within the wider Argentine memorial ecology and symbolism and examines their relationship with other forms of disappearance-related representation, such as silhouettes and rituals associated with the Day of the Dead. Da Silva Catela's focus is very much on the materiality of the images, which includes their deterioration and discarding; their simultaneous sacredness (in some contexts) and unsentimental utilitarianism (in others). Consequently, the materialities da Silva Catela engages with are often ephemeral, fleeting. But they are also telling of the continuous evolution and malleability of the photographs of the disappeared in Argentina.

Sharing da Silva Catela's ethnographic approach, as well as recourse to first person accounts, in Chapter 7, "An Impossible Scene: Towards an Ethnography of the (In)visible in the Memories of the Survivors of La Perla," Mariana Tello Weiss also turns to images that exist within the framework of the family, but in a particular and unusual way. The chapter tackles the difficult issue of the presence/absence and (in)visibility of the survivors of CDCs in Argentina's memorial and justice discourse. The stigma of survival is well documented, as are the material dangers facing those who decided to go public, especially when it comes to testimonies (Longoni 2007). Building on her long-term work with survivors, Tello Weiss analyses the role played by photographs in the construction and re-construction of survivors' private as well as public image. She offers an in-depth analysis of the case of Ana Iliovich, a survivor of La Perla CDC in Córdoba, and the family portraits taken at the point of Iliovich's temporary release from the concentration camp. With this as a starting point, Tello Weiss analyses the "practice that occurred among other survivors once their repressors started allowing them to contact their families: that of taking pictures of themselves as a way of proving they were alive" (p. 167). Using Rancière's concept of the *distribution of the sensible* as the framework, Tello Weiss asks what role such photographs – simultaneously showing someone who has appeared, while, technically, remaining disappeared – can tell us about the "connotation implicit in the term 'disappearance'" (p. 167) and the wider positioning of survivors in the memorial, and especially visual, discourse in Argentina.

Chapter 8, "What Appears and What Still Shines Through," acts as the collection's conclusion. In it, Ana Longoni draws together the themes running throughout the book. Ultimately and aptly, she situates them at the "intersection of the insistence and, simultaneously, the fragility of the photographs of the disappeared" (p. 188). She offers a final glimpse of the images' unique versatility and ability to be reinvented and re-used.

While *Familiar Faces* offers an insight into the specific Argentine situation, it also makes an intervention into how we think about photography more generally. This intervention goes beyond the considerations of representation, evidencing and registering violence (although these too, of course, play an important part). It offers a dialogical approach that conceives of images as at once autonomous from and dependent on their provenance and distribution. This is a dialogical dynamic whose meaning-making ability depends on a series of encounters (Azoulay 2008). Consequently, in many ways, *Familiar Faces* is intended as an exploration of the ways in which the specific Argentine context destabilises photographic discourse, especially in relation to indexicality, iconicity and materiality.

But neither is this intervention exclusively ontological. *Familiar Faces* is also a contribution to wider, global debates about the increasingly pervasive role of the photographic image in memorial and justice processes related to large-scale violence. Consequently, I hope that the diversity of the analysed material, approaches and voices in the collection contributes to putting the specific Argentine situation in dialogue with the uses of photography related to mass violence elsewhere, especially, but not exclusively, in the Global South. Zoe Norridge and Billy Kahora have shown the potential and importance of such dialogue in the special issue of *Wasafiri* on *Human Rights Cultures in Rwanda, Kenya, Colombia and Argentina* (2020). Key to this aspiration is the fact that the use of family album and institutional images in Argentina and Latin American has been foundational and included practices we can now recognise in many other contexts, including but not limited to, conflict and post-conflict situations in the Balkans, Rwanda, Cambodia and the Middle East. As Arnold-de Simine points out, "in South America [...] holding up photographs of the 'disappeared' as a performance [...] started as a form of civil disobedience." She goes on to add that "it has become a recognisable form of political protest and grassroot activism [...] that has caught on in various geo-political contexts" (2018, 190). *Familiar Faces* is in many ways a testament to how seemingly simple, personal images that never "intended 'to make history'" can transform into powerful tools of politics, activism and memory, while never losing their initial function as harbingers of love, kinship, affect and loss.

Notes

1 This chapter is an output of the British Academy funded project entitled "Intimate moments, public acts: photographs of the disappeared and memory politics in Argentina" (SRG20\200164).

2 In Argentina, the 1976–1983 dictatorship is commonly referred to as: la última dictadura cívico-militar. A direct translation would be: the *last* civic-military dictatorship. Throughout this book the word "last" is replaced with "most recent" as it gives a better sense of what is meant by the phrase in Spanish.

3 The junta operated on a rotational basis and included the representatives of the Army, the Navy and the Air Force. It is worth noting that in many places in the country, the repression against left-wing groups, activists and trade unionists began before the official date of the coup and that there are regional differences in how and when different parts of Argentina experienced violence and repression.

4 It was the longest dictatorship in the 20th century in Argentina but relatively short when compared with other countries in Latin America.

5 Like much else when it comes to Argentina's recent history and the memorial and justice discourse around it, citing the number of 30,000 disappeared and/or killed is, to an extent, a political statement. The figure is widely accepted, nationally and internationally, and endorsed by Argentina's human rights organisations. However, some of the outright revisionist discourse, as well as certain sectors of the political right, question the number. See Jelin (2021, 207).

6 When it comes to a comparative look at the nature of the dictatorship in Argentina, the regional and national context should be taken into consideration. Specifically, the dictatorships in Uruguay, Chile, Brazil and Bolivia, but also the role of the United States, its support for the dictatorship and its role in the destabilisation of the region through Operation Condor in the Americas' Southern Cone. See McSherry (2005) and Lessa (2022).

7 It is worth noting that many other targeted organisations and sub-organisations existed in Argentina at the time.

8 For a detailed account of the operation and impact of CDCs in Argentina, and the specific legacy of the concentrationary experience, see Calveiro (2001).

9 It is beyond the scope of this chapter to go into the details of the origin, modus operandi and, indeed, long-term impact of the 1976–1983 civic-military dictatorship in Argentina. This primer is designed to briefly outline the context for the chapters that follow, many

of which tackle specific practices of repression relevant to the material analysed. There exists a vast body of literature, in English and Spanish, about the different facets of the Argentine dictatorship. For a general overview, I would recommend Robben (2007).

10 For the origin of the symbol of the white handkerchief, see Longoni (2020). The Spanish pañuelo – in the context of the practices of the Mothers – is translated variably as headscarf, handkerchief and kerchief. These are used interchangeably throughout the book.

11 Other organisations have also been prominent in this activism and discourse from early on, such as, for instance, Relatives of the Disappeared and Detained for Political Reasons [Familiares de Desaparecidos y Detenidos por Razones Políticas]. For an in-depth history of the Mothers of Plaza de Mayo, see Gorini (2006).

12 Photographs and family albums were also often targeted in police raids (da Silva Catela 2001; Longoni 2010a; and Jelin 2021).

13 For a discussion about the complexities of using family images associated with moments of happiness to denote loss and violence, see Moreno Andrés (2019, 22).

14 Some writers have pointed out the importance of generational fault lines (parents, grandparents, children) when it comes to the preferred uses of different types and categories of images pertaining to the disappeared (Feierstein 2011).

15 The initial use of photographs by the Mothers and other relatives of the disappeared evolved and diversified relatively quickly. Starting (and often continuing) with the wearing of the photos on the bearer's body (da Silva Catela 2001; 2009), to the production of wooden banners (known as pancartas), to collectivising the photos into a banner with the help, initially, of the private photographic studio of Santiago and Mathilde Mellibovsky (Longoni 2010a; 2020; and Gamarnik in this volume).

16 Direct family ties were crucial in the formation of the resistance to the dictatorship. The main associations and human rights organisations still define themselves through their family connection to the disappeared: mothers, grandmothers, children. But it is interesting to note that the regime itself relied on the rhetoric of the family to advance its ideology. Jelin writes that "the military made extensive use of the family metaphor, from the 'grand Argentine family' to attributing responsibility to parents – especially mothers – whose sons and daughters (militants who were later disappeared) had 'strayed' from the path" (2021, 206).

17 To date, the Grandmothers have recovered 132 appropriated grandchildren. For details of all the cases, see www.abuelas.org.ar/caso/buscar?tipo=3. The year 2022 was seen as a bumper year. On 28 December, the confirmation of the identity of Grandson 132, Juan José, was announced. This followed over three years without new finds.

18 It is not unusual for "found" grandchildren not to go public immediately.

19 It is beyond the scope of this piece to chart in detail the evolution and changes that occurred in the human rights movement in Argentina. In her magisterial work on the subject, *The Struggle for the Past: How We Construct Social Memories* (2021), Elizabeth Jelin traces the initial role and objectives of the movement (85–86; 95; 164) and the way in which they developed over decades. This charting includes an invaluable taxonomy of the main slogans and demands.

20 I am thinking here in particular about recordatorios [reminders] that appear in the *Pagina 12* newspaper on the birthdays or anniversaries of kidnappings of the disappeared, usually accompanied by small, square photographic portraits. Da Silva Catela refers to them as "memory aides" (2001, 148).

21 See Grant (2003).

22 For an overview of the filmic and televisual output related to the dictatorship, see Grant (2003) and Feld (2010a and 2016). For an analysis of films produced by the sons and daughters of the disappeared, see Amado (2009) and Aprea (2008).

23 For the analysis of the images of human remains and mass graves that circulated in the Argentine press, see Feld (2015).

24 Víctor Basterra (1944–2020) was detained in ESMA between 1979 and 1983. During his incarceration he took and smuggled out photographs of other prisoners and of some of the repressors. Basterra's archive became one of the most prominent photographic collections showing life in Argentina's clandestine torture and extermination centres (Longoni and García 2013; and Feld 2010b). It was later joined by other recovered archives produced by the organs of the dictatorial state, including the Register of "Extremists" (see Chapter 3) and the reports compiled by the Federal Intelligence Agency (Tello Weiss and Tizón 2021).

25 For more on CoNaDeP and *Nunca Más*, see the glossary and Crenzel (2008 and 2009). For an analysis of the televised version of the Commission's findings, which aired in July 1984, see Feld (2009 and 2010a).

26 The 1990s were marked by a "profound clash" between human rights organisations and the state, especially when it came to the slow and imperfect process of trying to bring the dictatorial culprits to justice (Jelin 2021, 86–87).

27 Néstor Kirchner was Argentina's president between 2003 and 2007 and was succeeded by his wife Cristina Fernández de Kirchner, who was in office from 2007 to 2015.

28 Once it was reclaimed from the Navy, what to do with the complex that formed ESMA became the subject of a lively and sometimes fractious and public debate amongst Argentine human rights organisations. See Brodsky (2005).

29 For more about the impact of Macri's election and term in office on dictatorship-related public discourse, see Jelin (2021, 138–139) and Kaiser (2020, 71). *Familiar Faces* was written before the election of the right-wing libertarian Javier Milei to the Argentine presidency in November 2023. Judging by the incendiary rhetoric employed in the campaign, Milei and his vice-president, Victoria Villaruel, known for her long-held negationist views when it comes to the dictatorship, the number of its victims and the culpability of the perpetrators, are likely to destabilise the fragile consensus around memory politics in Argentina in the coming years, making the subject of this collection even more pressing.

30 See, for instance, Blejmar (2016) and Maguire (2017).

31 For more on H.I.J.O.S. and escraches, see Bonaldi (2006).

32 Brodsky is arguably the most internationally known Argentine visual artist working with domestic photography on account of his 1996 project *Buena Memoria*. One of the project's most recognisable pieces – *1st Year, 6ᵗʰ Division, Class Photo* – is Brodsky's school photo, annotated by the artist. Copies of the work have been purchased by MoMa in New York and Tate Modern in the United Kingdom.

33 As could be expected, many of the photographs related to disappearance in Argentina, as well as their multiple uses, have migrated online. The available analysis of this phenomenon is still relatively limited when compared with the richness of writing about the photographs of the disappeared more generally. However, some excellent work on the topic has been done by Agustina Triquell (2013) and Sebastian Bustamante-Brauning (2022).

34 A note on translation: the texts in *Familiar Faces* were originally written in Spanish and subsequently translated into English, and edited. For the most part, they follow the conventions of English-language academic writing but there are some instances, especially when it comes to the use of indented quotations, where the original presentation has been preserved. Most of the directly quoted secondary sources available in English are provided in that language. Where this was impossible, the Spanish citation has been translated into English by the translator (listed at the end of each chapter). Generally, if the source appears in English in the bibliography, it has been cited as published. If it appears in another language, it has most likely been translated.

35 Even though outside the scope of this volume, interesting work has been done on the application of the concept of postmemory in Argentine cultural production related to the dictatorship. See Blejmar (2016) and Maguire (2017).

36 An alternative translation here could be *Photos of You.*

2

Constructing the Image of the Mothers of Plaza de Mayo Through Press Photography

Cora Gamarnik

Press photography has been crucial in the construction of the image of the Mothers of Plaza de Mayo and, through them, of those disappeared by the most recent dictatorship in Argentina. After the 1976 coup, a close relationship developed between some Mothers and a group of photojournalists. This special bond resulted in the creation of several emblematic photographs, which continue to function as iconic images of resistance to the dictatorship to this day. This chapter traces the origins of this relationship and analyses how the image of the Mothers was constructed, and how it inscribed itself into the women's wider communication strategy for gaining visibility.

The visual material analysed here consists of photographs with little or no circulation at the time of the events depicted, as well as of a selection of images that are amongst the most commonly used when referring to the Mothers in books, films, press articles, exhibitions, commemorations, human rights activities and websites. The chapter also includes the analysis of a piece of Dutch television footage, shot during the 1978 World Cup, which proved key to the Mothers' worldwide visibility and recognition, and to the creation of an extensive solidarity network with their cause.

Mothers of Plaza de Mayo and their Struggle for Visibility

Once in control of the country, the Argentine military junta quickly recognised the power of images and, consequently and as part of a planned policy of cultural production, exercised strict controls over the circulation of photographs in the media outlets supportive of the regime. Mindful of the strong international condemnation of Augusto Pinochet's coup in Chile, the Argentine Armed Forces decided to launch a seemingly bloodless overthrow, while carrying out a clandestine repression policy that included a systematic plan of mass kidnappings, torture and murder. For the successful implementation of this strategy, the terrorist state required a clear censorship, disinformation and mass media manipulation policy.[1] While the regime spared no effort in creating a public image of the junta as an honest, professional, moralist "government" committed to bringing social harmony, it covertly developed a repressive plan, in conjunction with the implementation of various strategies for achieving social consensus.

The disappearances were accompanied by the negation of the existence of the detained-disappeared; a negation that also extended to the families who searched for them. It was as vital for the regime to conceal the disappearances and the fate of those kidnapped as it was to hide the Mothers who demanded to know what happened to their disappeared children. The negation took different forms. One was the absence of information about the kidnappings in the press, or a confusing, distorted or decontextualised presentation of such news. Another was a campaign of demonisation. The military regime tarnished the Mothers as "mad women," liars and mothers of "terrorists." In other words, "bad mothers." Specific campaigns were planned and conducted to discredit and shame them (Schoellkopf 2017, 278).

Forced disappearances enacted by the dictatorship prompted a series of spontaneous search efforts by family members and friends. These included many Mothers calling on police stations, military bases, hospitals, churches, state agencies and magistrates' courts in desperate attempts to obtain any news about their children's whereabouts. Full of despair and not knowing what to do or whom to turn to, the Mothers gradually began meeting each other during these excruciating pilgrimages. Anguish and hope, as well as the abuse and humiliation they often suffered, brought them together. The unorganised structure of their initial efforts is still apparent in their name, indicative both of their close relationship with the disappeared and of the place where they used to meet weekly to voice their claims, Plaza de Mayo. Initially they were a fairly small group.[2] Nora Cortiñas, a leading member of the Mothers of Plaza de Mayo – Founding Line, points out that:

No mother ever thought: I won't see them [the disappeared] again. We looked each other in the eyes and asked: When will this be over? When will they appear? In each meeting, in each bureaucratic formality, in each round of visits, that question was always present: until when?

(Szalkowicz 2019, 72)

The frustration felt after each unsuccessful search and the complete lack of knowledge about the fate of the disappeared in the clandestine detention centres (CDCs), of the actual extent of the repression and its effects, pushed the Mothers to take action that others regarded as rash or reckless, but which for them was just common sense: to appeal directly to the military junta outside the Government House for an answer to a simple question: "Where are the disappeared?" It should be noted that the lack of concrete information was also, in a way, a source of hope for the Mothers, fuelled by the lived experiences of previous dictatorships, when repression had not reached the extent and extremity of cruelty Argentina was witnessing now. They believed their children were still alive, held in detention. They just wanted to know where, so they could visit them, bring them some food and warm clothes. They were moved by love and despair, but also by hope; by the fact that their children – surely still alive somewhere – needed them.

Press Photography during the Dictatorship

The early 1960s in Argentina witnessed a radical shift in photojournalism. Images began to occupy a much more prominent place, particularly in the "pictorials" or illustrated magazines, leaving behind the merely decorative role they had played in the mass media until then.[3] Subsequently, a new generation of photographers – who emerged mostly in the heated milieu of activist and militant publications of the 1970s – appeared on the media scene, not only endowed with politically committed viewpoints, but also with professional training far superior to that of their predecessors. This resulted in a new type of photojournalism, both aesthetically and politically. But the development of the profession was thwarted by the 1976 coup. The working situation of the more socially and politically engaged photojournalists became far more unstable and hazardous.

During and before the dictatorship, the photographers of the so-called militant press were persecuted. Some were kidnapped and killed, while others were forced underground or into exile (Gamarnik 2020). As a result of the strict censorship initially imposed by the junta and the subsequent banning of many media outlets, hundreds of journalists – especially those actively involved in the labour movement and politics – lost their jobs.[4] The situation required a change of strategy, if one was to stay in the trade: some changed their line of work within the same publication or the kind of photography they did (e.g. shifting to advertising), while others moved to lower-circulation media. Consequently, despite the censorship and repression, several photographers managed to stay in the game, albeit under much stricter controls over what they did or what was possible to publish.[5]

At the same time, on the face of it, during the first years of the dictatorship there were no major events to photograph. On the political surface, nothing was happening, so photojournalists mainly covered military, sport and show business events. This apparent stasis prompted some photographers to seek opportunities that would allow them to take interesting or politically engaged pictures, despite the circumstances. The first strategy consisted in photographically capturing – during the events they were sent to cover – military officers, high church officials and civilians who actively cooperated with the regime, in gestures, attitudes or postures that ridiculed them or showed them in compromising situations. This approach produced ironic photographs of highly symbolic value. The second strategy consisted in taking photographs the photographers knew were definitely forbidden, or would certainly be censored, and keeping them in their private archives. Unpublished at the time, these clandestine images now serve as a record of the beginnings of the Mothers' struggle, as well as the struggle of other relatives of the disappeared. The images taken by Jorge Sanjurjo, who worked for *Crónica* at the time, are an example of such photographs. One early image is particularly emblematic. Taken on 12 August 1976, it shows a long line of people waiting for something outside a government building. In the photo, the relatives of the disappeared (for that is who the people depicted are) do not yet display any markers of group identification; no handkerchiefs on their heads or photographs of their disappeared children around their necks. There is no way of knowing from the picture itself what these people are waiting for or why they are gathered there.[6] And yet the image captures an important phenomenon which would become representative of the early days of the dictatorship when the relatives of the disappeared, and the Mothers in particular, would queue up for hours on end in front of the Ministry of Home Affairs, at 50 Balcarce Street, or outside other government agencies they were sent back and forth between – all part of the state's strategy of attrition and humiliation.

In October 1981, some members of this new generation of photographers organised the first Exhibition of Argentine Photojournalism. The purpose of the event was to show the photographs they had taken during all those years and that had remained unpublished or been explicitly censored by the big media.[7] It is worth noting that in 1981, the Mothers of Plaza de Mayo were still practically unknown in the country. They were more visible abroad thanks to the activities of groups of Argentine exiles, foreign journalists and the images Argentine and foreign photographers had managed to publish or broadcast in the international media.[8] In Argentina, only a relatively small group of people knew about the Mothers. Whereas public opinion in general ignored their existence, the dictatorship targeted, persecuted and harassed them. The Exhibition of Argentine Photojournalism disseminated – timidly in 1981, more robustly in 1982 and with a wide-ranging display in 1983 – the Mothers' image and showed their faces and fighting strategies to the Argentine public. Some of the photographs, regarded as the most iconic images of the Mothers, and, by extension, of the resistance to the dictatorship, were shown in the country for the first time.

The "Safety Net" and the Importance of Being Seen

French journalist Pierre Bousquet, the deputy director of Agence France-Presse in Argentina between 1975 and 1980, was the only foreign correspondent accredited to the Armed Forces at the time. Through denunciations made abroad, the French agency had become aware of the human rights situation in Argentina and gave its correspondent a carte blanche to investigate the story (Bousquet 1983; Gorini 2006, 87). Whereas local journalists ran serious risks when reporting on the topic, things were much easier for foreigners, given the military junta's interest in avoiding any open conflict with the international press. Bousquet and other foreign journalists created a "safety net" around the Mothers. They would go to the Plaza to ensure the women were not alone when confronted by the police; they publicised the Mothers' claims all over the world; and sometimes they even marched arm-in-arm with the Mothers as a form of protection from violent acts. Several photographers were arrested during the demonstrations organised by the group (Bousquet 1983; Gorini 2006, 87). It was also this cluster of foreign photographers and journalists who first helped the Mothers gain international recognition. Bousquet points out that "[i]n order to build a common front, the AP, Reuters, EFE, ANSA, Prensa Latina and Tass correspondents and I made a non-written agreement to exchange information" (Bousquet 1983; Gorini 2006, 88).

Quite early on, the Mothers themselves recognised they needed a mass media strategy if they wanted their claims to be heard and transcend national borders. From their first meetings, they had come to the realisation that the presence of foreign journalists and photographers offered them a certain amount of protection, but, above all, it gave them the visibility denied by the regime and national media. In the face of a dictatorship determined to discredit them, the Mothers' very presence was an irrefutable proof of the truth. Their anguished faces, their rounds and marches and the peculiar ways in which they made their claims were a constant denunciation that managed to break through the cloak of silence imposed by state terrorism. The rounds the Mothers made around the May Pyramid on the Plaza de Mayo, as well as the handkerchiefs on their heads, had been born out of pragmatic necessity but gradually became symbols of the struggle against the dictatorship. Through a combination of naiveté and courage, the Mothers dared to occupy a public space at the very centre of political-military power. "We became Mothers in the street, willy-nilly, becoming aware of it little by little," comments Nora Cortiñas, "the people who walked by the Plaza pretended they didn't see us, we were invisible; it was a time when people were afraid of even walking past our houses, of talking to us. Neighbours saw you and didn't dare to ask you anything. That's when you understand what state terrorism is" (Szalkowicz 2019, 73–74).

One of the communication strategies adopted by the Mothers was being present whenever an important international figure visited the country. "They wanted to be seen. It was an obsession" (Gorini 2006, 17). The first occasion when the strategy was implemented was the visit, in August 1977, of the US Undersecretary of State for Inter-American Affairs, Terence Todman, accompanied by several American journalists. The Mothers cried and waved their white handkerchiefs to attract attention. The event was reported in *Crónica*, and it was the first time a

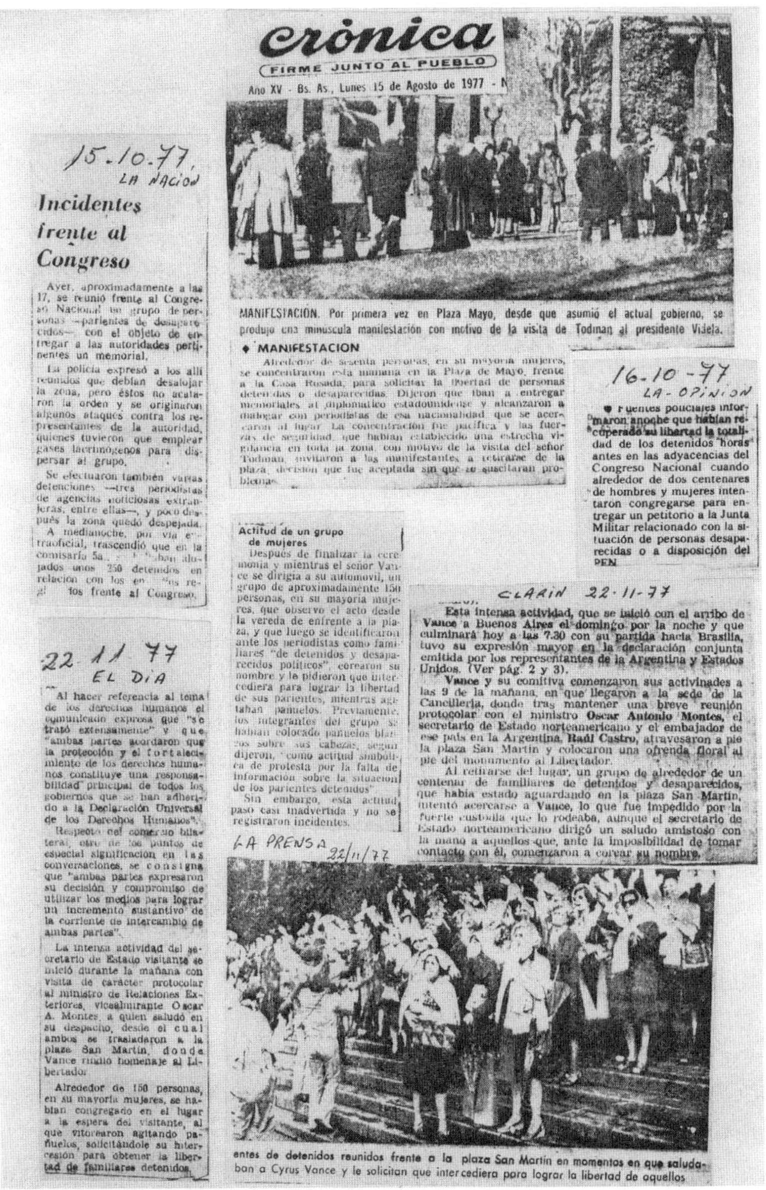

Figure 2.1 Newspaper articles related to the visit of the US Undersecretary for Inter-American Affairs, Terence Todman (August 1977) and the subsequent visit of the US Secretary of State, Cyrus Vance (November 1977).

Source: María del Rosario Cerruti Collection. Courtesy of the Memoria Abierta Archive, Buenos Aires.

photograph (Figure 2.1) of the Mothers appeared in a mass circulation paper in Argentina (Gorini 2006, 97).

This was a tremendous success and so the stratagem was repeated. The second opportunity arose with the visit of the US Secretary of State, Cyrus Vance. Hebe de Bonafini, president of the Association of the Mothers of Plaza de Mayo, later recounted:

When Cyrus Vance came, we went to Plaza San Martín. As they were laying down the wreath at the monument, we cried out and demanded that our disappeared were returned alive, and we also attracted the interest of the press. And there's a photograph of that which went around the world, in which we are seen shouting and demanding [the return] of our disappeared.

(de Bonafini 1988)

The photograph mentioned by de Bonafini was taken on 21 November 1977 by Eduardo Di Baia, a photographer for Associated Press (Figure 2.2). It was reproduced by other agencies and published in international media, including on the front page of *The Washington Post*. This was the Mothers' first international mass media success. The image is the epitome of grief: the photographed women's faces express anguish and despair. Four

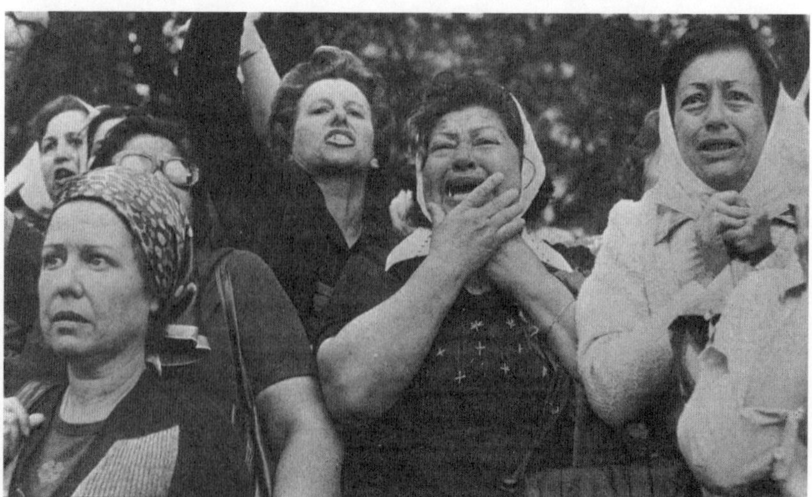

Figure 2.2 Mothers of Plaza de Mayo and other relatives of the detained-disappeared taking part in a protest during the visit of the US Secretary of State, Cyrus Vance. Buenos Aires, 21 November 1977.
Source/Author: Eduardo Di Baia/AP.

women are seen in the image, each of them reflecting in her gestures the suffering and distress they're going through: one is crying uncontrollably, one is imploring, one is captured in an infuriated shout of protest and demand, and another offers a tense, inquisitive and confrontational gaze. The photograph, reproduced in bulletins and on flyers, was used in solidarity campaigns organised by Argentine exiles. It was an image that allowed the viewer to identify with the plight of mothers searching for their children. Crucially, this image, and the emotions it evoked, bolstered the calls for solidary action abroad; an approach previously hindered by the armed struggle aspect of the resistance to the dictatorship. Due to the emphasis on the latter, many European organisations were reluctant to give their support to foreign revolutionary movements. The appearance of the Mothers removed this obstacle. Now, solidarity organisations were supporting a group of mothers who searched for their children, not an armed revolutionary group.

Di Baia preserved four other negatives, which were not reproduced at the time but which have great historical value today (Figures 2.3, 2.4 and 2.5).

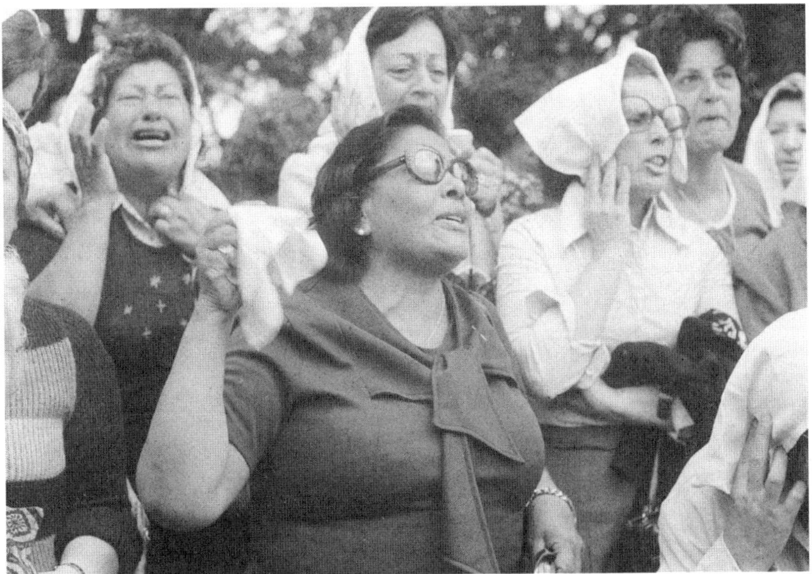

Figures 2.3, 2.4 and 2.5 Mothers of Plaza de Mayo and other relatives of the detained-disappeared taking part in a protest during the visit of the US Secretary of State, Cyrus Vance. Buenos Aires, 21 November 1977.
Source/Author: Eduardo Di Baia/AP.

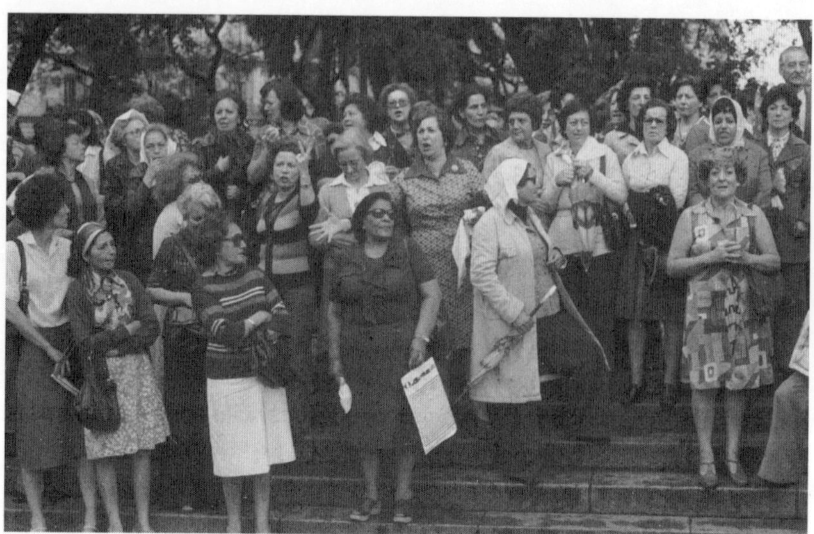

Figure 2.4

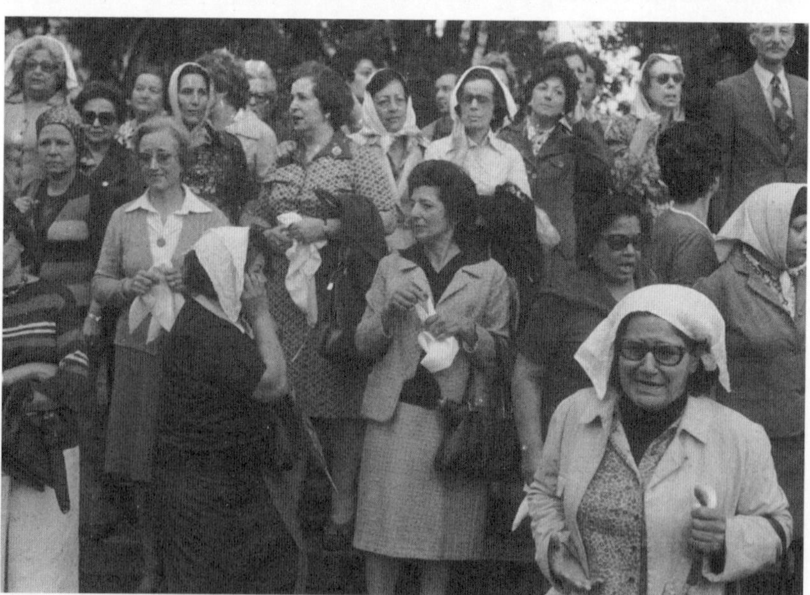

Figure 2.5

As can be seen in these images, not all the Mothers wore the handkerchief tied at the neck yet; some wore a napkin, a diaper loosely covering their head or held in their hand so that it might be more readily seen when waved.

The Mothers' presence at Plaza de Mayo and other conspicuous places gradually became even more effective and visible. However, they soon began to suffer personal consequences of this exposure: they were beaten and suffered brutal acts of repression by police officers who prevented them from demonstrating and, in some cases, detained them. Three Mothers, including the first president of the group, Azucena Villaflor de De Vincenti, suffered a tragic fate: they were abducted, tortured and dropped into the sea from a plane.[9]

The Mothers and the Photographs of their Children

The photographic documentation of the Mothers' public actions became an integral part of the demands they were making and the Mothers recognised this. Daniel García, a photographer for the Noticias Argentinas agency, recalls the moving messages of gratitude that the members of the group used to leave in the visitors' books at exhibitions, when they often saw themselves portrayed as symbols of the resistance to the dictatorship for the first time. Roberto Gómez, the director of *Acción* newspaper during the years of the dictatorship, points out:

When we talk of the struggle against the military dictatorship, a universal symbol comes up: the Mothers of Plaza de Mayo, but what were and are the Mothers of Plaza de Mayo other than a photographic image? It's impossible to separate the highest political symbol of the struggle against the dictatorship from its visual image. Those white headscarves, those sorrowful figures walking around the Plaza, are one of the photojournalists' greatest contributions. Without them, that symbol would have never been fully constructed.

(2001)

These photographs helped create and amplify the symbolic dimension of this movement, as Nora Cortiñas remarks:

Photographs helped us to identify ourselves as a group, we always encouraged the presence of journalists in our activities and called the newspapers to let them know about the things we were going to do [...] The photographers' role was of great help at a time when you couldn't put into words what the real facts represented. The images of repression in the streets, the soldiers with their guns provoking us, all of that helped make the tragedy we were going through here known to the whole world. We've always been grateful to photojournalism. Each year, they included in their exhibitions information about how the human rights issue was evolving.

(2009, personal communication)

Several photojournalists point out that, during those years, they documented the actions of the Mothers and other relatives by taking their pictures in secret, sometimes in direct opposition to the instructions issued by the newspapers or media agencies they worked for, often at serious personal risk.[10] When these photographs eventually appeared in the media, they were not only made available to a wider public but also seen by the Mothers themselves, and, in turn, impacted the Mothers' self-perception.

But photographic representations of the Mothers weren't the only images that played a crucial part in their struggle. Almost from the very beginning of their search, the Mothers and other relatives of the disappeared carried with them photographs of their children, husbands, grandchildren, etc. This act returned to the disappeared a face, an identity, a history and a social tie that rescued them from the invisibility they had been condemned to. Inevitably, the images photographers took of the Mothers often also featured the images of their disappeared children. The photographs thus exposed the state's attempt at double concealment – that of the disappeared and that of their relatives looking for them. They refuted it with double visibility.

The nature of the photographs employed by the Mothers to increase their public visibility was particularly effective. They ranged from images initially taken for different purposes and in other contexts: ID portraits, school photographs or images of family gatherings, such as weddings, baptisms and birthdays. These photographs made the disappearance visible and allowed the Mothers to reconstruct the identity of the disappeared person, to give them a face and recover them in their personal, familial, historical context. Da Silva Catela remarks that "while the category of the disappeared encompassed all individualities, without distinguishing sex, age, trajectory, photographs made it possible to show an individual existence, a biography. Image allows the formation of the notion of a person, making them come out of death's anonymity, in order to recover an identity and a life story" (2009, 341). In their different uses and formats, these photographs have since become one the main forms of representation of disappearance.

From its beginnings in the 19th century, photography has always been an effective antidote to oblivion. Portraits – one of photography's most widespread applications – have been historically employed to vivify the dead, to remember those family members that passed away, to establish a link between life and death. Therefore, the use the Mothers made of their children's photographs was based on previous traditions to which they now added a political dimension. They used photography not only to remember, but, essentially, to search for their disappeared children, to denounce their disappearance and make them re-appear in the public space. The same pictures were later taken to the meetings with the survivors of CDCs in the hope that they might shed some light on the fate of fellow inmates (da Silva Catela 2009, 343). Also relatively early on, photos became an instrument of international denunciation. Exiles, survivors and human rights organisations that supported the cause circulated the photographs of the disappeared, and of the appropriated children, around the world. Simply as a direct result of their practical use, those photographs became an instrument of political counterpropaganda that denounced the clandestine actions of a terrorist state which not only abducted people but also denied their disappearance.[11] What's of particular interest here is the use of these images by the Mothers in public: attaching the images to their own bodies, hanging photos around their necks, or carrying them as placards or banners. Those pictures allowed the Mothers to carry their children with them, to somehow have them close by again, and to show them as still alive.[12]

However, the Mothers' attitude towards the photographs of their children was not homogenous. The different relationships they established with photography were marked by the same political disagreements that affected the movement and that finally caused its split into two factions in 1986: Mothers of Plaza de Mayo – Founding Line; and the Association of the Mothers of Plaza de Mayo, led by Hebe de Bonafini. Initially, all the Mothers carried the images and names of their own children. After the split, the Mothers under de Bonafini's leadership decided that they would stop individualising the photographs of the disappeared – they did the same with the headscarves, stopping the practice of embroidering the name of the disappeared person on them – and proposed that each Mother carry any placard, not necessarily one with the photograph of her own child. De Bonafini comments on the issue:

One day we met and had a long talk and said that what we should do was to socialise motherhood and become everybody's mothers [...] We took off the child's name from the headscarf and no longer carried the photograph with their name. [...] So that, when asked by someone, the mother could say: 'Yes, we are mothers of the thirty thousand' [...] When we went to the Plaza we would exchange our children's placards. I started with that idea so that each mother could realise that socialising motherhood is such an amazing act of love, with a multiplying effect.

(Di Marco 2006)

In contrast, Nora Cortiñas points out that, for her, using her own children's photographs with the corresponding identification was crucial:

During the first marches, when we would go with the picture and the name, we discovered that many schoolmates of our children who, in those early days when we began going to the Plaza still didn't even know that their schoolmates were disappeared, joined us [...] Sometimes they [the schoolmates] only knew them [the disappeared] by their nickname, so when they saw their picture and name, they found out [that they were missing]. The same thing happened with the name on the headscarf. That's how they identified us, they knew: this is so and so's mother. And the photograph played a fundamental role in this.

(2009, personal communication)

Cortiñas also recalls the origins of the idea of carrying the photographs as placards and banners:

One day, a father who was working with us and who was always thinking about things to do, Santiago Mellibovsky, came up with the idea of reproducing every photo and enlarging them (he had a small photography studio in his house). And we did it [...] The first time we went out with the enlarged photos it was a tremendous shock. My husband [...] broke down when he saw the column approaching; we were marching along Diagonal Street, with the photos bigger than us. It was really overwhelming.

(2009, personal communication)

Santiago Mellibovsky and Matilde Saidler de Mellibovsky – the parents of Graciela, a young economist disappeared in 1976 – were active members of CELS (El Centro de Estudios Legales y Sociales) [Centre for Legal and Social Studies], of the Jewish Movement for Human Rights and of the Mothers of Plaza de Mayo – Founding Line. The collection they built consists of 3,238 high resolution photographs of the detained-disappeared, compiled over thirty years (Figure 2.6). These images make up the long banner unfurled by human right organisations in the demonstrations held every 24 March in Buenos Aires.

Santiago Mellibovsky, who, in his small photographic studio, reproduced, developed and enlarged each photo brought to him by the Mothers, recounted the profound emotion that overcame him when, with each new photograph he developed, he saw one of the disappeared "appear" in the processing tray (Cortiñas 2009, personal communication). Between February and April 1983, the Mothers and other relatives began affixing those photographs to a piece of cardboard and mounting them onto wooden T-shaped structures which served as a handle, thus transforming them into placards. This idea created a powerful visual resource that,

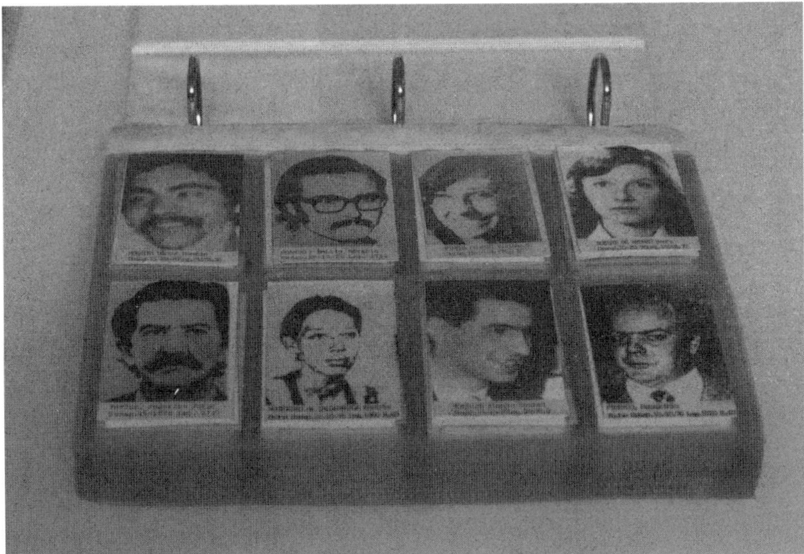

Figure 2.6 Archival photographs of those detained-disappeared by the dictatorship used to make the banners created by Santiago Mellibovsky.
Source: CELS Collection – Santiago Mellibovsky. Courtesy of the National Memory Archive, Buenos Aires.

brandished in the hands of the Mothers and other relatives, managed to reverse, at least partially, the invisibility generated by the disappearances. Those black-and-white, ever-young faces are part of a material dimension of memory and have become paradigmatic icons of disappearance. Ana Longoni writes that:

The simple device of the banners had a powerful impact and proved very effective, and they've been carried in human rights demonstrations again and again ever since [...] Mellibovsky's idea marks a crucial turning-point, a watershed between personal use and public reach: the photos detach themselves from the intimate (family) circle to become a visual device available to the crowd. The presence of those who were absent rose powerfully and touchingly to a height from where many more could feel "addressed" and "looked at." This transition implies two important questions, one of a practical nature (the existence or creation by human rights organisations of a, more or less centralised, archive of photographs of the disappeared), and another that entails the definition of a visual policy (the incisive awareness of the impact that those faces marching through the crowd, or above it, would generate among the witnesses).

(2013)

Todorov (2000) claims that identity is constructed through the images of the past that individuals have at their disposal, whereas Stuart Hall argues that identity "is always constructed through memory, fantasy, narrative and myth" (2000, 704). In the hands of the relatives of the disappeared, photography became a medium of an identity narrative, a body of irreplaceable images for recreating the relationships between mothers, fathers and children; between comrades and friends. Those photographs went far beyond the family and private sphere to become visible presences in public spaces, and in that displacement, they managed to reverse one of the objectives of the military regime. The photographs of the disappeared, reinserted into the public sphere by their families, were not only a powerful instrument useful in neutralising the effacement and testifying to the absence, but also a way to give the disappeared back social ties, a face, a name, and the reasons for their political struggle that the regime had tried to obliterate. This new use of the photographs carried as placards by the Mothers and other family members also gave rise to a visual display that photojournalists deftly capitalised on and helped to expand (e.g. Figures 2.7, 2.8, and 2.9).

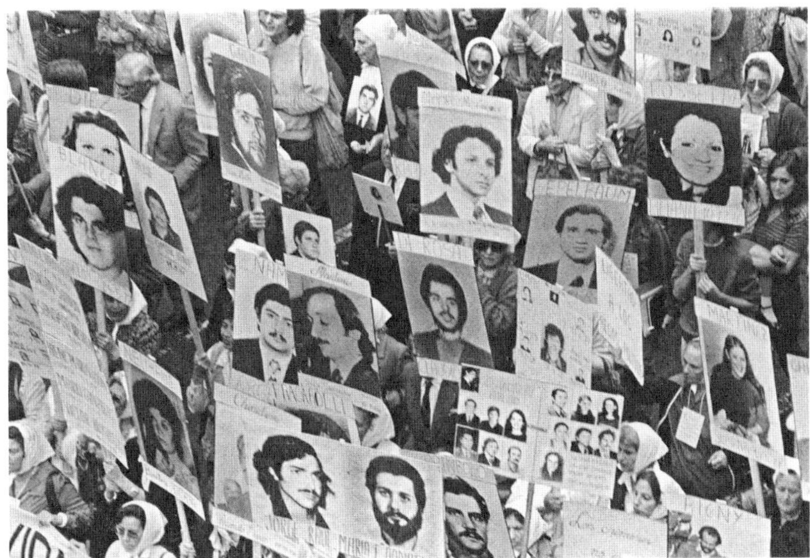

Figure 2.7 Plaza de Mayo, Buenos Aires, 4 May 1983.
Source/Author: Silvio Zuccheri/CIFHA.

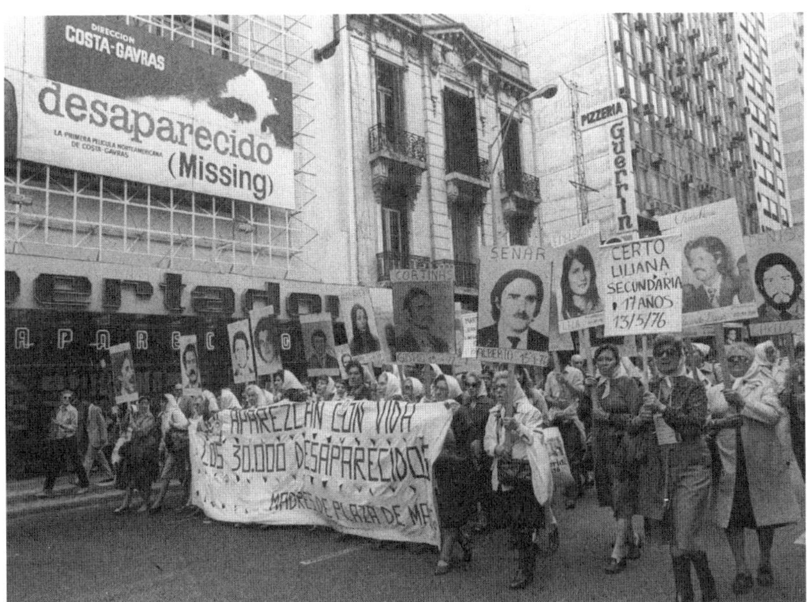

Figure 2.8 A march with banners through Buenos Aires, 1983.
Source/Author: Dani Yako.

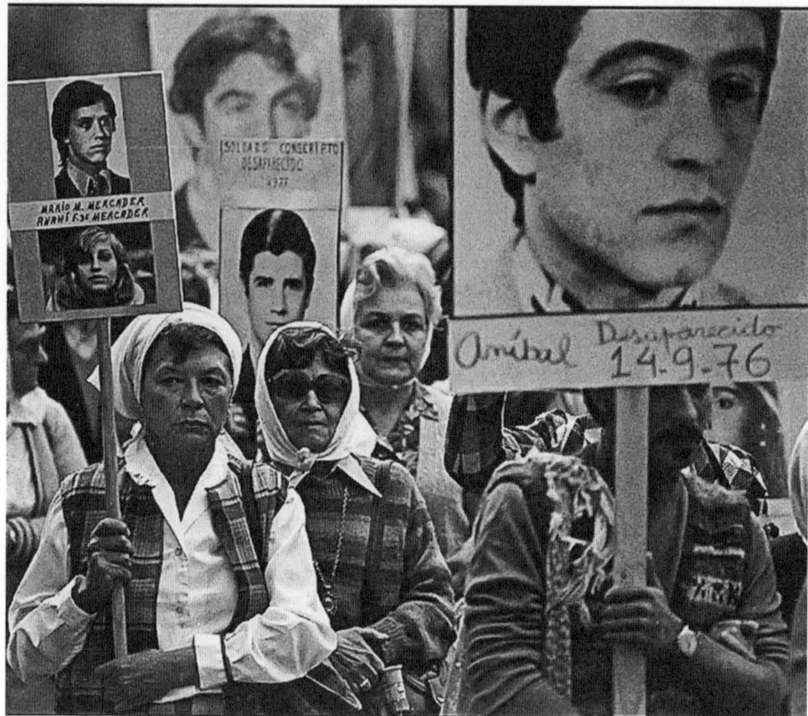

Figure 2.9 A march with banners. Plaza de Mayo, Buenos Aires, April 1983.
Source/Author: Daniel García.

Giorgio Agamben (2007) examines the actions of political subjects and the ways in which these are mediated by imagination and representation. He queries the political capacity of images, understanding it as the activation of a dialogical process between the subjects' reflections and their environment. In the case of the disappeared, the fracture between body, name and identity necessarily implied, on the part of the relatives, a search for a reconstruction. Photographs served as a support for re-establishing the devastated identities. The political capacity of images in the hands of a mobilised group expanded their power and impact.

The Mothers and the World Cup

Alongside the use of repressive policies, the Argentine Armed Forces carried out numerous operations aimed at building social consensus.

Probably the most important and successful one was the hosting of the 1978 World Cup. As a way of countering what they called the "anti-Argentine campaign" launched abroad (in reality, international denunciations about human rights violations committed in the country), the military junta used the event, which they dubbed "The Cup of Peace," as an attempt to gain legitimisation from the international community and as a political propaganda operation to deny human rights violations.

In France, the Committee for the Boycott of the World Cup in Argentina (COBA) was created. The slogan of this initiative, which extended to other parts of Europe, was: "Will the World Cup planned for June 1978 in Argentina take place amid concentration camps?" The campaign called for a boycott of the World Cup hosted by a country where human rights were systematically violated. The Argentine dictatorship hadn't been repudiated internationally as strongly as the regime headed by Pinochet in Chile, in part due to the different characteristics of the coups in both countries and the governments they toppled. In the Argentine case, two other factors made international condemnation problematic. One was the serious internal conflicts that divided the Peronist party. Another was the already-mentioned difficulty that European institutions faced in expressing solidarity with revolutionary organisations that supported armed struggle. Therefore, the World Cup boycott campaign proved instrumental in denouncing and raising awareness about the human rights situation in Argentina.

For the Mothers, the World Cup was a fresh opportunity to attract the attention of the international media and the tourists who visited the country to participate in the event. One of the actions the Mothers settled on was to simply walk along Florida Street, a crowded pedestrian area in downtown Buenos Aires, carrying little handwritten signs with the phrase: "My child has disappeared." They alerted a few photojournalists about the day and time of the planned walk. Mario Manusia, who at the time worked for *Atlántida*, received the tip off and went to cover the Mothers' action. At one point, two armed men in civilian clothes tried to kidnap one of the youngsters who accompanied the Mothers. In the ensuing tussle, Marta Vázquez, one of the Mothers, tried to, successfully, save the boy and prevent him being taken away. Manusia managed to take two photographs of the incident, when he was suddenly hit from the back and fell. The armed men asked him for the camera. Manusia carried two cameras and surrendered the one that didn't have the photographs he had just taken, while he remained lying on the floor, covering the other camera with his body. Once the men vanished, Manusia rushed to develop the photographs; two photographs (Figures 2.10 and 2.11) that recorded an attempted kidnapping in the street by two armed civilians and, at the same time, captured what the Mothers were going through (Manusia 2011, personal communication).

Although eventually historically important, Manusia's photographs were not published at the time. What viewers all over the world did see, however, and what had a massive impact in the media, was a TV interview by a Dutch journalist, Jan Van der Putten. Van der Putten – a correspondent in Latin America for different Dutch and international media

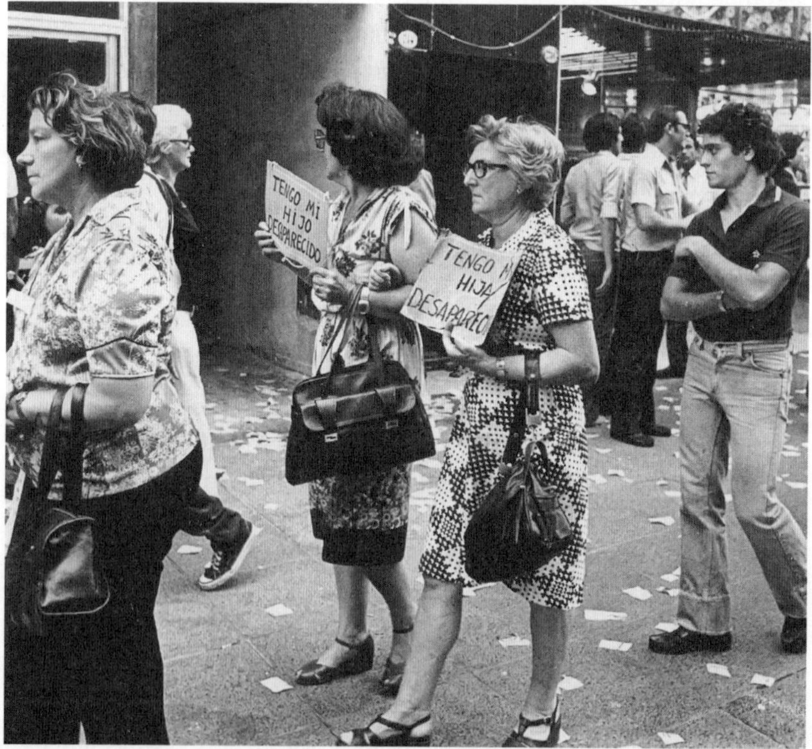

Figures 2.10 and 2.11 A demonstration of Mothers of Plaza de Mayo on Florida Street, Buenos Aires, 28 December 1979.
Source/Author: Mario Manusia.

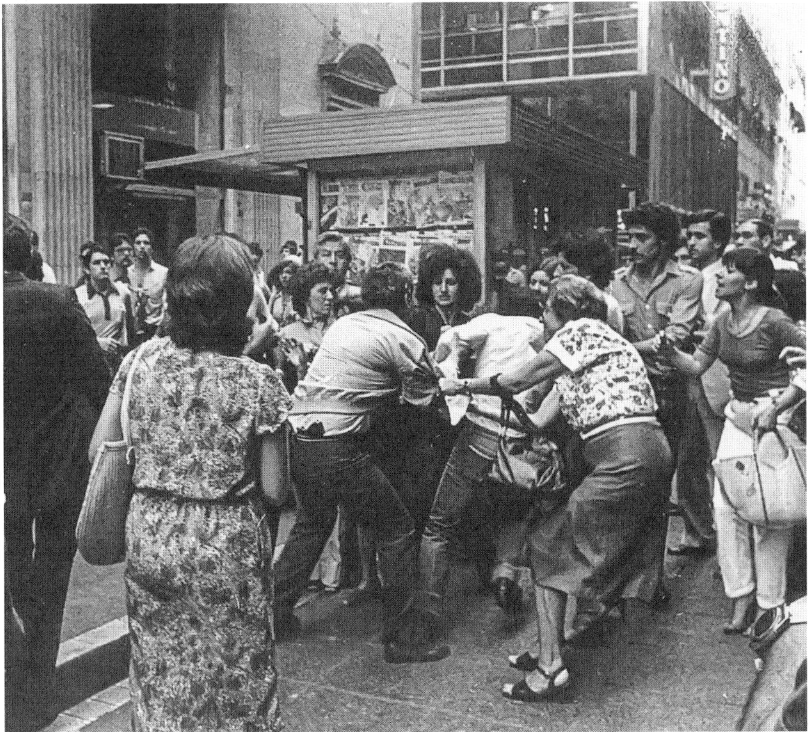

Figure 2.11

between 1971 and 1987 – had left Argentina in 1976, fearing for his life, and returned two years later for the World Cup, using it as a pretext, but determined to show what was really happening in the country. He was officially accredited with free access to the stadiums, but he did not attend any soccer matches. In fact, he watched the final on television at a Buenos Aires café (González Cezer 2020). On the World Cup's opening day, the Mothers went to Plaza de Mayo, like they did every Thursday. While the rest of the country was anxiously awaiting the opening ceremony, they decided they would walk around the Plaza as usual. On the same day, Van der Putten also went to the Plaza with a Dutch television team. The city was totally deserted. The government had declared a public holiday to allow everybody to watch the opening ceremony. Curiously enough, the event was scheduled to take place at exactly the same time as the Mothers' weekly round. Van der Putten interviewed the Mothers on that day. In the footage, we see him approaching the Mothers and asking: "What's the matter, madam?"[13]

The Mothers start to answer all at once in a spontaneous, bewildered, ad-hoc manner, without prepared speeches, without hierarchies; their voices overlapping one another: "We want to be told where our children are, whether they are alive or dead." Van der Putten then asks them: "How many are you?" "Thousands", they answer. Suddenly, one of the Mothers, Marta Moreira de Alconada, who has so far been listening at the back, steps closer to the microphone and takes over. She had had no news of her son, Domingo Roque Alconada Moreira, for over a year. He had been kidnapped in December 1976, while studying law at the University of la Plata. He was a member of the Peronist University Youth and twenty-three when he was kidnapped. Marta gradually comes closer to the microphone, holding a small slip of cardboard in her left hand. As she starts to speak, the camera zooms in on the note that reads "We want to know where our children are." Marta asks her fellow Mothers to let her speak and delivers a speech: "We just want to know where our children are, alive or dead [...]. They say that the Argentines abroad are giving a false image of Argentina, we who live in Argentina can assure you that there are thousands and thousands of families who are suffering much grief, much anguish, much despair, sorrow and sadness, because they do not tell us where our children are, we know nothing about them. They have taken away from us the most precious thing a mother has: her child." The Dutch television camera then takes a close-up shot of the list of the disappeared the Mothers have brought closer for the journalists to see and returns to Marta's face. She continues: "Anguish, because we don't know whether they are ill, whether they are cold, whether they are hungry. We know nothing. And despair, sir, because we no longer know who to turn to, consulates, embassies, ministries, churches. They all have closed their doors on us. That's why we implore you, we implore you, you are our last hope. Please, help us, help us, please. You are our last hope." Marta makes a great effort to keep on talking; she wants to cry but holds back her tears; her voice changes, breaks. The scene is extremely moving. Marta's phrases still reverberate in our memory in spite of the decades that have elapsed since they were uttered.

The Dutch television decided to broadcast the World Cup and the interview with the Mothers of Plaza de Mayo on a split screen.[14] The interview had a massive impact and, the following Thursday, correspondents from other European countries also went to Plaza de Mayo to talk to the Mothers. The interview made the Mothers known to the world almost overnight. During the Mothers' 2,087th march, when they were accompanied by a delegation of the 1978 Dutch football national team, Hebe de Bonafini thanked the players and commended their decision not to attend the ceremony organised by the dictatorship after the final game they lost against Argentina, pointing out that: "We were a very small group of desperate women, with our three best mothers murdered, raped, tortured and dropped alive into the river. Nobody knew us, nobody talked to us. From that moment, the world knew us" (Paredes 2018).

This interview represented a quantitative leap in the Mothers' international visibility and in the world's awareness of the human rights violations committed by the Argentine dictatorship. It was a great media success. While the dictatorship had organised the World Cup as a self-legitimation propaganda campaign, the Mothers' presence and voice were enough to break through the iron wall of censorship and make their children's disappearance internationally visible. As Bram Daanen points out: "The World Cup was crucial. During the competition, the Mothers became known [...] this event radically changed the solidarity campaigns" (2021).

Images of Resistance, Will, Perseverance, Sorrow and Grief

In the final part of this chapter, I would like to briefly focus on the last years of the dictatorship, between 1982 and 1983, when the Mothers were photographed by dozens of Argentine and foreign photojournalists during marches and public actions. The resulting photographs, published with increasing frequency in local and international media, and showcased during the Exhibitions of Argentine Photojournalism, were a key element of a visual identity that gradually turned into a symbol. The Mothers used these images in their activities, sent them to exile groups, and included them in their own publications. The Mothers' grief, resistance, way of dressing and presenting themselves, as well as their activities, became the clear focus of the photographs. Taken with a solidary and empathetic gaze, the images constituted a counternarrative to the "mad, subversive, anti-Argentine" stereotype the dictatorship used to demonise the Mothers in the country and abroad.

Recently declassified documents prove the control the dictatorship exerted over the Mothers, whose activities were under constant surveillance. The information thus obtained was then used as the basis for repressive and psychological warfare. A document declassified in 2021, entitled *Special Report on the Mothers of Plaza de Mayo*, compiled by SIDE (La Secretaría de Inteligencia del Estado) [The Secretariat of State Intelligence] in February 1983, concluded that:

Within the sphere of OOSS (Solidarity Organisations), the Mothers of Plaza de Mayo have been acquiring – since 1977 – growing prominence, to be finally regarded, by late 1982, as the most influential and well-known entity thanks to a series of characteristics: they have exploited the emotions and feelings associated with *the image of the helpless mother persecuted by the powers of the state*.

(Ginzberg and Bertoia 2020; emphasis added)

The document added that [the Mothers] "have had the perseverance to make a weekly appearance at Plaza de Mayo, demonstrating internal cohesion, managing to interest indifferent publics, sensitising them in support of their claims" and "they have contributed with their constant preaching to the destabilisation of the PRN [The National Reorganisation Process] and to the questioning of the Armed Forces about their actions in the anti-subversive struggle" (Ginzberg and Bertoia 2020). The report clearly shows that the intelligence apparatus of the military dictatorship itself recognised that the Mothers' actions had contributed to the destabilisation of the regime.

Moreover, the persecution the Mothers suffered was visible in images, increasingly circulated from 1982, which, effectively, served to broaden the social base for their claims. An analysis of the photographs from that period allows us to identify three recurring representational axes: 1) Resistance to Repression, 2) Will and Perseverance, 3) Sorrow and Grief.[15] A selection of examples of the images falling into these categories is presented here, alongside the words of some of the photographers who took them, to contextualise the relationship that existed between the bearers of the message and those whose work amplified it.

The Resistance to Repression part of this taxonomy includes photographs in which the Mothers – while pictured with expressions of sorrow, fear and innocence on their faces – appear to be confronting the mounted police that the dictatorship employed to intimidate and suppress them. In the two photographs reproduced here (Figures 2.12 and 2.13), prominence

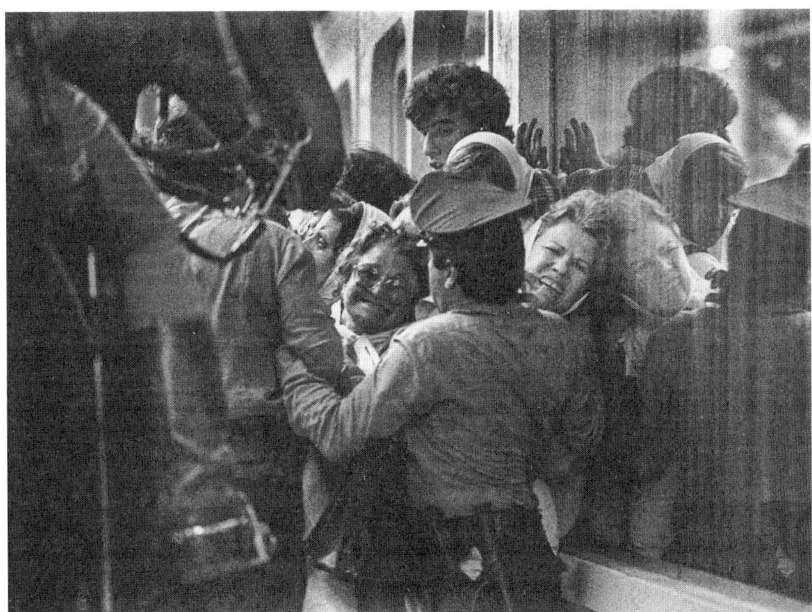

Figure 2.12 The March of Resistance, Buenos Aires, 10 December 1982.
Source/Author: Daniel García.

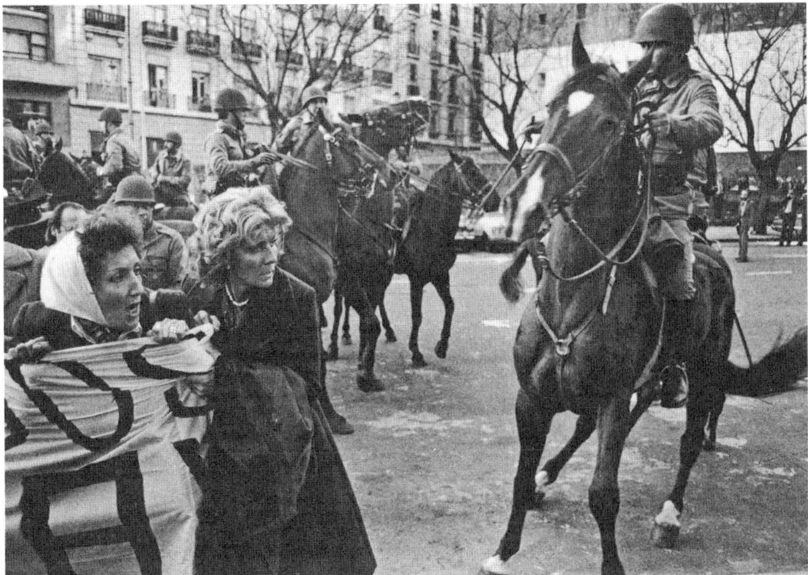

Figure 2.13 The March for Life, Buenos Aires, 5 October 1982.
Source/Author: Eduardo Longoni.

is given to the horses in the foreground. This compositional choice results in clear messaging: no matter how overwhelming the repression, the Mothers will confront it. The first image (Figure 2.12) is by Daniel García, taken during the March of Resistance, on 10 December 1982. The Mother seen reflected in the windowpane is Lilia Orfanó. García recalls that a police cordon had been set up earlier that day to prevent the Mothers from entering the Plaza. Aware that the Mothers had decided to try to break through, García placed himself behind the cordon in order to shoot the Mothers head on. As a result of this photo, García established a personal relationship with Orfanó, and subsequently carried out photographic work related to her life and her disappeared children. "I cannot speak for everybody, but some of the relationships were of a solidary, ideological, and affective nature. We ended up building up an inevitable emotional relationship" (García 2009, personal communication).

The second image (Figure 2.13) was taken by Eduardo Longoni during the 5 October 1982 demonstration. In the photo, two Mothers try to protect each other as a mounted police officer charges at them. One Mother appears to be wrapping herself up in the banner for protection. Some more police officers on horseback can be seen in the background. This kind of direct engagement with the political reality of the time, the decision to be close to the Mothers at the risk of police repression, is a recurring theme in the testimonies of several photojournalists active in those years. Longoni, for instance, remarks:

The Mothers of Plaza de Mayo, with their headscarves and the marks of the disappeared in the wrinkles of their faces, fought at government offices, in their homes, in the streets. On the day of the March for Life, they wanted to reach their Plaza, but a retreating power wanted to prevent it. At the corner of Diagonal Norte and Piedras, they confronted the mounted police with a sign and with their dignity. [...] I needed to be within range of the policemen's batons, almost under the steaming snouts of their horses, that's where they were, trying to keep afloat. Only from that closeness could a photo emerge that showed their pain, their impotence; an image of their rage.

(Longoni cit. in Cerolini and Reynoso 2006, 181)

The second representational theme – Will and Perseverance – is strongly present in images of the time related to different manners of fighting and resistance. For instance, in another one of Daniel García's photographs (Figure 2.14), the Mothers are standing in the rain, with their feet under water. The photographer recollects: "It was a Thursday. I remember

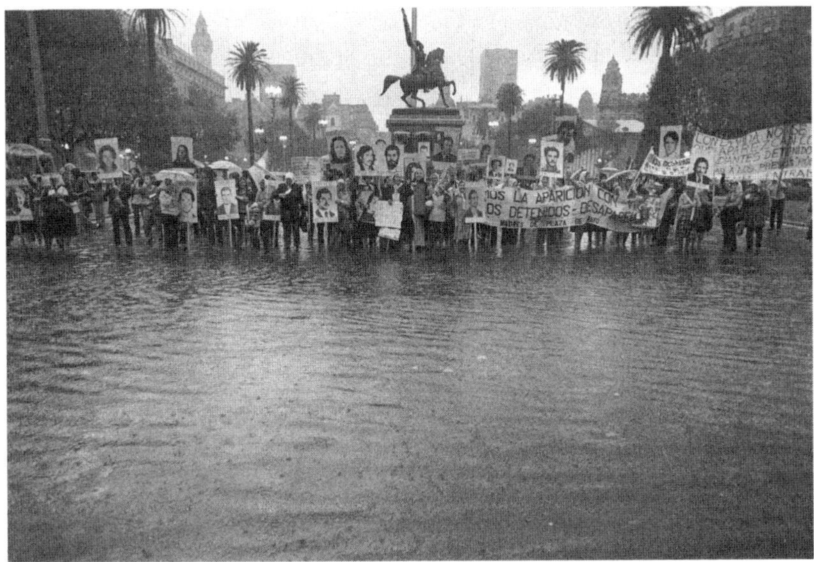

Figure 2.14 The Mothers of Plaza de Mayo standing in the rain, Buenos Aires, 28 April 1983.
Source/Author: Daniel García.

it was the only time in my life that I saw Plaza de Mayo covered with water [...] Maybe the military had blocked the drains for the Plaza to get flooded, so the Mothers couldn't go." García goes on to recount:

I had bought [new] shoes that Thursday morning, 1983, at a famous shoe shop on Florida Street [...] Like almost every Thursday, I went to Plaza de Mayo to be there just before half past three in the afternoon. Although the situation was more relaxed, we still preserved some instincts from the time of the "hard dictatorship," and we were used to going a little earlier to appraise the atmosphere. [...] I looked in two directions: forward, [I saw] all of them [the Mothers] without any protection or shelter, making their claims before a power that did not listen to them. Shouting out for the return of their disappeared. [...] There was no one else in the entire Plaza, just a handful of journalists. The problem was that [to take the photo I wanted] I had to get close enough. [...] There is a photo taken by Pichi Martínez in which I am seen walking towards the Mothers holding the camera with the wide-angle lens on it, calculating the distance, with the water up to my ankles. [...] Ever since that afternoon, I've asked myself many times why I decided to step into the puddle. The question was not money [spent on the new shoes], the question was whether "stepping into the puddle" was committing oneself, whether or not it meant telling what was happening in a better way, and getting a more convincing photograph.

(2016)

In Adriana Lestido's image, taken on 25 November 1982, a Mother and her daughter fuse in the same screaming gesture of rage (Figure 2.15). It is the husband/father who is missing. The little girl sports a white headscarf, similar to her mother's. There is a clear metaphor in the image: the fight will continue, passing on from one generation to the next. This is an example of an image that speaks of persistence, of grief transformed into perseverance. Lestido was twenty-four when she took the photograph. She had started to work as a photojournalist for *La Voz* only a week before. She recounts:

As the demonstration began, the little girl who was with her mother burst into tears and the photographers rushed towards them to take pictures. It kind of embarrassed me to take pictures of the little girl crying, but at one point the mother lifted her up in her arms, the girl stopped crying and then I took the photograph. She is an atypical Mother of Plaza de Mayo, because she is demanding her husband's re-appearance, not her child's, and the girl is demanding her father's re-appearance, that absent man that has somehow been the central axis of all my work.

(Bossini 2018)

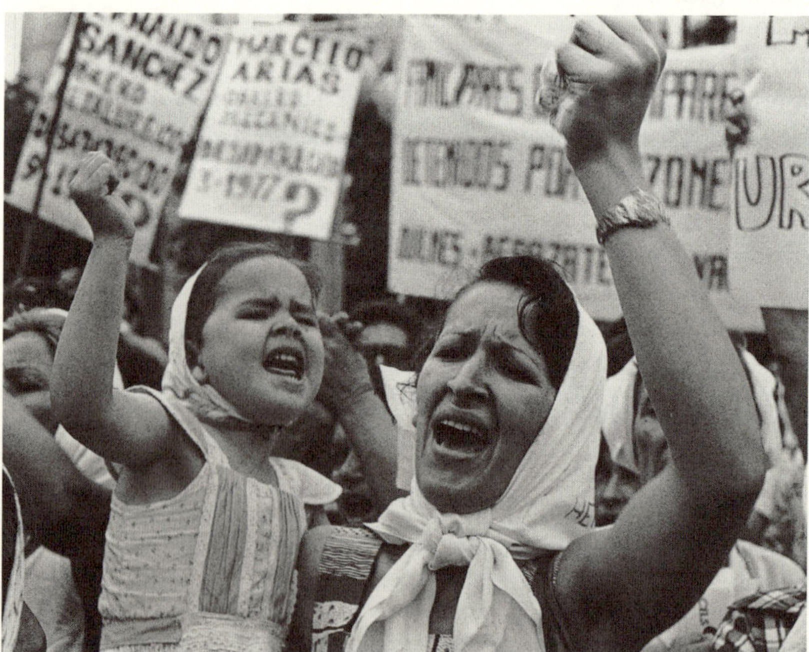

Figure 2.15 Mother and daughter in Plaza de Mayo, Avellaneda, 25 November 1982. Source/Author: Adriana Lestido.

Another photograph, taken in 1982 by Omar Torres, shows six Mothers seen from the back, with their headscarves on, as they walk towards the Government House. It was published on Monday, 4 October 1982, in *La Voz* to illustrate an article about the demands of human rights organisations. *Clarín* published it again in April 1983.[16] Torres recounts:

That afternoon, the Mothers, as always, had walked around the May Pyramid demanding [to know] the whereabouts of their children. Once the round was over, they talked among themselves, and when I asked them what they were going to do, they told me that they intended to deliver a denunciation document to the Pink House. Then, they began to walk towards the building, and I realised that I had never seen a photograph of them taken from behind, walking towards the Pink House. The sun favoured me, for as it shone on the white headscarves it highlighted them against the architecture of the Government [Pink] House.

(Bianco 2007)

Two significant details stand out in this statement. On the one hand, the photographer talks to the Mothers, who inform him in advance of their intended movements, so that he can plan his photograph. On the other, Torres chooses the angle, measures the light, selects a framing he'd never seen before. But he also remarks on how the sun, as it shone on the headscarves, highlighted the Mothers against the Pink House's façade. His gaze creates a synthesis, providing the necessary metaphor. The headscarves, with all their vulnerability but accompanied by the bright shining sun, confront the structure that embodies the power of the terrorist state.

The last group of images in this taxonomy centres on the representational theme of Sorrow and Grief. The first example is an image by Pablo Lasansky, a photographer from Noticias Argentinas (Figure 2.16). The crying Mother, the only one whose face is clearly identifiable, is surrounded by anonymous men wearing hard, black helmets – faceless symbols of an oppressive power. In contrast, the Mother is wearing her white headscarf, soft and tender, and drying her tears while still holding the banner. The image is made up of oppositions: frailty/hardness, light/shadow, sharpness/blurriness, identifiable face/namelessness.

Daniel García's photograph (Figure 2.17), on the other hand, while also an image of grief, shows this emotion accompanied by solidarity and love. The crying Mother, almost in a prayer-like pose, is being comforted by a woman who kisses her tenderly while firmly holding a placard that

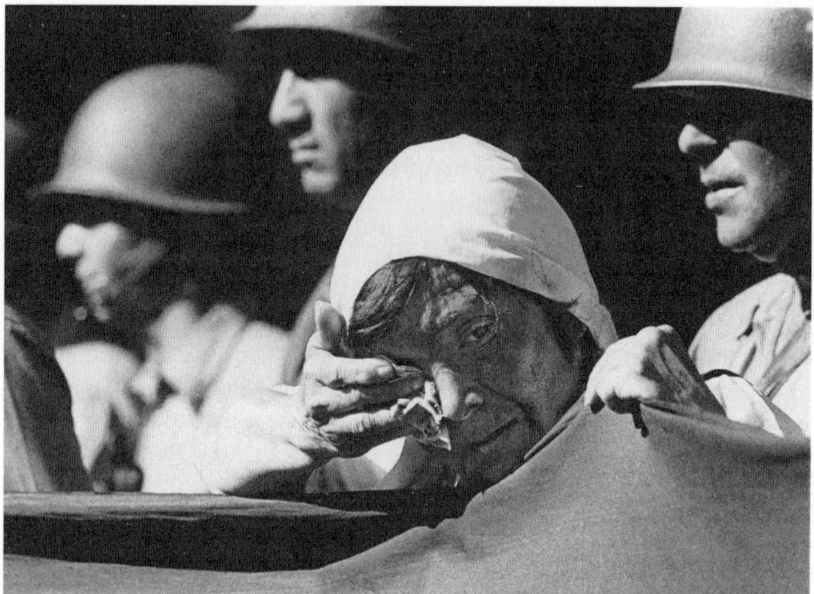

Figure 2.16 The March of Resistance, Buenos Aires, 21 September 1983.
Source/Author: Pablo Lasansky.

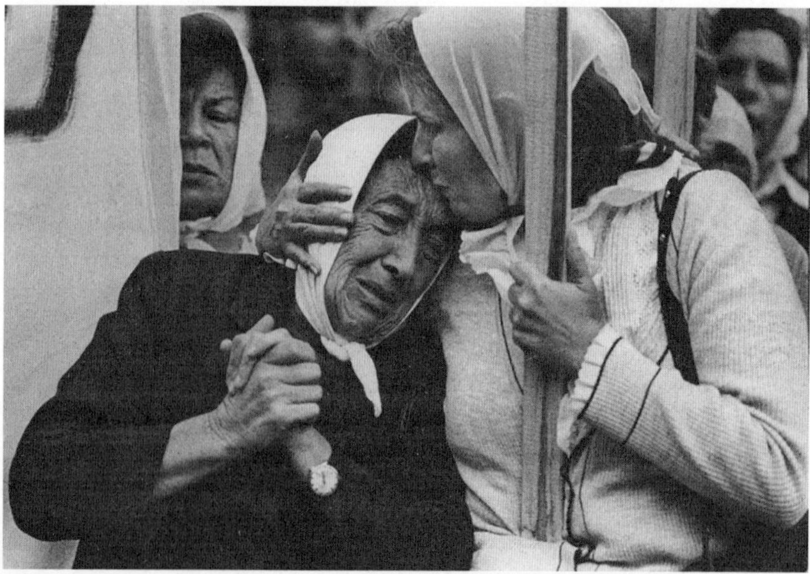

Figure 2.17 Plaza de Mayo, Buenos Aires, 1983.
Source/Author: Daniel García.

most likely bears the face of a disappeared child. The image signals tenderness and suffering, but also perseverance and solidarity.

It is important to note that while photography was used to amplify the Mothers' claims, it was also used against them. In 2008, the archive of the former Intelligence Bureau of the Buenos Aires Province Police [La Dirección de Inteligencia de la Policía de la Provincia de Buenos Aires] was discovered. Under the heading 'Subject: Mothers of terrorists,' came to light the reports about the Mothers compiled by that office. The Provincial Commission for Memory later organised an exhibition entitled *Stolen Images, Recovered Images* with some of the photographs kept in the archive. Among them were photographs of each of the Mothers, as well as images of their walks at the Plaza and other activities. In one of the images, a group of Mothers is pictured coming out of the Quilmes Cathedral. The photograph was taken in December 1981, after a hunger strike. The figures in the photo have numbers written above them. On an attached sheet, each number is accompanied with a Mother's name. Many photographers relate that it was not uncommon in those years, when documenting the Mothers' struggle, to come across alleged "colleagues" – in reality the regime's stooges.

Most of the women searching for their children were housewives who had no professional training or experience in political militancy. A certain underestimation on the part of the dictatorship and a belated recognition of the significance of their movement would later allow the emergence of what would eventually become one of the main pockets of resistance and opposition to military power in Argentina. "The delay in perceiving the Mothers as a political force also had its roots in the very essence of these women: neither did they, in their beginnings, conceive of themselves as a political movement" (Gorini 2006, 26). According to the dominant, sociocultural imaginary, every mother has the responsibility to protect her child and strive to secure their safety and well-being, and this was precisely what these women, who, for the most part, shared this conception of an ideal family, did.[17] How, then, could anyone question them? These Mothers did nothing but fulfil their duty, a duty that, moreover, coincided with the dominant conception of what a model family should be.

The main feature of the Mothers' image was precisely that, their maternal role and duty. Simple women, housewives who indefatigably walked around in sandals or low-heeled shoes, carrying a handbag or a shopping bag, and who were seen, with all their fragility and innocence, confronting policemen on horseback, surrounded by armed soldiers, marching together in the rain, arm-in-arm. Women crying and comforting one another. Women resisting. The image of the Mothers, which the professional gaze and work of photojournalists helped to circulate, inspired empathy, aroused compassion, promoted solidarity and provoked indignation against the regime, even in those who ignored the real dimension of the government's campaign of repression.

Conclusion

Not all the mothers of disappeared children became part of the Mothers of Plaza de Mayo. In fact, only a small number formed that group. Most did not go beyond the boundaries of individual search. Helplessness, the impossibility of assuming a new social role, denial, illness, death and suicide were in fact the predominant reactions to what happened to them (Gorini 2006, 25; Melicchio 2019, 163). In some cases, they accepted their children's disappearance as a "punishment" imposed by the dictatorship. Nevertheless, the idea of the fighting Mothers is the pervading image that dominates the period. The circulation of highly symbolic photographs taken by photojournalists helped create this image which would subsequently influence the movement and the view the Mothers began to have of themselves.

When the Mothers started to come out and show themselves in their walks at the Plaza, with their heads covered in white and carrying their children's photographs, a visual display emerged that was later amplified and enhanced by the work of photojournalists who shot highly symbolic, moving photographs. In turn, through these images, the Argentine photojournalists could show their creative potential and professionalism that had been thwarted and stifled by the 1976 coup. This helped a whole generation of young photographers in eroding the dictatorship that had persecuted, oppressed and censored them. As the dictatorship quickly perceived the impact of these photographs, photojournalists became a target of repression during public demonstrations.

For the Mothers, these photographs were an instrument of visibility that enabled them to reach out to a broader segment of the population, enhance people's identification with their cause, expand their denunciations internationally and undermine the policy of concealment implemented by the dictatorship. This series of events – production of photographs, their circulation in the media and people's recognition of the events portrayed in the images – is what allowed those same photographs to transform into a testimony that helped propagate knowledge about and raise awareness of human rights violations in Argentina under state terrorism. The images were a key element in gaining support for the Mothers' claims. Their faces, their sorrow, their solidarity, their resistance, in short, their images were the counterpoint to the "mad and subversive women" label the regime tried to pin on them. The photographs were a powerful communication tool that contributed to spreading the Mothers' search and their claims for truth and justice, transforming them into an icon of international significance. The photographs of the Mothers and other relatives carrying images of their loved ones helped to break a double concealment: that of the disappeared and of those who searched for them.

At the same time, a considerable number of younger, politically engaged photographers, contemporary with many of the disappeared and aware that it could be their own mothers searching for *them*, supported the cause while producing emblematic images that gained them both legitimacy and social and professional recognition. Those images were also an important contribution to the human rights struggle in Argentina, becoming an effective instrument of protection, communication and defence for the Mothers. But they went beyond that. Giorgio Agamben writes:

But there is another aspect of the photographs I love that I am compelled to mention. It has to do with a certain exigency: the subject shown in the photo demands something from us [...] Even if the person photographed is completely forgotten today, even if his or her name has been erased forever from human memory – or, indeed, precisely because of this – that person and that face demand their name; they demand not to be forgotten.

(2007, 25)

The photographs of the Mothers emphasised symbolic and metaphorical elements, and created new meanings about disappearance and state terrorism that were still in dispute, shedding a new light on sorrow and grief, but also on the imagination, solidarity and creativity that the Mothers brought to bear in their long walk towards justice and truth.

Translated by Jorge Salvetti

Notes

1 Even if there were differences between individual print media outlets, all the national press unambiguously supported the coup. One exception was *The Buenos Aires Herald*, published in English, under Robert Cox's direction. All radio and television stations were under military control.

2 Fifteen people (mothers and other relatives) attended the first meeting. Gradually, this number increased. In a statement to the press in 1981, Laura Armendáriz de Rivelli and Hebe de Bonafini spoke of 2,500 members at the time. By 1983, the Mothers had branch offices in Calilegua, Libertador General San Martín, Concepción del Uruguay, Concordia, Gualeguaychú, Mar del Plata, La Plata, Junín, Chacabuco, Punta Alta, Bahía Blanca, Zárate, San Rafael, Mendoza, Río Cuarto, Villa Mercedes, Salta, La Rioja, San Juan, Neuquén, Alto Valle, San Miguel de Tucumán, Catamarca, Luján-Mercedes and, later, Rosario (Gorini 2006; Zubillaga 2019).

3 For a history of photojournalism in Argentina in the 1960s and 1970s, see Gamarnik (2020).

4 Before 1976, María Estela Martínez de Perón's government had closed *El Mundo* and *Noticias* (a bomb was planted in the latter's offices). After the coup, many other newspapers and magazines were taken over by the military or closed altogether (Ulanovsky 1997).

5 In the print media of the time, photojournalism was, without exception, under the control of the editorial board. In general, photographers had no say in what images were published.

6 This photograph was first published in 2006 (Cerolini and Reynoso 2006, 101).

7 For a history of this exhibition, see Gamarnik (2013).

8 Miguel Martelloti and Alberto Rodríguez from *Crónica*, and Enrique Rosito from the DYN agency, were three photographers who sent undeveloped rolls of film to exile groups in Europe. The rolls were carried by a passenger departing from Ezeiza airport (Rosito and Martelloti 2021, personal communication). This method of getting material out of Argentina became more commonplace in the run up to and during the World Cup.

9 Between 8 and 10 December 1977, twelve members of the group that used to meet at the Santa Cruz church (Buenos Aires) to organise the search for the disappeared were abducted and murdered by the Navy. Among them were Azucena Villaflor de De Vincenti, Esther Ballestrino de Careaga and María Eugenia Ponce de Bianco. In 2005, the Argentine Forensic Anthropology Team was able to identify the remains of the three founding Mothers, buried as unnamed bodies after they were found on the coast off San Bernardo and Santa Teresita between December 1977 and January 1978. It was also proven that they had been dropped into the sea from Naval Air Force planes during a Death Flight.

10 They included, amongst others, Aldo Amura, Bécquer Casaballe, Eduardo Di Baia, Daniel García, Pablo Lasansky, Eduardo Longoni, Daniel Merle and Carlos Pesce.

11 The photographs of the disappeared also played an important role in the creation of archives and databases, and more recently, numerous blogs and websites, where it is possible to identify the disappeared and learn their personal histories. Needless to say, these photographs continue to retain an inalienable, personal meaning and are used in family homes.

12 The use of family photographs also resulted in another kind of visibility, related to the activism of the Grandmothers of Plaza de Mayo who searched for their grandchildren

(either kidnapped or born in captivity and appropriated by the terrorist state; often given to families associated with the regime). The public presence of these images allowed many people to identify themselves or be identified by others as the possible child of a disappeared person. Many recovered grandchildren describe the experience of looking for a family resemblance in the photographs displayed on the Grandmothers' official website.

13 The interview can be viewed here: www.youtube.com/watch?v=OBlVz3VO09k

14 Van der Putten and his team were threatened in the days following the interview. They contacted the Dutch Ministry of Foreign Affairs and were told that, if anything happened to them, the Netherlands would withdraw their national team from the final (González Cezer 2020).

15 There also exists a prize-winning and often reproduced photograph from that period that falls outside of this taxonomy. It is an image used to suggest an alleged reconciliation between the Mothers and the repressive forces; a reconciliation that never took place. The image shows a false embrace between a police agent and a Mother. The photograph won the King of Spain Award for the best news image in 1983, awarded by the Ibero-American Cooperation Institute and the EFE Agency, often regarded as the most important Spanish language journalism award. The photograph was taken on 5 October 1982, during the March for Life, and is an image repudiated by the Mothers. For a history of this photograph see Gamarnik (2021).

16 The image was also chosen to illustrate the cover of *La rebelión de las Madres. Historia de las Madres de Plaza de Mayo, Tomo I (1976–1983)* [*The Rebellion of the Mothers: the history of the Mothers of Plaza de Mayo, Volume I (1976–1983)*] by Ulises Gorini.

17 For more details on this, see Filc (1997).

3

Ways of Looking: Violence, Archive and the Register of "Extremists"

María Eleonora Cristina
in conversation with Piotr Cieplak

For me it is a matter of different kinds of gaze. It's about the eyes that take the photo; the eyes that look at the camera; and the eyes of whomever looks at the photo afterwards.
– María Eleonora Cristina, Director of the Provincial Memory Archive in Córdoba

The Provincial Memory Archive [El Archivo Provincial de la Memoria] (APM) is located in the heart of Córdoba. The narrow, cobbled Pasaje Santa Catalina separates it from its grand neighbour, a 16th century cathedral. The APM's façade is adorned with a plexiglass displaying the names of those disappeared and/or killed by the Argentine state before and during the most recent military dictatorship.[1] The names wind and contort to collectively form the shape of a fingerprint. The importance of leaving a mark of identity – stolen, denied, reclaimed – spills out onto Córdoba's streets. As one approaches the names, it's possible to look inside through one of the windows, into the Room of Lives to be Told – a chamber full of the portraits of the disappeared and killed in the 1970s and 1980s.

The APM shares the building with the Provincial Memory Commission and the site of memory: ex-D2.[2] Until the 1980s, it housed the headquarters of the Central Police as well as the notorious Department of Information D2 – one of the main cogs in Córdoba's state terrorism machine. Many of those detained at D2 would be eventually transferred to one of the local clandestine detention centres (CDCs), including La Perla and El Campo de la Ribera – now also reclaimed as designated memory sites. In this conversation, María Eleonora Cristina talks about the APM and ex-D2 as a space that's "liminal," in many ways. Its surroundings are also far from

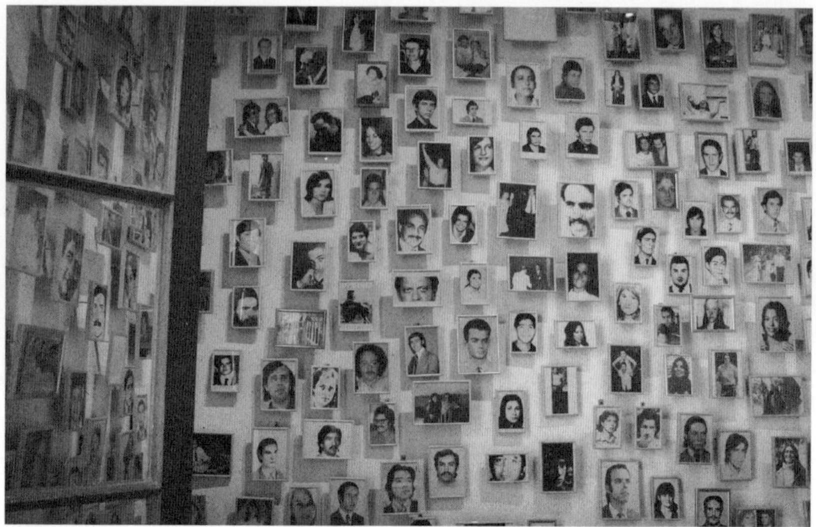

Figure 3.1 The Room of Lives to be Told at the Provincial Memory Archive, Córdoba.
Source: Piotr Cieplak.

neutral. Pasaje Santa Catalina was associated with "violence against the 'other' since the 16th century."

María Eleonora Cristina has been the director of the APM since 2015, having previously worked in its Investigations Department. A daughter of a disappeared father and a long-term activist of H.I.J.O.S., between 2006 and 2008 she was the Secretary of the Provincial Memory Commission, which represents the views of Córdoba's human rights organisations.

Cristina shares her unique insight into the curatorial processes and discussions about using the photographs of the killed and disappeared in narrating and mediating a space as difficult as ex-D2. She explores their role as "bridges of meaning" between the brutal past and the present, which, for some groups and individuals, continues to be brutal. She also addresses the relationship between different types of photographs: those donated by friends and family members and those produced as a tool of oppression by the terrorist state.

The APM is the custodian of a unique collection of over 130,000 negatives of images taken by Córdoba's Provincial Police between 1964 and 1992. Amongst them are photographs of over 5,000 people detained as "extremists" – a designation given to them by the Police – before and during the dictatorship. The process of trying to understand and contextualise the collection was both complicated and enriched by the mysterious appearance of the Register of "Extremists" – a ledger listing the names (and corresponding photographic negatives) of those the Police considered to be politically subversive and thus a danger to the regime and its vision of what Argentina should be.

Some of the images in the collection are brutal. Created as mugshots, they show people who have been beaten up, sleep-deprived, exhausted, blindfolded. There are images of pregnant women. There are looks of resignation but also of defiance. Cristina, who participated in the process of the restitution of these photos to the people portrayed in them or their family members, talks here about the collection's horror but also about its potential. She focuses on the crossover of functions, uses and meanings of these images as: parts of an institutional archive; memory and commemoration aides; and (originally) tools of oppression. She talks about the uniqueness of being able to consult the uncropped negative, which shows the prisoners but also, sometimes, the oppressors. She also explores the more pragmatic uses of these images such as, for instance, research into deciphering the key features of the spatial arrangements of ex-D2.

Crucially, Cristina reflects on the curatorial processes and discussions that preceded the 2012 exhibition – *Moments of Truth: Photographs of the Register of Extremists from D2* [*Instantes de verdad. Fotografías del Registro de Extremistas*] – which used the images across the memory site. She frames the Register as an active, "live" tool that oscillates between its evidential, judicial and memorial functions – including the transition from the institutional to the personal; from disappearance to view.

Piotr Cieplak

Piotr Cieplak: *The most recent Argentine dictatorship shares such a complex relationship with photography. What do images mean to you, especially in the context of the continuing fight for justice and memory?*

María Cristina: My first encounter with the relationship between photography and state terrorism is connected to what happened to my father. At one point, I realised that, in my head, my dad and my aunt – both disappeared – were photographs. I remember visiting my grandmother Antonia's house in Buenos Aires and seeing their likenesses displayed alongside the photos of other family members who weren't missing, including myself. It was as if my father's corporeal form was connected to a photograph. My memories of him were anchored in images.

When I started my activism in H.I.J.O.S., photos were a constant presence at marches and protests. It was soon after the return of democracy and at that point the photos of the disappeared became bearers of denunciation and memory; a way of contrasting absence with presence; numbers with individual identities; disappearance with faces and looks. They originated from the home. Most were either photographs from a family album or institutional images: passport or other identity document photos. At some point, they were forced to leave the family space and began to have public lives, in public places. It wasn't a linear journey; there were many stops on the way. The same photograph of my father that was displayed in my grandmother's living room also appeared during a protest; as part of a tribute to him at the Light and Power [Luz and Fuerza] Syndicate in Córdoba; *and* was the basis for a mural at the University of Buenos Aires. It appeared in all these different places that featured in my father's life and, at the same time and through this image, my father was present in these places, too. And that's just one photo; as we know, there are thousands.

The images of the disappeared form a complex network because they had and continue to have so many different functions. After the marches and protests, they made another set of transitions: to the archives, memory sites, public tributes and multiple other memorial contexts. But the presence of images is as important as their absence. There are families who have albums and albums full of photos and there are others who have none – with the few images of their loved ones that had existed, destroyed during the dictatorship. Ludmila da Silva Catela, the founding director of the APM has written extensively about the complex and varied trajectories of some of these photos (2001).

PC: *Tell me about your work at the APM and the role the photographs of the disappeared play in it.*

MC: Unlike other similar institutions, the APM was created without documents, but with the legal power to request them, take custody of them and make them accessible to the public. The APM is housed in three colonial mansions located between the City Hall and the cathedral – in the former headquarters of the Central Police. The APM's location in the heart of the city is a daily reminder of the thinness of the folds between what is clandestine and what is public. Since the beginning of the 20th century, these buildings were home to police units linked to the persecution and repression of social, political, cultural and trade union activity, including the D2 Information Department.

Today, the APM is a memory site – open to the public – as well as an archive where documents linked to state terrorism and the fight for the defence of human rights are preserved. In many ways, it is still a space where different things overlap. Ever since we took over the buildings, we have strived to narrate what happened here in a respectful and inclusive way. The photographic image plays a preponderant role in this narrative, physically and virtually, just like it has done in the human rights movement in Argentina over decades. One of our first major actions was to ask local organisations – The Relatives of the Disappeared and Detained for Political Reasons [Familiares de Desaparecidos y Detenidos por Razones Políticas] and H.I.J.O.S. – for the images they used on their placards and banners. For more than ten years now, we have been displaying these photos in Pasaje Santa Catalina at the beginning of each trial and the announcement of each sentence related to state abuse of power in the province. The photographs now also form part of the extensive collection included in the virtual memorial, *Presentes*.[3]

A lot of our work is about finding ways of creating what I would call bridges of meaning. This is especially important as time passes. In the specific case of the photographs of the killed and disappeared, there initially existed a certain hegemony – a tendency to think about them primarily as tools of search and denunciation. But, over time, the photos and their uses began to change. They became less fixed. This allowed for all sorts of interventions that were previously unthinkable such as: enlargement, projections, use in collages and audio-visual projects, addition of colour and flowers to the images, and use in memory workshops. Working with memory is about generating questions rather than certainties. An important part of this process is the development of new languages of remembrance and, to a certain extent, desacralisation. But it's a process, not a singular burst.

PC: *Thursday Photos is one of the APM's longest-running initiatives involving the photographs of the disappeared. The portraits are hung in Pasaje Santa Catalina on most Thursdays, bringing the memory and its burden out of the walls of the site and into the city. What lies behind this ritual?*

MC: In 2007, we had 200–300 photos. Today, after fifteen years of work, we have more than 1,000. The initial images were donated by Córdoba's human rights organisations from their own photographic collections. We arranged them into banners and hang them on the façade of the APM every Thursday – the day of the round of the Mothers here in Córdoba, as well as in Buenos Aires. The idea behind this is twofold. First, to create an accompaniment ritual. Second, to mark the presence of the disappeared in the Pasaje; a place historically associated with terror. This tiny street has been linked to violence against "the other" since the 16th century. It is here that the indigenous people forced to build the cathedral were shot at. And then, in the 1960s and 1970s, Pasaje Santa Catalina was almost synonymous with state terrorism. That's what it meant for that whole generation. Being able to have the photographs of the disappeared present in this particular public space, in the very centre of Córdoba, was very powerful.

In addition to the Thursday displays, the photos also travel. We take them to the courts; we take them to the openings of other memory spaces or to activities connected to things like introductions of new laws in the legislature. In each articulation of this ritual, especially those involving different institutions and groups, we use our photos to encourage whoever is involved to collect and display their own. There is something extremely powerful and important about how the act of bringing the photos together, grouping them, affects individual images.

PC: *This tension between the individual and the collective is felt strongly in another part of the permanent exhibition at the APM, The Room of Lives to be Told. In this powerful space, one is faced with framed portraits of the murdered and the disappeared. They are slightly different to* Thursday Photos *in that they're more like photographs you would see in a family album or on the living room wall. They feel individually more intimate and, at the same time, collectively more tragic.*

MC: *Thursday Photos* had already been used as public tools: on banners, at marches, in missing persons reports. In many families of the disappeared there are other images that never leave the private sphere. Or at least they don't make this journey through marches and banners. When people started donating photos directly to the APM, we strived to facilitate and encourage the choice of different kinds of images: important family moments, even moments of laughter and happiness. This is closely linked to the multiplicity of functions that the photographs of the disappeared played at different points. Their initial role was to identify; to know if someone has seen the disappeared; to use the image as something that jogs someone's memory and results in concrete information, data.

When we started asking for more photos to put together The Room of Lives to be Told, we had to explain to people that these new devices, often connected to memory sites, are no longer just about the idea of recognition but also about the idea of finding ways of "knowing" a person; "knowing" what they were like. While *Thursday Photos* referenced

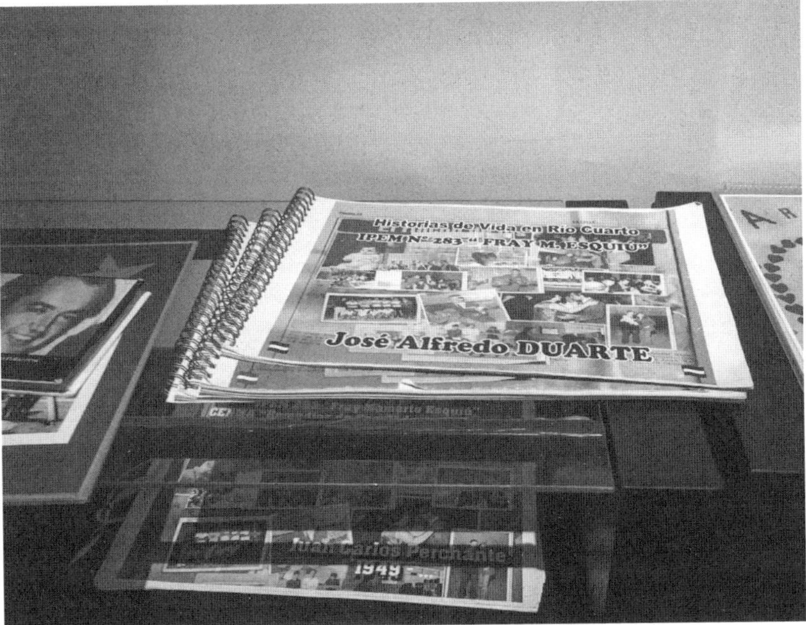

Figure 3.2 "Family albums" on display at the Provincial Memory Archive, Córdoba.
Source: Piotr Cieplak.

the marches and the placards, as well as marking the presence of the individuals, the images in The Room of Lives to be Told are more akin to those seen at home, something more familiar, something linked to a different kind of record of life.

PC: *The APM is the custodian of a unique collection: The Register of "Extremists" and the photographic negatives that accompany it. What is it and how did it come into the APM's care?*

MC: The Register of "Extremists" is a logbook. It records – alphabetically and chronologically – 5,548 arrested and photographed people who were considered extremists by the Provincial Police between 1961 and 1977. As well as the usual information such as the date of the taking of the photograph, first name and surname, each entry also includes the number of the negative and the number of the folio. These refer to the images taken and kept in police archives. The accompanying photographic collection consists of 136,242 negatives taken by Córdoba's Provincial Police between 1964 and 1992. Amongst them are images of the people who appear in the Register.[4]

How did we know about the existence of the Register? Before it was ceded to the APM by the Federal Judiciary, H.I.J.O.S. already had access to it. It was left on the doorstep of the office of a human rights lawyer and passed on. I remember it well; it was a tremendous find. It was 2010, when the trials of some of the oppressors were beginning in Córdoba. For much of our society, the period and the idea of state terrorism was this black hole that had just sucked people in. It often wasn't clear to people what had been real and what had been a fantasy construed by the

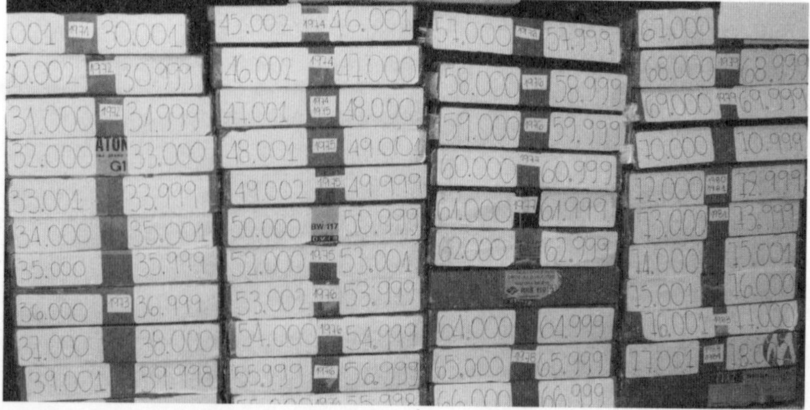

Figure 3.3 Boxes containing the negatives from the Register of "Extremists."
Source: Provincial Memory Archive, Córdoba.

repressive apparatus of the state. And then, suddenly, we had something that was a real piece of evidence.

H.I.J.O.S. arranged for a copy of the Register to be deposited in the APM. The arrival of the boxes with the photographic negatives, which happened later, was another powerful, seminal moment. I think it had to do with the materiality and the sheer scale of what appeared before us. But also with the fact that these were images, not written documents.

Photographs are fascinating because of where they can situate the viewer and the subject: somewhere between the moment of capture and the fact that this moment is no longer; doesn't exist. More pragmatically, having this collection meant that we had the ability to shed light on some of the stories we'd already gathered. It was another tool in the task of solving the enigma of this repressive labyrinth. A treasure. It reminded me of the words of John Tagg:

What we have in this standardised image is more than a picture of a supposed criminal. It is a portrait of the product of the disciplinary method: the body made object; divided and studied; enclosed in a cellular structure of space whose architecture is the file-index; made docile and forced to yield up its truth; separated and individuated; subjected and made subject. When accumulated, such images amount to a new representation of society.

(1988, 76)

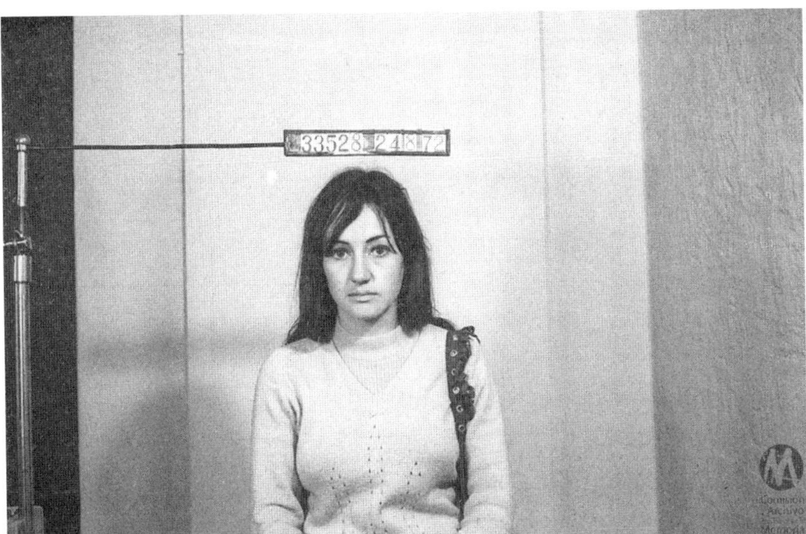

Figure 3.4 An image of a female detainee from the Register of "Extremists."
Source: Córdoba Provincial Police – Section 3. Series: Register of "Extremists."
Collection: Provincial Memory Archive, Córdoba.[5]

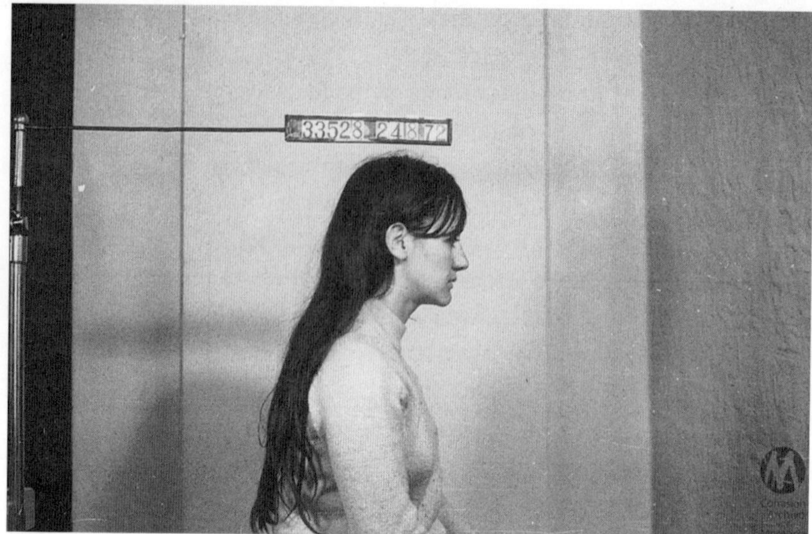

Figure 3.5 An image of a female detainee from the Register of "Extremists."
Source: Córdoba Provincial Police – Section 3. Series: Register of "Extremists."
Collection: Provincial Memory Archive, Córdoba.

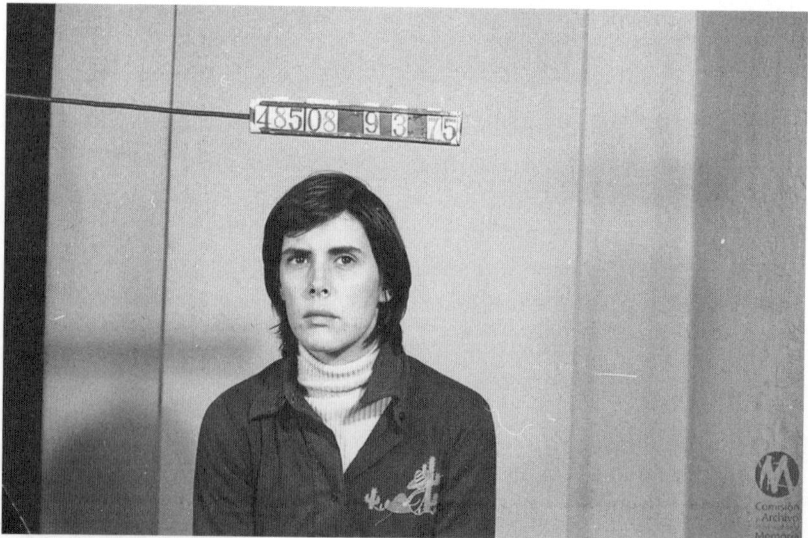

Figure 3.6 An image of a female detainee from the Register of "Extremists."
Source: Córdoba Provincial Police – Section 3. Series: Register of "Extremists."
Collection: Provincial Memory Archive, Córdoba.

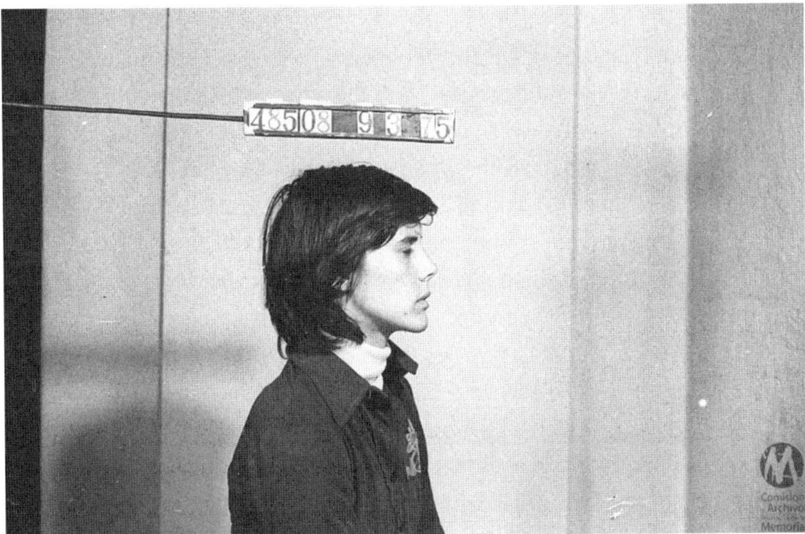

Figure 3.7 An image of a female detainee from the Register of "Extremists."
Source: Córdoba Provincial Police – Section 3. Series: Register of "Extremists."
Collection: Provincial Memory Archive, Córdoba.

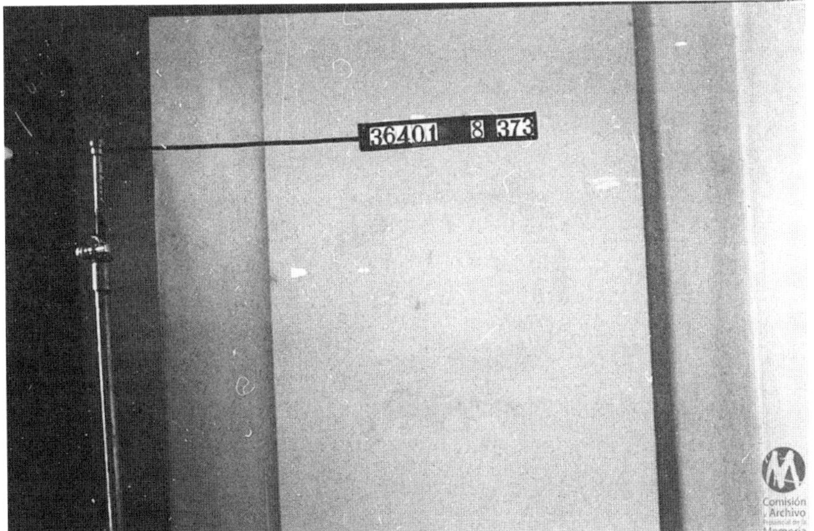

Figure 3.8 An image of the "comb."
Source: Córdoba Provincial Police – Section 3. Series: Register of "Extremists."
Collection: Provincial Memory Archive, Córdoba.

PC: *What is the aesthetic of the photographs in this collection?*

MC: Structurally and aesthetically, they're mugshots, police booking photographs, front-view and profile – with the number of the negative and the date written on what was commonly known as the "comb" (Figure 3.8).[6] We're talking about all the images of alleged criminals taken by the Police between 1961 and 1977 – so a massive collection of negatives. Of course, our work centres on the specific links to state terrorism and the persecution of the political "other." But it's important to remember that state terrorism also ended up being an excuse for the exacerbation of violence against gypsies, the poor and other minorities; against whomever the state saw and constructed as the "other." The fact that the collection spans such a long period allows us to ask precisely that: who did the Police think of as "other" over decades?

There are also other kinds of images amongst the mugshots. For instance, there are images of people sitting together, leaning on each other; not able to keep themselves up. People with blindfolds covering their eyes, wearing 1970s clothes. These images tell us how the detainees inhabited this space. But in truth, when we found them, we were often lost for words. They're so explicit. They seemed almost like a movie. The extremity of the truth which these images record almost transforms them into fiction.

The Register itself provides many clues. For instance, prior to 1974, all photographs were taken in the City Hall. Between 1975 and 1976 – when the majority of the photographs of the "extremists" were taken – the location moved to the Department of Information D2. This tells us something very specific about the inner workings of the Police. It speaks directly to the thin line between the clandestine and the public I mentioned before. Let me explain. The Police was headquartered in the City Hall. Anyone suspected of committing a crime was transferred to the studio on the first floor to be photographed. So when we begin to see the same kinds of images but taken in other places (particularly in D2), this means that the photographer and the camera moved. There are also markers of difference in the collection other than the location of the shot: blindfolds, the kind of "comb" used, wide open eyes of someone who was unaccustomed to the light on account of being blindfolded (many testimonies of those detained at D2 mention this), marks of violence on the photographed bodies, groups of people waiting for their photos to be taken next. So these images, especially the negatives, tell us not only about the disappeared and the detained, but also about the Police and how it functioned.[7] They tell us about what was deemed "official" business and what happened under more clandestine conditions.

Each time we approached the photographs, a spiral of anxiety and questions emerged. Who is the person in the image? Where was it taken? The architectural as a trace allowed us to draw a spatial map of the dynamics of D2 as a place. It was forensic, detective work and a lot of it was done by David Schäfer and Alejandro Frola.[8] The Register's negatives weren't only for looking at people's faces, but also at other things such as, for example, the background. From these little details, we would very slowly begin to piece together when and where a particular photo was taken. It is important to remember that D2 was a liminal space in more than one way. More than anything, it was a space of distribution; of passing through. When CoNaDeP came to Córdoba, they didn't go to D2; they went to La Perla and to La Ribera. Generally, the periods of detention in D2 were relatively short. Many people who were detained in La Perla and La Ribera would talk about these sites, not about D2.

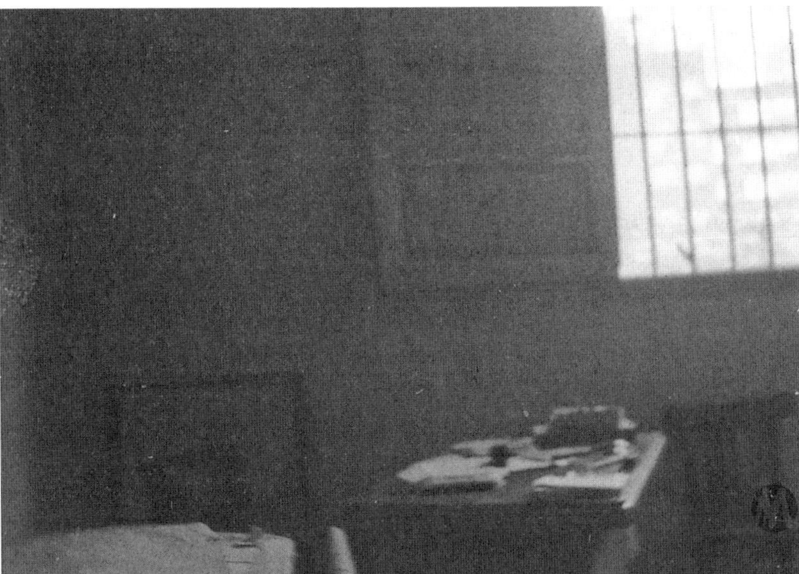

Figure 3.9 An "accidental" image from the Register of "Extremists."
Source: Córdoba Provincial Police – Section 3. Series: Register of "Extremists."
Collection: Provincial Memory Archive, Córdoba.

When the APM took over, the buildings, as well as what precisely took place where, were a mystery. The often-overlooked aspects of the photos – does it show this door, this staircase, this wall, this floor? – played a crucial part in our ability to understand the spatiality of D2. It's horrible to speak in those terms, but this kind of work was really fascinating. As I have already mentioned, it was a painstaking job. It meant studying the negatives and looking for details: marks on the walls, signs of air-conditioning units, benches, patterns on the floor and so on, and trying to match them to specific spaces. To complicate matters even further, the building had changed significantly between when it belonged to the Police and when the APM took over.

PC: *The APM's remit includes the return of the photographs from the Register to the people who appear in them or, if that's no longer possible, to the surviving relatives. What kind of reactions have you witnessed in these complex encounters?*

MC: It's different for everyone. But I remember a few instances vividly; they stay with you for a long time. I remember a woman whose mother was a militant. In 1975, she left her children with their grandmother and disappeared. The next thing the six-year-old daughter – now the woman who came to the APM seeking information – knew was that her mother had been murdered. Now, all these years later, the woman had children of her own and wanted to tell them about their grandmother. So she came to us. During the research, we found a record of detention at the beginning of 1975. We also discovered a record of a photo taken at D2. This was before we received all the negatives, so we made an application to the Ministry of Justice for the release of the materials. They arrived but were incomplete. One of the photographs missing was the photograph of the "militant grandmother."

I also remember a man who filed a request for the release of information about him available at the APM. He was particularly interested in photos and, for one reason or another, felt obliged to clarify why. He said: "It's going to seem funny to you. The thing is, I didn't have access to cameras back then. I started my militancy very young and that meant not taking or keeping any photos that could involve others. I don't have pictures of me from when I was young, from that time in my life. That's what I'm looking for."

Another person that comes to mind is a woman who worked on issues linked to the recent Argentine past. This is to say that she was in contact with the generation of survivors, their stories, and their experiences. She was a survivor herself; she'd been interviewed; she'd even written about her experience. In many ways, she knew what was coming. She had already seen some photos of herself. But when we asked her if she would be prepared to release her images, she became paralysed. She said: "Not really. I would like to consult with my daughter first. I don't have a problem with releasing them, but my daughter looks very much like what I looked like; and she's the same age now. I wouldn't want her to be faced with this image and feel seen by everyone who can associate her with it."

This difficult process of restitution is varied and differs from individual to individual. Some people are unable to recognise themselves in the image and the situation. They say: "It's not me." But our research tells us that it is them. Others look at a photo and say: "This is me," while we know that that's impossible. It's not them. It's important to understand that the impact of the existence and discovery of these photographs was colossal – an explosion of different emotions, even for people who came very well prepared.

There is so much emotional expectation when it comes to seeing, meeting these photographs under such circumstances. So much meaning. It can get even more complicated and heart-breaking when the meeting doesn't happen; when we can't locate the photograph of a particular person who wants to see it. Just imagine someone who was detained at D2 three times and there is no record of that in the photos corresponding to the Register. People begin to wonder why that is. What does it mean? Sometimes they even interpret this lack of photos as a way of putting the very fact of their detention – their experience – into question. We just patiently explain that there are many possible reasons for photos missing.

The Register we have is only volume one. Volume two has not been found. A lot of things need to fall into place for us to be able to locate the precise photograph. Firstly, the person had to have their photo taken – not all the detainees were photographed. Secondly, the photograph must be in one of the boxes we have at the APM – some boxes are missing. Thirdly, the person in question must appear in the Register. If the latter is not the case, all that's left to do is to offer the person who seeks information the opportunity to review all the photographs we have from the year of their arrest and hope that they will recognise themselves. There are pragmatic practicalities associated with this: all the relevant photos must be digitised; there needs to be a computer available; and a member of staff to accompany the search. It's very resource-intensive and time-consuming. Hundreds of people have reviewed the collection, and many recognised themselves. Occasionally, incredible things happen in this process. One man who came in to consult the archive had such an incredible memory that, while looking for photographs of himself, he recognised and identified about twenty others: all part of one mass arrest.

We need to remember what the Register is and where it comes from. It is imperative not to fetishise it. Many of the annotations are wrong. There are errors. The Police were not the most careful keepers of data. But that's hard to explain to someone who has summoned all this courage to come and ask and look.

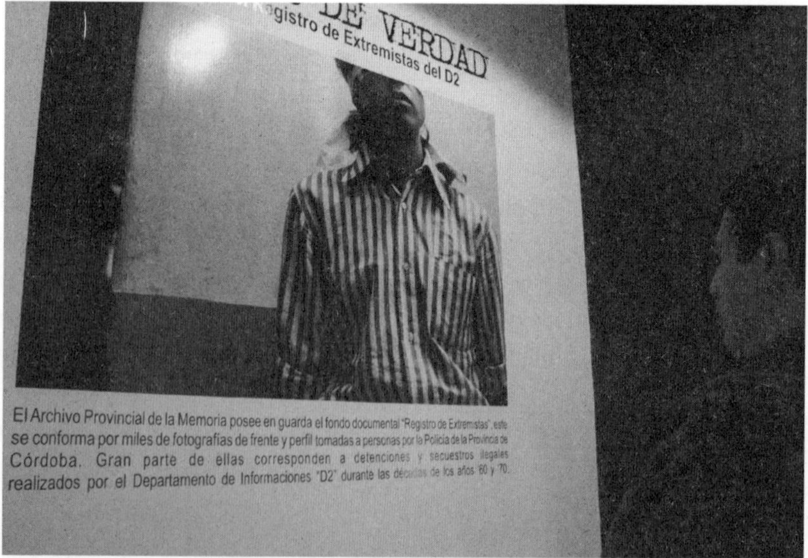

Figure 3.10 Moments of Truth: Photographs from the D2 Register of Extremists.
Source: Provincial Memory Archive, Córdoba.

PC: *In 2012, the APM used the photographs from the Register in an exhibition:* Moments of Truth: Photographs of the Register of Extremists from D2.

MC: The initial impulse behind the exhibition was our everyday work with the collection and the relationships we'd developed with each person who came to request information about themselves or their relatives. We witnessed first-hand and were very aware of the anxieties associated with finding yourself or your loved one; or being reminded of the moments and places captured in these photographs. At the same time, we also knew the power of these images to open doors to the memories and experiences that had been negated; to the memories of others who had been detained; to identify captors; to present a "reliable proof" of what was experienced. The photographs associated with the Register had the power to become tools to relay all this memory and experiences. It is like Feld and Stites Mor write, "images construct meaning for events, help to remember, allow to transmit what happened to the new generations. They collaborate to evoke the lived experience and to know what wasn't experienced directly. They are, in short, valuable instruments of social memory" (2009, 25).

We were clear from the beginning that the exhibition had to be open to the public. We had the institutional mandate and duty to "reverse the burden" of these images; to make the invisible visible; to make the clandestine public; to advance the practice of restitution to those who were never thought of as the true owners of these images. Being able to do this with documents that shed light on the machinery of terror also speaks of a chink in this totalitarian system. It presents the possibility to see what lies beyond the visible; to look through the "keyhole" to the clandestine detention centre. At the same time, the exhibition had to include and acknowledge the various complex feelings that we were very aware of in our work. We were determined that the exhibit shouldn't just reproduce horror.

The text in the exhibition brochure explains what we were seeking to do with the images: "In this oscillation between the visible and the invisible, between what we can see and what they do not show, lies the force of the truth they transmit" (Córdoba Provincial Memory Archive 2012). The parallels between photographic practice and what we sought to convey were very illuminating when it came to framing the exhibition. At the forefront of our minds were photography's ability to capture an instant, a second of reality; to focus; to reveal and develop an image; and to, in many ways, cast light; to capture a minute of life or an instant of death that has passed and will not return.

In Andreas Huyssen's words: "If there is an obligation, individual and social, to remember the traumas of history, then there must be images. There is no memory without images, there is no knowledge without the possibility of seeing, even if images cannot provide complete knowledge" (2009, 15). In the hundreds of photos we looked at, the same questions arose again and again: how was it possible to construct an "other" that deserved torture, extreme humiliation, death and disappearance? And how had all this become so unquestionable that the authorities didn't even feel the need to disguise it in the photographs? Photographs – known for their ability to preserve things in time. These questions fed into the conceptualisation of the exhibition: "The cruelty exerted by the repressors was intended to render inert, powerless, immobile those whom they considered enemies. With beatings, torture and humilia-tion, the enemy, once threatening, was debased, bloodied, disfigured. The cruelty presented here shows that, beyond the defeat of the other, what was intended was the denial of their humanity" (Research Dept. of Provincial Memory Archive 2012, 36).

Moments of Truth was divided into seven parts, or moments. These moments ran along three main thematic axes: Origins of Violence, Banalisation of Evil and Denial of Humanity.

Moment 1: "From negative to positive." It was important to begin by telling what this collection consisted of, how it came to us and the "artisanal" work that made it possible to convert it into an exhibition or deliver the photographs to their owners. That's what the first part was about. It also helped with signposting the photographs as sensitive material. We wanted people to be able to decide whether to continue; to be able to decide how much they wanted to see.

Moment 2: "Focus" invited the visitor to come into a room called Escrache.[9] Part of the permanent exhibition, this space had been the office of the head of D2. Inside, we presented our research on the agents who worked in the precinct. The idea was to shift the focus on those who operated the machinery of terror in Córdoba and thus highlight the context in which the photographs had been taken.

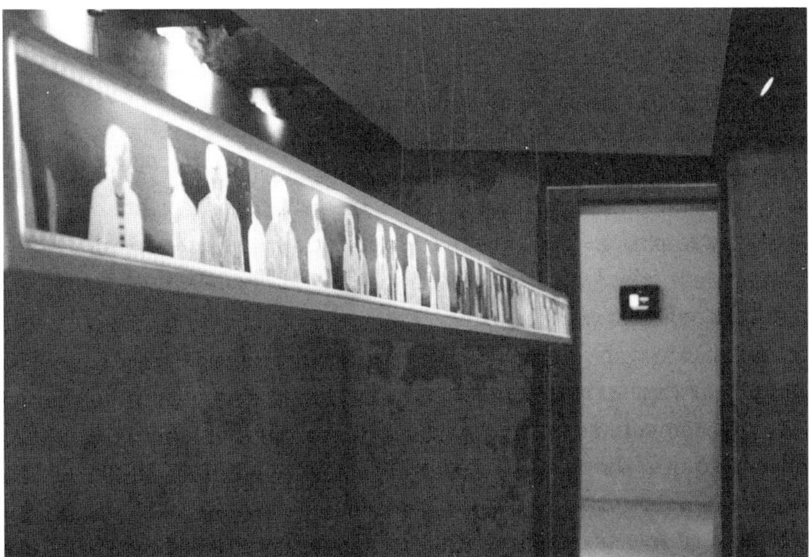

Figure 3.11 Photos from the Register of "Extremists" in the "Tram."
Source: Provincial Memory Archive, Córdoba.

Moment 3: "Facing images" positioned the visitor face-to-face with what happened at D2; with the images of the detained (Figure 3.11). We decided that the most appropriate place to do this was the "Tram." When we took over the space in 2006 and did the first tours with survivors, one place kept being mentioned: the "Tram." People talked about a narrow, corridor-like space, with an octagonal roof, and cement benches on each side, facing each other.

Subsequent research discovered that the "Tram" was where people were thrown after having been tortured or between torture sessions, usually beaten and blindfolded. Some remained there for a long time, sometimes days, without being able to move. The survivors spoke of the cold of the cement benches; of the absolute prohibition of physical contact with those they knew lay beside them; of the proximity of the screams; of how the time spent in the "Tram" felt endless; of the darkness of the blindfold; of the policemen passing by and hitting the prisoners waiting in line for their turn.

In terms of the exhibition, it was logical to face what happened at D2 in this charged space. We chose to present the images from the Register in strips that resembled the strip of a photographic negative; a rectangular artefact that stretched across the length of the "Tram." It hung from the ceiling, on the visitor's eye level, and was illuminated by a backlight – which gave the impression of it being looked at on a light table in a photographic laboratory. In the chosen images themselves, it wasn't possible to tell the identities of the people photographed (to ensure their privacy) but, at the same time, it was clear what the images were showing.

Moment 4: "Register of Extremists" took the form of a short audio-visual piece placed next to the "Tram." It consisted of many fast-edited images from the collection, changing at a pace that made them look almost like a piece of animation. Every now and then, the pace would slow and focus on a singular photograph. The purpose of this was to create a clash between the devastating numerical extent of the people photographed and kept in these negatives and the uniqueness, individuality of each of them.

Moment 5: "Moments of Truth, D2 in photos" showed a selection of entire photographs in various sizes. How to present images in this section was preceded by many difficult discussions. At first, we planned to use a single photograph that would condense and transmit the essence of what we wanted to say to the visitors. The proposed image was of a pregnant woman, handcuffed, sitting at the entrance to the "Tram;" her oppressor standing next to her, holding a "comb" and a blindfold. The image would speak of totalitarian and gender violence, of vulnerability. It would also highlight the presence of the agent of this violence. The focus on a single image would address the concerns about preserving the privacy of those captured in the photographs – only the authorisation for this particular image would have to be obtained. It was also argued that such an approach would evade the danger of trivialising the photographs, anesthetising the gaze through an overload of images. On the other hand, there was an unease about the exhibition team being the ones with the power to (re)censure what is being shown; about the potential of choosing just one image that would then become an omnipotent object capable of transmitting all the complex processes and emotions that had to be transmitted.

Following this discussion, we decided to include multiple images. The next question was: what images should be included, how should they be presented and arranged? We decided to stage the room as a photographic lab, where the images begin to take form, reveal themselves, on paper. Here, we selected photos of people at the point of arrest, prior to subsequent kidnapping, disappearance, or murder. The effect of making out silhouettes emerging on the photographic paper was that of a disappeared/murdered "appearing." To individualise the people in the images, each was accompanied by a few paragraphs about the life of the photographed, including the date the photo had been taken and the date of the subsequent disappearance. These individual stories opened the possibility of talking about different groups of victims: men and women, young and old, married, single, parents, students, workers, militants, disappeared in Córdoba, in Tucumán.

Revealing the photographs in this way allowed us to zoom in on the repressive apparatus. For instance, there was an emphasis on people who had been photographed multiple times, during separate detentions. Each image of the same person told us about a different moment; not only in their life and experience but also in the operation of the authorities: the context, the place where the photo had been taken, the body, the way of looking at the camera. The selected photographs also allowed us to put into play something that we had noticed in several cases: photographs taken by the Police later being published in the newspapers. Only the press photos would be cropped. They no longer had the policeman holding the blindfold and smoking a cigarette next to the detainee. All that appeared in the media was the detainee's face in the standardised format of the mugshot.

In the exhibition we sought to explore what it meant that these records had been left behind – with the certainty of timeless impunity. We sought to reflect on the machinery put in place to achieve terror, silence and social consent for a political project carried out with blood and fire. Da Silva Catela's words on the concentrationary experience and narrative were important in thinking about our approach:

To be narrated, the practices of violence suffered by the bodies of the kidnapped during the last civic-military dictatorship require images and the ability of the witness to place their memories in territorialities that act as material supports of memory. Being kept in a CDC, blindfolded, ended up sharpening a memory of the senses, touch, smell and sensations of cold, heat, humidity [...] hunger or thirst [...] Acts of violence are, in this way, narrated with the body and punctuated by images loaded with stories and feelings.

(da Silva Catela 2010, 86)

Think of an image of the body of a female detainee, with eyes opened wide after days of existing in the darkness of the blindfold. In the background, we can also see a policeman in his uniform, waiting to pass with freshly washed coffee cups in his hand. Or an image in which the person who's holding the "comb" over the detainee's body is also smoking a cigarette, trying to disguise the weapon that peeks out of his pocket. All these details visible in the negatives gave us the ability to show that the world continued to spin while this was happening. That, beyond showing the faces and the profiles of the detainees, these negatives could tell us so much more about what happened inside the D2.

Moment 6: **"The photo of my parents"** consisted of excerpts from two audio-visual interviews with the children who received the photos of their parents as part of the APM's work to return the photographs associated with the Register to their rightful owners.[10] It seemed important to include in the exhibition the effect photographs had on them. It highlighted the intrinsic memory connection between the past and the present. As Martín Caparrós writes:

Photography, goes through history, against time: photography is an always vain attempt to stop time, to postulate errors in its passage. In each photo, what is no longer and will never be is presented as if it still was: with the lasting freshness of wallpaper flowers. For a moment, there appears the perplexity of being faced with what has been lost: the emotion of this encounter. Then, sadness. Photography is always cruel.

(1997, 16)

Moment 7: **"The construction of the other"** closed the exhibition. Located in a small room, it consisted of a framed mirror made to look like a polaroid, with a flashing flashlight. It was accompanied by a brief text that outlined the journey from the Law of Residence of 1902 all the way to the Anti-Terrorism Law of 2011. The intention in this final section was to encourage a reflection on the construction of the "other," which the state conjures and each of us individually sustains: the anarchist, the extremist, the subversive, the terrorist. The role played by the security forces in this process preceded the period of Argentine state terrorism in the 1970s and 1980s, and many practices continue to be perpetuated to this day.

PC: *What impact do the photos in this collection have on you?*

MC: A lot of these photographs are very hard, almost obscene – especially photographs of physical injury. When I look at some of them, my brain does something strange, as if it is trying to fictionalise what I'm looking at; transform it into an image from a film.

Different images affect me for different reasons: the sadness of the look or the eyes that challenge the gaze of the camera. I am also moved by images of women. It's hard not to think about the misogyny of the violence and abuse; of the fact that many of the women were or would be pregnant. These are all stories that are not immediately evident from the Register itself. Lastly, I am always fascinated by the images that are not there, that are absent. I'm reminded of a very powerful story related to an anniversary of the Cordobazo[11] and The Guevarist Youth [La Juventud Guevarista].[12] There exist testimonial records of the arrest of four people: two men and two Jewish women. The men survived. The women are still missing. We know that all four passed through D2. There are accounts of the women in La Perla. The only photos we could find are of the two men. I can't stop thinking about what happened to these women. Why don't we have their photographs?

What matters to me is how we can contribute to contextualising some of the extreme experiences that happened here. Things are messy and complex and documents, especially those created by the state, are never something pure or definitive. The APM's role, alongside other institutions, is to tear down this wall and try to reach something more complex. For instance, how can we talk about the notion of betrayal? In some circles in Argentina, it is difficult to discuss the links between detainees and repressors or what detainees within the CDCs were forced to do. The wickedness and complexity of these experiences should not be subject to moral judgment. They must be seen in their extreme context.

PC: *We've talked about all these different kinds of photographs of the disappeared. Is there anything that connects them – from family portraits to the police mugshots?*

MC: The capture of an instant of life. What makes them different is the eye behind the camera. A photo taken by your dad, your partner, your son or daughter, your fellow militant is one thing. Even a photo taken to process a document, with your consent, is a totally different thing to an image produced by the security forces in a context of persecution. It is a violation of privacy. These are not consensual acts.

Therefore, for me it is a matter of different kinds of gaze. It's about the eyes that take the photo; the eyes that look at the camera; and the eyes of whomever looks at the photo afterwards. What does a child look for in a photo of their parent? What does a lawyer look for? What does someone from The Argentine Forensic Anthropology Team look for in a photo? What are the Grandmothers of Plaza de Mayo looking for? If you start asking these questions you stop seeing a photograph and start looking, almost hypnotically, into a kaleidoscope.

There's a family in Córdoba who chose a photo from the Register to be displayed in The Room of Lives to be Told. They did it because it was the only photograph of their disappeared in which he was visible from the front. They cropped it so it no longer has the "comb" in it, just the face. Photos are malleable and sturdy. They can adapt to what we want them to be.

Córdoba/London, 29 April and 27 May 2021

Translated by Piotr Cieplak

Notes

1 Violent repression in Córdoba began before the 1976 coup – which extended it to the whole country.

2 For details of the site and information about APM's work, see: https://apm.gov.ar

3 The virtual memorial *Presentes* can be accessed here: https://apm.gov.ar/presentes

4 Most of the images in the collection are of people detained on suspicion of criminal activity (often petty, such as pickpocketing) and not for political/ideological reasons. This is why the accompanying Register of "Extremists" is such a crucial tool in the task of deciphering this vast collection of photographic negatives, especially in the context of state terrorism.

5 The specific captions for the images from the Register of "Extremists" have been provided by the APM.

6 El peine in Argentine Spanish slang (for its resemblance to a comb) stands for a narrow, metal mugshot plate detailing (varyingly) the date of the detention and other numerical identification pertaining to the detained (what was included and how it was expressed differed regionally and institutionally).

7 The presence of the negatives is important here as they present the whole picture, so to speak. Printed images were often cropped much more closely to include just the face of the detained and the number above it. A lot of the contextual information mentioned by Cristina (including, in some cases, the face of the functionary holding the "comb") is only present in the unmodified negatives.

8 David Schäfer and Alejandro Frola were researchers external to the APM. For the account of their work on the Register, see Schäfer (2017).

9 For an explanation of the term, see the glossary.

10 The video from this part of the exhibition can be accessed at www.youtube.com/watch?v=cp1u6VzFkek

11 Cordobazo was a 1969 civil uprising of workers and students in Córdoba. Its aftermath marked the beginning of the brutal and coordinated repression of perceived dissent that continued during the dictatorship.

12 A leftist student and worker organisation.

4

Political Landscapes and Photographic Artefacts in Post-Dictatorship Argentina

Natalia Fortuny[1]

Disappearance often makes the healing of bereavement impossible. It is a suspension of death, a wait, pure pain. Disappearance implies a triple condition: the absence of a body, the lack of a moment of mourning and the impossibility of a burial.[2] Argentine photographic art has responded to these dictatorship-related deprivations – exacerbated by protracted legal, political and symbolic struggles – with artefacts that fuse the aesthetic with the political; personal memories with collective histories. Indeed, photography in Argentina has become the political emblem of the disappearance of bodies, as well as a way of engaging with the ontological complexity of the phenomenon. This chapter examines photographic work related to the Argentine dictatorship that focuses on countering disappearance by striving for the visibility of traumatic pasts. In doing so, it explores the tension associated with the duality of the medium: as both an index and a construct; a crafted artefact and a record, a trace of the world as it is (or as it was). In other words, it investigates the consequences of situating photography somewhere between art and archive.[3]

The artists whose work is concerned with Argentina's recent past are, of course, unable to photograph the bodies that were the objects of the violence of forced disappearance. And yet, they insist on (re)presenting that which is no longer alive but whose death cannot be evidenced precisely because of its very absence: the disappeared body. Nelly Richard points out the dramatic nature of the fight "against the *disappearance* of the body," of "having to incessantly produce the social *appearance* of the memory of this disappearance" (2007, 144; original emphasis). Consequently, it is the production of visual and verbal language that breaks the traumatic silence, complicit in oblivion. Numerous photographic artefacts produced in the country since the return of democracy in 1983 fit into these parameters: aesthetic manifestations that construct memory by opting for the fragmentary and the small, often built on what can be seen as leaning towards fictions, chiaroscuros and duplicities. I am thinking here about the early photographs of city spaces and the still-visible remnants of repression in the series *¿Dónde están?* [*Where Are They?*] by Res (1984). Or the work of Paula Luttringer (1995, 2012), Fernando Gutiérrez (1997), Helen Zout (2009) and Inés Ulanovsky (2011), which evoke the tools and technologies employed by the repressive state apparatus, such as the Ford Falcon, the planes of the Death Flights and the clandestine detention centres (CDCs), where detainees were tortured and murdered.[4] Several artists with close family ties to the disappeared have also produced another vast body of photographic material by reutilising the photographs from their own family albums as prompts for constructing new sets of images. Amongst these are Marcelo Brodsky (1997), Gabriela Bettini (2003), Camilo del Cerro (2005), Gustavo Germano (2006) and Lucila Quieto (2011).

These photographic works conjure a common traumatic history, with no documentary claim. In the very processes they use to *construct* reality, they constitute themselves as photographic memories of the past, drawing on photography's dual capacity to offer itself as the trace of a world *and* the representation of newly constructed worlds.[5] It is precisely as artefacts – that is, as constructed objects – that they visually question the notion of a photographic record, while emphasising their own, crucial adherence to the world they try to reach, as well as their potential to intervene in the present. In the midst of *becoming a document* that characterises much of contemporary art, what are the possibilities offered by photography, haunted, as it has been from its very inception, by its documentary quality? What can a photographic artefact say about history?

Photography interacts with the world in a dual movement of estrangement and irruption. An antithesis of a reflection, the photographic image honours distance (created by the photographic act itself), that hiatus that Aby Warburg conceives as *Denkraum*, or room for thought (Burucúa and Kwiatkowski 2014). In fact, it can be argued that photographs are "the first place we know of where humans actualise that distance, the first civilising record" (Santos 2014, 19). At the same time, photography fuses with the things that surround it in a unique way. It can bring us, for instance, to the world of politics, to conflict, with an insistence that emerges abruptly to disarrange or disconcert.

The images examined in this chapter are artefacts that, insofar as they construct unique photographic landscapes, offer a distance from which to decipher the painful collective experience of Argentina's recent history. They are conceived and considered here as photographic memories and political landscapes – in Warnke's terms (1994) – and grouped into three thematic lines of enquiry. The first is the *natural landscape* that opens up like an abyss to evoke, through exposure to the elements suggested in the images, the bleak desolation, wilderness and "shelterlessness" of disappearance. The second is the *urban landscape*, which explores the deliberate reconstruction and the artifice of photographic practice. Here, photography's supposed ability to record the world is questioned because the very world that is to be recorded is absent. Lastly, the *familial landscape* develops its potential through collage, which, by working with the materiality of the photographic medium, allows the artist to create imaginary worlds that allude to and gesture towards other worlds, ones that were denied the chance to continue existing. The architecture of the images, their details and visual strategies, allow us a glimpse into the relationship between, firstly, photography and what surrounds it, and, secondly, photography and the recent history of political violence in Argentina.

Natural Landscape (Wilderness and Desolation)

I would like to begin with a double photograph of Jorge Julio López; double because it consists of an already existent and circulated image re-inserted into a new context that produces an altogether new photograph. It is part of Gabriel Orge's series *Apareciendo* [*Appearing*] (2014–2015). The series began as an urban intervention, with a sunset projection of a photograph of López onto a street corner in the city of Córdoba, on Thursday, 18 September 2014. On the same date, eight years earlier, López had disappeared for the second time.

López's first disappearance took place during the dictatorship. Involved in the local militancy of the left-wing Peronist movement, he was kidnapped from his house in Los Hornos – in the outskirts of La Plata – on 27 October 1976, and remained detained-disappeared for five months.

López was kept in the CDCs that operated under the command of Miguel Osvaldo Etchecolatz, a known repressor and, at the time, the head of the criminal investigation department of the Buenos Aires Provincial Police. López was later "whitewashed," imprisoned without trial in La Plata Detention Centre Nº 9, and eventually released on 25 June 1979.[6] His second disappearance took place on 18 September 2006, at the age of eighty. It happened soon after López had testified in the trial for crimes against humanity committed by Etchecolatz, despite receiving threats designed to convince him not do so. The day after López's second disappearance – and partly due to his testimony – Etchecolatz was handed down a life sentence. After years of investigation, and despite being heard in court in 2015, the case of López's second disappearance remains unsolved. Ever since, a seat has been kept empty during the Truth Trials held in La Plata as a marker of López's "presence."

What happened to López embodies the risks – which include the potential loss of life – faced by those who decide to testify in trials related to the dictatorship. To be a witness and/or a claimant in Argentina can be dangerous. López's disappearance has been clearly meant to instil terror in others.[7] The act of testifying – far from simply implying the possibility of being heard – places survivors in an uncomfortable position, exposing them to criticism and dangers. It often leads to questioning and suspicion – all because they managed to survive. Ana Longoni proposes that what happened to López shows that: "the threat of punishment that hangs over the few survivors of clandestine detention and extermination centres is fulfilled." She goes on to add that the "unprotected" survivors "bear today the terrible historical responsibility of telling – over and over again – the horror suffered, while at the same time being suspected and stigmatised for having survived when thousands of others were disappeared forever" (2010b). Returning from disappearance isolates survivors in an after-life that, all too often, also condemns them.

In his response to López's second disappearance, the Córdoban photographer Gabriel Orge worked with the photograph taken by Helen Zout for her series *Desapariciones [Disappearances]* (2009). As mentioned before, the first projection was an urban intervention on the exact date of López's disappearance eight years earlier. After months of projecting it in the city, Orge eventually took Zout's photograph out into nature – into the landscape of his childhood – and recorded that projection in a new photograph, a double image (Figure 4.1). The resulting piece – "Making López appear in the Ctalamochita river" – won the "Acquisition" First Prize in Photography from the National Gallery of Visual Arts.

Zout took the original photo in 2000 (Figure 4.2). It was part of a series of interviews she conducted with López, accompanied by photographs. In 2012, this particular image was also granted the "Acquisition" Grand Prize by the National Gallery of Visual Arts. The portrait is a paradigmatic, symbolic and emblematic image that resonates in the visual memory of protests and demands for justice for that second disappearance. It has been displayed in numerous demonstrations, publications and tributes. In *Desapariciones*, Zout examines, retrospectively and with a survivor's gaze, the traces of the repressive policy and actions of the dictatorship. In the book's pages, we see black-and-white photographs of Ford Falcons, the planes used by the Armed Forces in the Death Flights, the bone fragments recovered by the Argentine Forensic Anthropology Team (EAAF), the escraches of the H.I.J.O.S., and several portraits of survivors. A militant herself, and a friend of many of the disappeared from her home city of La

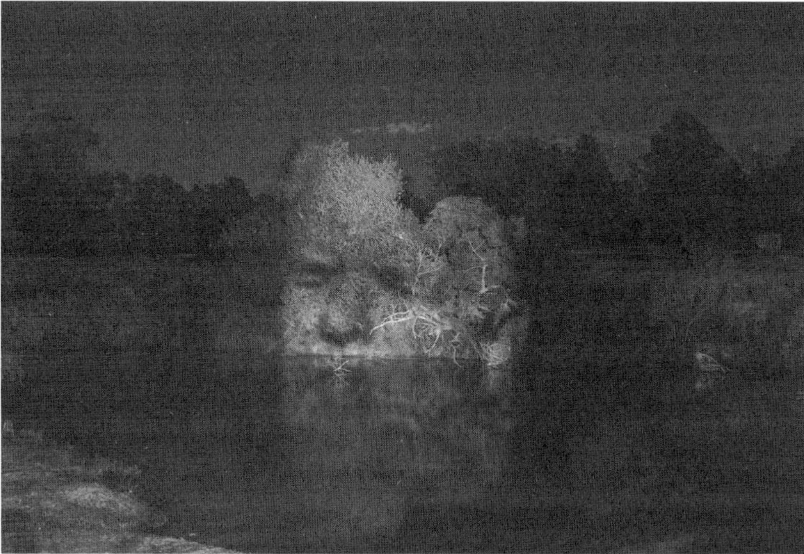

Figure 4.1 Making López appear in the Ctalamochita river.
Source/Author: Gabriel Orge.

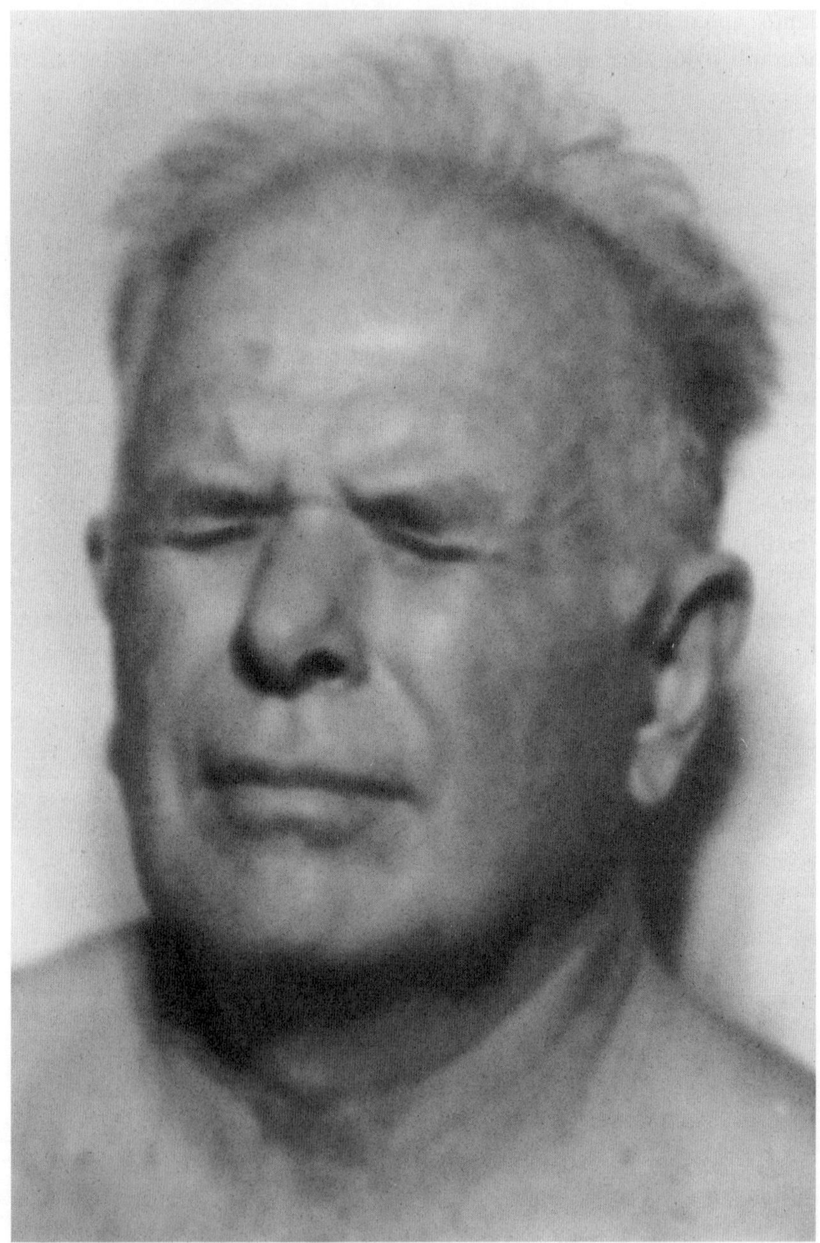

Figure 4.2 Portrait of Julio López with eyes closed.
Source/Author: Helen Zout.

Plata, Zout managed to evade capture by going into hiding. Her photographs embody a clear generational and biographical perspective: "my place is the place a disappeared person would have occupied: a tortured person, someone dropped into the river. Each one works from their own place" (Zout 2011, personal communication).[8]

Double exposure is a frequent technique used in Zout's work of representing survivors. Her portraits of Nilda Eloy and M., for instance, show doubly-exposed, overlapping faces – in one of the images, a second pair of eyes appears superimposed over a cheek. By resorting to simple strategies, such as blurred, overexposed and superimposed images, Zout opts for visual incertitude to portray the survivors in their unceasing suffering. The blurred image, with its vagueness, confusion and lack of clarity, possesses an ambiguous ability to defy contour, depth and duration. This expressive aptitude alludes to *zero degree* not only of photography but also of movement: "the shudder" (Bellour 2009, 91). The shudder occurs between the mobile and the immobile and produces a *durée*, establishes duration, a temporality that is not sequential but that co-exists between the temporal dimensions of the present and the past. It is also a phenomenological time, a temporality that frustrates the idea of time as a unidirectional succession of singular moments (van Alphen 2014). On the other hand, if there is time, there can be a story, and in this sense Zout's blurred images are, effectively, narrating something. Time, both stuck and mobile, endows those photographs with a power of dramatisation, of fiction. The eye does not register the movement itself and therefore the blurred image acts as the transmitter of a moving presence before the camera and, in this, it certifies the photograph as a construct. According to Bellour, photographic blur "is one of photography's clearest techniques for pointing to itself as artifice, and appointing itself as art," and for capturing an effect of the real without taking it as reality (2009, 87). Even when it is the result of different techniques – long exposure, a moving subject or the image being out of focus – the blur in the photograph always exposes the image's artificiality.

Zout employed this approach when she photographed López. Two portraits of him are particularly well-known, one with the eyes open and one with the eyes closed (Figure 4.2). In the latter, López is photographed in black-and-white, in a close-up that includes his bare neck and upper chest. The epigraph accompanying the image reads: "Jorge Julio López, a survivor of the Arana clandestine centre. La Plata, 2000" (Zout 2009). The image is slightly blurred. The closed eyes, as if in pain, suggest a refusal to see or to remember. They also create a *caesura* or an interference in the recognition of López's humanity, for a portrait, by definition, implies the gaze of the sitter. Zout has said that she photographed López on several occasions but that she chose this photograph because of his concentrated gesture, a gesture of recalling and giving testimony (Zout 2011, personal communication). According to Res, in this picture López looks as though he is about to be shot (Res 2011, personal communication).

In Gabriel Orge's photograph, López, twice-disappeared, also appears twice, duplicated through the insertion into a completely different context and, in a way, dissociated from the original photograph. The original image is familiar to us – we know its history; it is symbolic – and this results in an even deeper estrangement as we now see it appear in nature. The clear, light background of Zout's portrait is replaced by the darkness of the night and the drama of the sunset. The serene sky, with the line of trees silhouetted in the background, is clear but dark. A tiny cloud looks like it could be part of López's head, almost as if something has become detached. It makes one question where the projected image begins and where it ends.

Orge's photograph enhances Zout's image. The record of the projection magnifies it with its phantasmagorical vegetal intervention. Something happens to the landscape once López's image emerges. He re-appears; a vegetal López; a ghostly, bodiless López; a sunken López; a projected López. With white veins and his mouth partly underwater, submerging. López's face both touches and is reflected in the water. The two-dimensional photograph expands to make the unpalpable palpable: an image of that which has disappeared. López is maimed, he's sinking, submerged like those *non-human* prisoners – without thought, without language – described in Primo Levi's testimony (2006) and examined by Giorgio Agamben (2000).

The return to nature is not a sign of harmony but of the loss of the human condition, of *bare life*. López closes his eyes, no longer on painful memories as in his portrait as a witness, but on the new horror, on the new condition of loneliness and helpless desolation in the landscape, on the condition of being a sheer, bodiless image; a condition he is subjected to for the second time. The closing of the eyes in the original photograph is here aggravated because the depicted person gradually disappears, sinks down into the water and will soon be gone completely when daylight arrives. López closes his eyes to this second disappearance. Faced with what is happening to him, he shuts down his own gaze.

Zout's acumen as a portraitist is accentuated in Orge's photograph, suspended as it is between vegetation and water: water that is neither that of a lake nor of a lagoon but of a river that hints both at the passing of time in its unstoppable flow and at La Plata River, into which living people were dropped during Death Flights. That's where López is "appearing," between units of time and contemplation, in the Narcissus-like reflection in the water, in the smallest gesture reinserted into a vital and yet anomalous situation.

However, the evanescence and immateriality of López's presence is not enough to speak of an actual, complete re-appearance. Rather, the gerund form used in the title "Making López appear" clearly implies that these photographs simply document an ephemeral projection.[9] Orge understands this image as a record of his fleeting intervention in the landscape, of his futile and temporary attempt to make López appear by the means of light in the face of the obvious irreversibility of his actual disappearance. The image highlights the performative quality of the photographic act, the practice and the event alike. Considering that images are capable of acting beyond human intentions, it is important to note their performative potential, their capacity to have a life of their own that can result in actions and effects. Going beyond the artist's foresight, the visual configuration of images does things; carries out *image acts*. Despite their inorganic materiality, images can be endowed with a certain agency, particularly in the realm of visual memories about a conflictive past (Bredekamp 2014). Consequently, the performative, precarious, evanescent installation of Zout's photograph in the water is the real labour in this piece of work.

But why in a natural landscape? Firstly, it is worth noting that in that same year, 2015, the National Gallery of Visual Arts also presented the "Acquisition" Grand Prize to Gabriel Díaz for his series *Flores en la ESMA* [*Flowers in the ESMA*] (2016), a group of images of flowers taken with expired polaroids. This means that in the same year the National Gallery honoured two series that took the recent history of the dictatorship and its relationship to nature as their subject. Secondly, it is not the first time

Orge deals with this theme. In his 2012 series *El Paisaje crítico* [*The Critical Landscape*], he conceived geographical terrain as an effect of the action of a community and showed the historical marks of agricultural production in the countryside and of the global crisis in the city. Based on the notion that landscape is somehow "human" in relation to space, Orge believes that every peaceful landscape hides something. Consequently, Orge's work endeavours to decipher the violence inflicted on the earth in order to "find beauty in the tragic" (Molas 2013). Part of this intention is also visualised in the landscape with López, where the portrait disrupts the peacefulness of nature.[10]

Orge takes inspiration from the desolate, the unsheltered outdoors where one is exposed to and at the mercy of the elements, but also from the work of artistic conceptualism of the 1960s that used the public space as a place for experimentation. The latter may explain why in his first intervention Orge projected the photograph in the city. He later moves to natural sceneries, and this is where his personal memories emerge powerfully, and in particular an event that deeply affected him in his childhood. The banks of the Ctalamochita river in Bell Ville not only represent Orge's birthplace. According to the artist, "that river area is a very significant place for me, it is where I learned to swim against the current, encouraged by my uncle Ovidio, and it was also there, when I was six, that I saw the first scene of violence in my life" (Máximo 2015). Thus, Orge chooses natural sceneries because of their significance to his own life. Nature here is chosen as a framing space for violence, as a landscape of history and danger. Water is summoned because of its active quality: it brings its own aquatic memories.

Photography, as a double – just like its precursor, the silhouette – is particularly well equipped to conjure the past thanks to its indexical quality and its contiguity with the human body.[11] Orge's work is part of a larger trend of employing the projection of family portraits to evoke the memory of the disappeared.[12] Like in other pieces of similar nature, there is a performance here in the photographic capture, a staging that flows towards the future. We witness the enactment of an already seen photograph. By presenting this altered incarnation of the original, Orge invites us to see something new. By changing the scene that receives and contains López's image, Orge raises the question of the photograph's materiality, prompting us to ask: what exactly constitutes the image of the disappeared? What is its material basis? Following Deleuze and Guattari's allocutions in *A Thousand Plateaus* (1987) – specifically in "Follow the plants" – Michael Marder invites us to "engage in irreverent thinking of the plants, which will set us on the path of becoming-plant" (2020, 44). Orge's photograph underscores the non-identitarian, rhizomatic aspect of a twice-disappeared López. By de-automatising the way of seeing a known photograph, the image creates a memory gesture aimed at and coming from a former detainee-disappeared of the dictatorship, who disappears once again after having testified. This dual photograph reveals some of the uncertainties that continue to surround Jorge Julio López's disappearance. And thus, in its double and vegetal artificiality, it bears testimony.

Other artists, such as Hugo Vidal and Lucas Di Pascuale, also ciphered the struggle for López's re-appearance into their work. Vidal radically changed his production process in order to focus on different tools designed to give publicity to the case and call society's attention to it by, for instance, substituting López's name for his own on the business cards he gave out. Or by creating a stamp that allowed him to alter, in a subtle and almost imperceptible way, the label on the bottle of the popular López wine with the inscription demanding "Julio's appearance alive."[13] For years, Vidal carried out this alteration on the supermarket shelves, with the tampered-with bottles kept in commercial circulation. In turn, Di Pascuale evoked the fragility of López's second disappearance by creating an ephemeral reminder: a sign made with light wood strips bearing just one word: "López." This piece has been set up and replicated in different cultural spaces in Córdoba and other Argentine cities. Completely devoid of light and colour, Di Pascuale's signs are overshadowed, almost to the point of invisibility, by the surrounding light pollution. As they are left exposed to the elements, they quickly deteriorate and a new call for collective action must be launched to replace them and to revitalise the demand (Longoni 2015). La Brecha Collective's posters, made ten years after López's disappearance, are also interesting to consider here. López's photographic portrait appears modified with drawings in order to create five other identities also likely to be subjects of disappearance. This is how López becomes a shanty town kid, a travesti, an indigenous person, a female victim of human trafficking and a piquetero.[14] Another powerful and significant image of López is the photograph taken on 11 October 2011, during the Camps Circuit trial, when the video of López's testimony, recorded during a previous trial in 2006, was projected *as testimony*. It was the first time in a trial for crimes committed by the dictatorship that a witness testified while remaining disappeared.

There has also been work that specifically addresses the natural world and landscapes of absence in relation to López's testimony. In *Imágenes en la memoria* [*Images in Memory*] (2011), Gerardo Dell'Oro, photographer and brother of a young woman disappeared together with her partner a few weeks after their daughter's birth, in November 1976, uses his sister Patricia's images from the family album to create others that, together with text and other media (drawings, school report cards, short stories, letters and judicial testimonies), trace the complex path through the experience of absence and the search for justice.[15] "Trees", the book's third section, consist of night scenes full of overgrown vegetation captured with long exposure and a trembling hand. The lack of illumination makes time flow with the movement within the images: light comes from an always imperfect flash, or from a car's headlights, or the sun breaking on the horizon. All this is part of the last stretch of the photographic journey though Patricia's life and disappearance. She was murdered in the Pozo de Arana CDC a month after being apprehended. The family only found out about the circumstances of Patricia's death in 1999, thanks to Julio López's testimony. Coincidentally, Dell'Oro photographed, "intuitively," as he puts it, the trees near the last place his sister lived in. They are images of rage and fury which Dell'Oro included in his book to evoke "the ups and downs in the search for justice, the hope and defeat. Some are dark and blurred; others shaped like graves, like silhouettes, and even like an upheld fist" (Meyer 2008). These are photographs of the traces of the horror left out, exposed in nature. The trees, also present in some of Zout's photographs, and of course in Orge's, represent the dramatic corroboration of life's continuity, even where horror took place. Dell'Oro documents this terror by visually exploring these sinister sceneries and interspersing them with Julio López's testimony about the torture inflicted on his sister and brother-in-law during their last days, and the account of their murder. "There exists the belief that trees breathe the breath of the people who inhabit buried cities" proclaims a phrase by Miguel Ángel Asturias that functions as an epigraph for this series. Photographs and texts travel from the forest to the concentration camp (the CDC), in a two-way journey between what is seen and what has transpired in those places, between what *can* be seen and what *can* be said – especially when the testimony for which Patricia's family had awaited took decades to materialise. In these photographs, trees fuse with the concentration camp, and it is no longer possible to tell where one begins and the other ends.

The artefacts considered and analysed here appeal to nature to find in that outdoor space a key to understand and express disappearance and absence. The natural horizon appears in them as a *political landscape* (Warnke 1994). Landscape, in turn, – understood as aesthetically-seen-nature (Simmel 2014) – is a territory of multiple exchanges and has in common with photography the fact that it is just a piece, a segment, a section (Cortés Rocca 2011). The photographic landscapes, then, seek to shift the focus of the *magisterial gaze* of a viewer distanced from the terrain. Someone who walks away to look in from the outside and who captures an arresting natural horizon on a magnificent scale; practices linked to travel and establishing dominion over terrain (Boime 1991). The gaze of the photographic work considered here distances itself from that outlook that regards the human as the measure of the landscape. The question asked is no longer one about finding a fixed viewpoint where one might situate oneself, outside of what one is looking at, but about unfolding a voice and a gaze that may become part of the terrain and allowing oneself, in turn, to be affected by it.

If there is a remnant of truth in the landscape, it will only be found by addressing the gaze towards what remains there, unsheltered and exposed to the elements, and conversely by listening to – and this includes looking at – the testimony of the very voice of the mineral and the vegetal wilderness. This is precisely what these photographs explore: the relationship between terrain and the past, the remnants of history and politics that remain there.

Urban Landscape (the Artifice)

While the previous section of this chapter demonstrated how, through Julio López's case, various photographic memories can be inscribed into the natural and vegetal world, here I turn to an image – artificially true – situated within the city limits. The photograph – "Calle 30 Nº1134" ["Street 30 Nº1134"] (Figure 4.3) – by Hugo Aveta raises questions about what is real and what is not when dealing with the intersection of memory and urban landscape. More specifically, the image probes the possibility of creating – inventing – the (photographic) remnants of the recent past.

Among the few traces of the last dictatorship that remain in Argentina's urban spaces is a house in La Plata that still retains the original marks of its destruction – the consequence of an attack by the Armed Forces. The building used to house – under an elaborate disguise – the clandestine press that printed the publication *Evita Montonera*. On 24 November 1976, a task force launched an assault on the site. Five members of the Montoneros died, and a three-month-old baby, Clara Anahí, was kidnapped. Her whereabouts are still unknown. The site has been turned into the House of Memory and declared a National Historical Monument of the Buenos Aires Province.

The building is conjured in Aveta's image. At first glance, one sees a house with dilapidated walls and the garage door riddled with bullet holes.

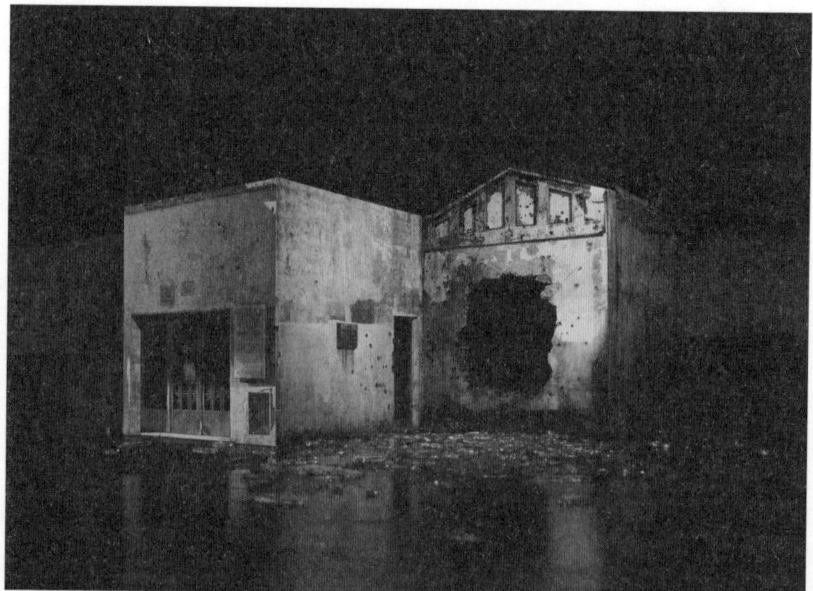

Figure 4.3 Calle 30 Nº1134.
Source/Author: Hugo Aveta.

Where there must have been a window, there is now a wide gap, as if a bomb had blasted the whole structure apart, an assumption corroborated by the pieces of broken glass on the floor. An empty frame indicates that a door has also been ripped out. The whole scene is lit in a strange artificial light: more in line with cinema lighting than with natural night light or streetlamps. Moreover, the house stands between a homogeneous black sky above and a very even long strip of black floor below. This produces the first feeling of estrangement, something that breaks the automatised perception ready to decode any documentary photograph of a devastated site. At a second glance, other details, such as the freshly fallen pieces of glass on the floor or the impeccable reflection of the pavement, confirm our suspicion that something is out of place in this image.

There is a simple reason for this discomfort: the photograph is not a shot of the actual building but an image of a scaled model of the house, specially constructed for the purpose of being photographed. We may then wonder what is real and what is not in the illusion enacted by this piece. Two simultaneous readings are possible. Firstly, this is a photograph that shows what is in front of the camera and therefore shows *something* – the scaled model of the house – that *was really there*, in Barthesian terms. Secondly, however, what the photograph shows is a model, a mock-up, with a level of accuracy and verisimilitude similar to that of a model railway. The effect of this is complex and unstable. It reminds us of the processes involved in the construction of reality, especially when it comes to representation. Aveta points out that he created this image "from the double track of reality and fiction, working on perception, memories and history, without upholding any truth, nor rejecting all deception either [...] Spaces are deconstructed and reconstructed (in scaled models) into new settings, linking them to social history, architecture, and their codes of legitimisation and validity" (Aveta 2016). Thus, the photograph shows the fictitious traces, the invented markings of a documented event that actually took place. Ultimately, it is the indeterminacy between the scaled model and the real house that creates the expressive effect of this image.

Aveta has a sustained record of work related to urban settings, the passing of time and the way these spaces can act as support for memory. "Calle 30 N°1134" is part of a series entitled *Espacios sustraíbles* [*Subtractable Spaces*] (Aveta 2015), composed of eighteen images of specially produced scaled models. The mock-ups of emblematic urban sites, completely devoid of people, are presented in dark, rarefied atmospheres. The images are of deserted urban spaces that convey a feeling of dereliction and, in their own construction, allude to an aesthetic-political charge of past times. Strange and estranging images that exhibit the fictitious traces, the invented marks of events that really happened and places that once existed. For instance, the apathy and negligence evoked by the medical histories of the Santa María Hospital in Córdoba – created for the treatment of tuberculosis and later used as a psychiatric hospital – or the emptiness of La Perla's (a former CDC, also in Córdoba) architecture. The very idea of a subtractable space is akin to a space related to an absence, a lack. Aveta offers *created remnants* of a traumatic past. As if we could only allude to certain events from the ambiguous vantage point between something created and something documented, thus exposing the fiction and construction present in each photograph; in harmony with the constant and active work of memory.

Aveta's photography does not speak exclusively of the past. Rather, in order to speak of the past and, more fundamentally, of the possibility of constructing memories about the past, it speaks of the process involved in the creation of the real – including of what can be understood as the photographic real. Drawing on Walter Benjamin's ideas, Didi-Huberman proposes that some photographs have the:

Extraordinary ability to fuse with things. But what does it mean, to fuse with things? To be in place, undoubtedly. View to observe, while knowing that one is observed, concerned, *involved*. And still more: to stay, to linger, to live for a time in that gaze, in that involvement. To make that experience last. And then to make of that experience a form, to deploy a visual work.

(2013; original emphasis)

It is, perhaps, the combination of the construct and document that underscores and permits photography's interlacing with politics. Jorge Ribalta (2018) argues for this approach when it comes to contemporary photographic work: a molecular realism, a new articulation capable of surpassing the opposition between document and fiction and operating in the realm of micro-politics. By inscribing itself within that fluctuating tension, Aveta's work burns with the real; in other words, it acquires and enhances its political charge.

The Familial Landscape (the Collage)

Particularly notable among the photographic artefacts that evoke the dictatorial past by unfolding political landscapes is the work of Lucila Quieto, constructed out of family images. From the beginning of her career, Quieto has worked with photography and collage. Her photographic series *Arqueología de la ausencia* [*Archaeology of Absence*] (2011) is made up of manually constructed photographs of herself together with her father, Carlos Quieto, disappeared by the dictatorship before Lucila was born. Urged and haunted by the lack of photographs of the two of them together, and by the need to visually reconstruct an unattainable moment, Quieto conceived the idea of creating impossible family portraits both of herself and of other children of the disappeared (Figure 4.4). The photographs were initially produced to make up for the absence that exists not only in the daily life of the family of disappeared people but also in the family album: the disappearance of a body magnified by the absence of its portrait. "I clung to the image because it was something that I always missed about my father and something that always amplified the void created by his physical absence" (Bullentini 2010). Many children of the disappeared are affected by this lack of images.[16]

It is important to note that Quieto's series was part of – and helped to inaugurate – a broad field of cultural production by artists who are family members – especially sons and daughters – of the disappeared and who re-use the photographs from their own family albums in their work. These visual pieces and fictions expose the absence in an ambiguous territory, where the public and private spheres contaminate each other. By being exposed in the public sphere, these family photographs are, as it were, transplanted and their previous functions transformed. And this movement denounces and exposes in the public sphere a fragment of the family life before it was fractured by state violence. The singular stories and trajectories intersect in a complex way in each of these images. As photographic memories, these portraits' function consists in narrating the tragic absence of the loved one, the singular lack of *that* particular person.

In a 2007 series, Quieto created powerful and heterogeneous scenes by combining drawings taken from the comic *Sargento Kirk* [*Sergeant Kirk*], by a disappeared writer Héctor G. Oesterheld, with photographs of the Cordobazo, the organised labour and student uprising in the city of

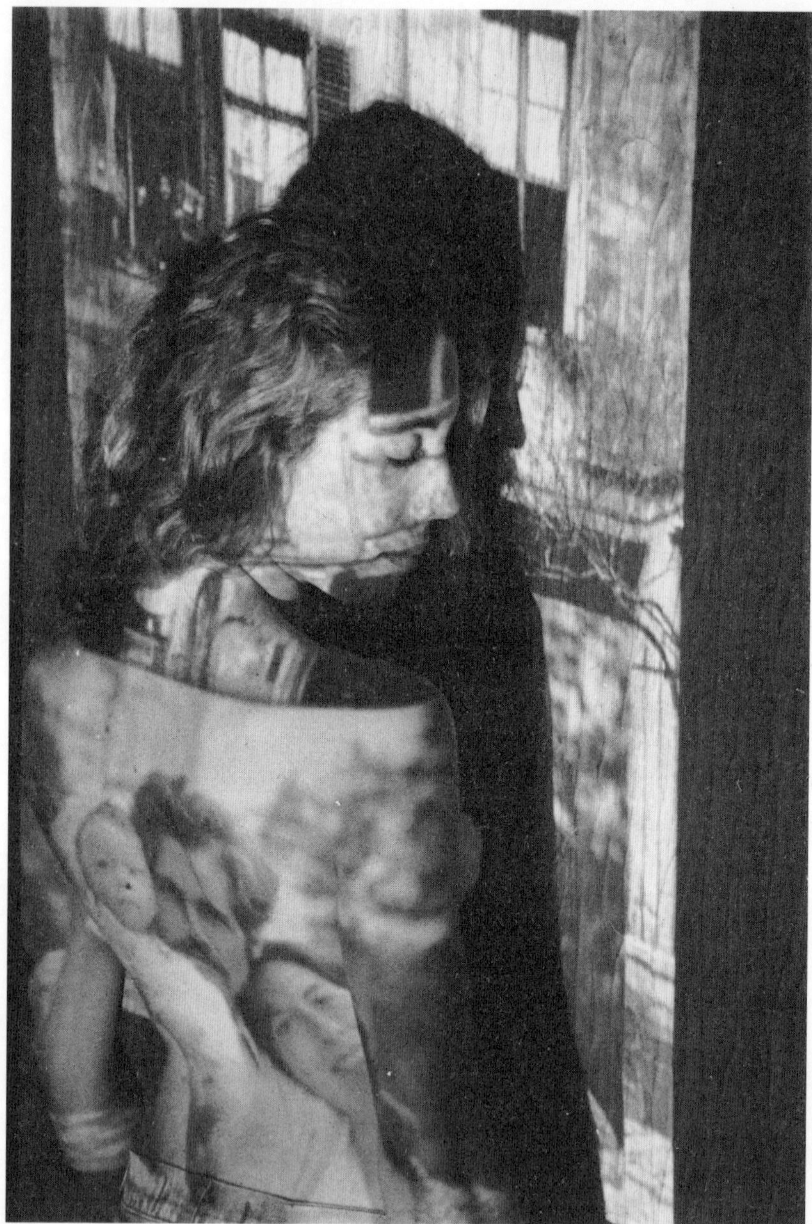

Figure 4.4 Image from *Arqueología de la ausencia*.
Source/Author: Lucila Quieto.

Córdoba in 1969. In another set of images, between 2008 and 2009, she reproduced several police photographs from press archives, by drawing and colouring them with tiny bits of glossy paper. She presented in this way armed men, a clandestine gun and, among others, four detained militants from Tucumán, including the infiltrator who gave them away. In response to the repressive actions taken against the families that had built their precarious dwellings in Indoamerican Park in Buenos Aires, in 2010, Quieto copied press photographs using colour pencils and crayons, creating beautiful and simple drawings of the women and the tents in which they had temporarily settled.

Continuing the exploration of handmade images, in 2013 Quieto produced the series *Filiación* [*Filiation*]. In it, she adorned portraits of her father with dried leaves and flowers, drew foreboding skulls on old family photographs and created overlapping genealogies with cut-out photographs and crayon drawings. At the root of theses collages lies the desire to find the skeletal remains of her father, a reference to the search for the remains of the disappeared that the EAAF has been carrying out for decades.

Lately I've had the opportunity to experience the burial of the parents of many of my companions. Children who recovered the bones of their parents, after thirty-five years, and buried them [...] The appearance of our parents after thirty-five years is a political event [...] I began to think about the possibility of finding or not finding my father's bones. I took the photographs of my grandmother, my father, his brothers and sisters, of my cousins, my son, my cousins' children. Some physical resemblances are there and visible, although I think that if, one day, he is found buried somewhere, it's going to be like seeing him for the first time.

(Máximo 2014)

This collective horizon of a (painful) experience and of making artwork with her peers is always present in Quieto's outputs. A long-term member of H.I.J.O.S., she was one of the promoters of the The Collective of Children [Colectivo de Hijos]. This organisation emerged in 2010 with the purpose of reconsidering its members as children of the disappeared, and of placing them at the centre of the traumatic situation, rather than focusing exclusively on the suffering of their parents. It would be no longer a question of dealing with the absence of the mothers and fathers but of shifting the focus towards their own condition and reviewing their lived experience as victims, especially in the light of the fact that some were kidnapped and remained temporarily disappeared in their own childhood. The images they tried to rescue from oblivion were no longer only those of their parents but also of them as children and as subjects of that experience. Several works addressed this theme: María Giuffra's paintings and comics – mainly her series *Los niños del Proceso* [*The Children of the Process*] (2005); the literary pieces by Ángela Urondo Raboy – in particular, her contributions to blogs about the restitution of her identity and the experiences of a childhood under the dictatorship; and Mariana Eva Perez's recently republished *Diario de una princesa montonera* [*Journal of a Montonero Princess*] (2021). Collage was also employed to explore this new imperative. The periodical meetings of the Collage Club [Club del Collage] (CdC), promoted by the Collective of Children, created a space where images were produced collectively with the use of this technique. Jordana Blejmar highlights the importance of the CdC and writes that "Quieto points out in this respect that collage is an accessible egalitarian language that anyone can use to say something." Blejmar also cites Quieto recounting that "maybe in a meeting (of the Collective of Children), where we are discussing an idea or an issue, not all of us can or have the capacity to take the floor and say something. So the idea of holding these collage meetings was to give everyone a chance to speak" (2013, 175–176).

Quieto's own photomontage images in *Filiación* take us to the realm of manual arts, of handicrafts and collage, of DIY. The visions captured in these images, created by cutting out, painting and reimagining old family photographs, playfully convey a painful history that is at once collective and intimate. These are fictions that recompose the family home and fill in, in an impossible way, the holes in its narrative, if only with a red crayon and photocopies. Each of these collages is an attempt to bring closer and strengthen the link with the absent parent, the brief and unique shared history. Does cutting photographs with one's fingers run the risk of ruining memories? Is there a danger of hurting oneself in the process? Although the joints in each assemblage are always noticeable, Quieto cuts the photographs to reunify broken things. Playing with history and politics, she situates her work in handcrafted photography, in montage and in working with paper. She cuts and assembles photographs, knowing that once re-assembled the joints will always remain there as markings.

Quieto's collages show landscapes created with the stroke of a crayon. But also with plants, leaves and flowers stuck with glue around the portrait of her father as a child (Figure 4.5). Just as the leaf remains green for a while after being plucked from the tree, these photographs underscore that which never grows old. The chlorophyll-green shade accompanies the portrait of the young man; youthful vigour and freshness stopped in time. The plucked leaf remains, like the photograph, preserved in formaldehyde, frozen. The photographs promise a *forever*. That promise is duplicated in the green areas that surround the image: the plucked green warns us that things are not what they appear to be, that they are no longer what they seem, that now they are but a sheer evocation of what is missing.

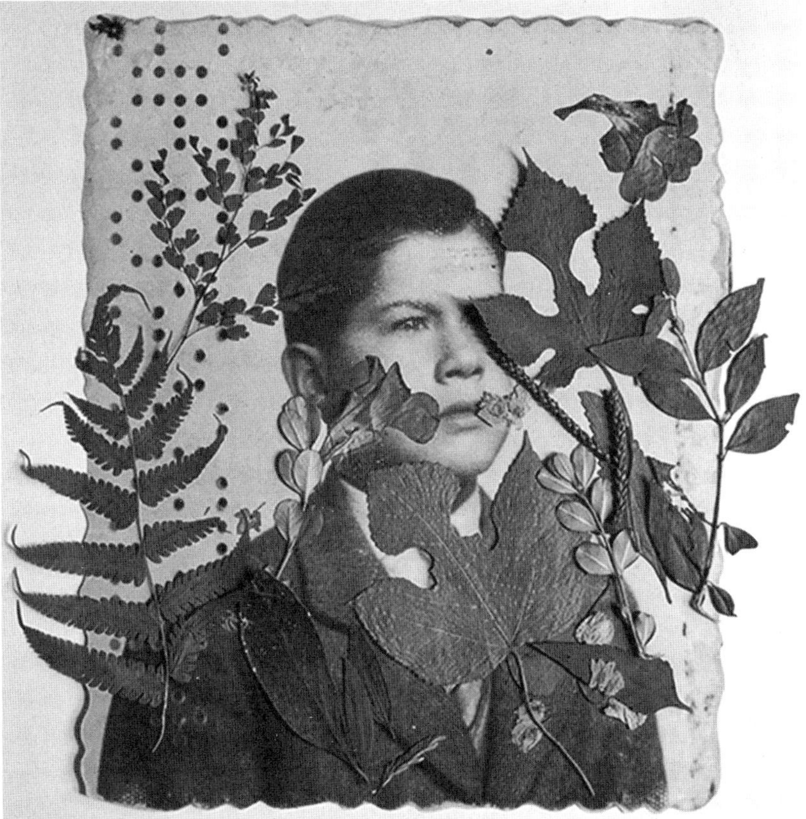

Figure 4.5 Image from *Filiación.*
Source/Author: Lucila Quieto.

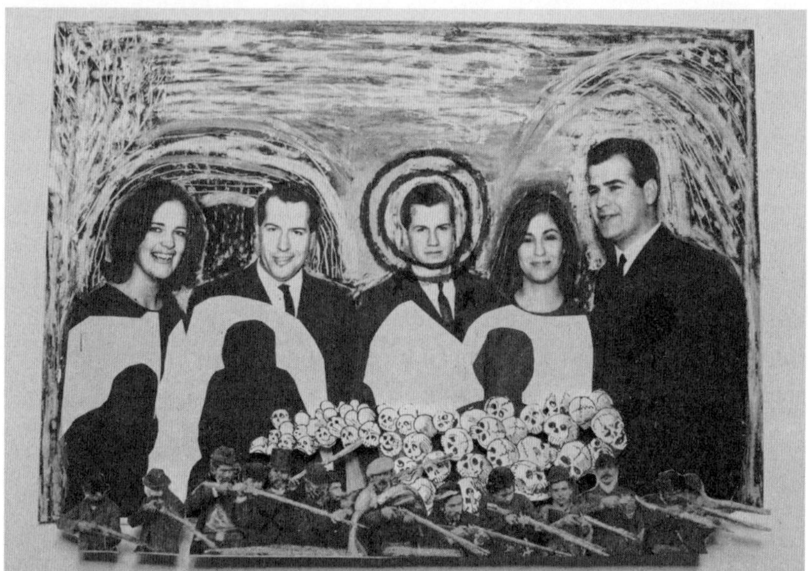

Figure 4.6 Image from *Filiación*.
Source/Author: Lucila Quieto.

The family tree is also green: what trait or feature of the unknown father's face can be detected in the eyes of Quieto's son, the cousins, the uncles and aunts, the nephews and nieces, the grandmother? Like in the branching of any family tree, filiations are multiple and the straight line is useless to understand the confusion of bones, features, faces and remains. The family, sitting in armchairs in the middle of the thicket, has their future members floating over their heads, like birthday party balloons. It is a "montage of heterogeneous times forming anachronisms" (Didi-Huberman 2008b, 39). By overlapping layers, Quieto skips timelines, sees the future. Not today's future, but the future of that past. In this, she does not trust the young girl's smiles. She draws the future with a red pencil around the portraits, draws the (as yet) unshed blood over the heart, surrounds a face with a circle turning it into a target to shoot at. In this world of photographs and photocopies, she draws bones, cuts and pastes a sea of skulls: a huge skull, like the heavy balancing rock one must visit before it falls. The translucent foreboding bones make us wonder how the people that appear posing next to them can be smiling. It is not always easy to tell what Quieto adds to the images and what was there before: timelines overlap, merge and intermingle.

All these playful games make one think of bones, of features and characteristics: the ways of recognising one another. Quieto assures us that, if she ever recovers her father's bones, they could give her an idea of her father's physical build. In the meantime, she looks at the faces and reconstructs images. She studies which of the genes have prevailed over which, who inherited whose bone structure. She imagines the bones underneath the skin to be able to know, above all, what the skin and smile must have looked like and to be able to recognise them the day she recovers her father's remains. In these images, the skeletons form a lineage as well as a hope.

In *Filiación* there is a photograph that appears twice: the picture of a girl in a school uniform and with a stern look (Figure 4.7). The girl seems reluctant to smile for the photograph. Perhaps something has annoyed her. She is wearing an eye patch, of sorts. The gaze in one of her eyes is blocked by a photocopy of the image of her father. Other, identical copies of the same paternal photo float around in the image, which has a holiday seaside and a national postage stamp for a background. A *pattern*-father, a sequence of identical men in black-and-white. When she was little, Quieto used to dislike this photograph of herself, because it made her look like a boy. Until she saw another photograph, of her father at the same age, and found out she wore her hair exactly like he had done, the same haircut, and the same stern look that only a child, boy *or* girl, can sustain. "We are alike", she thought, and she reconciled herself with the girl portrayed in the image, the protagonist of this series.

Collage underscores the tactile quality of photographs as objects that can be broken and recombined. It undoes the mimetic desire and amazes us with the artifice. Rancière highlights the critical tradition of this visual form: "The artistic and political success of collage and photomontage [derives from] the clash on the same surface of heterogeneous, if not conflicting, elements" (2010, 31). Willy Thayer (2003) emphasises the political character of collage in that it assimilates, by activating the heterogeneous, otherness without identity.

With their repetitions and different approaches to the search for the absent and lost time, Quieto's photomontages and collages focus on the

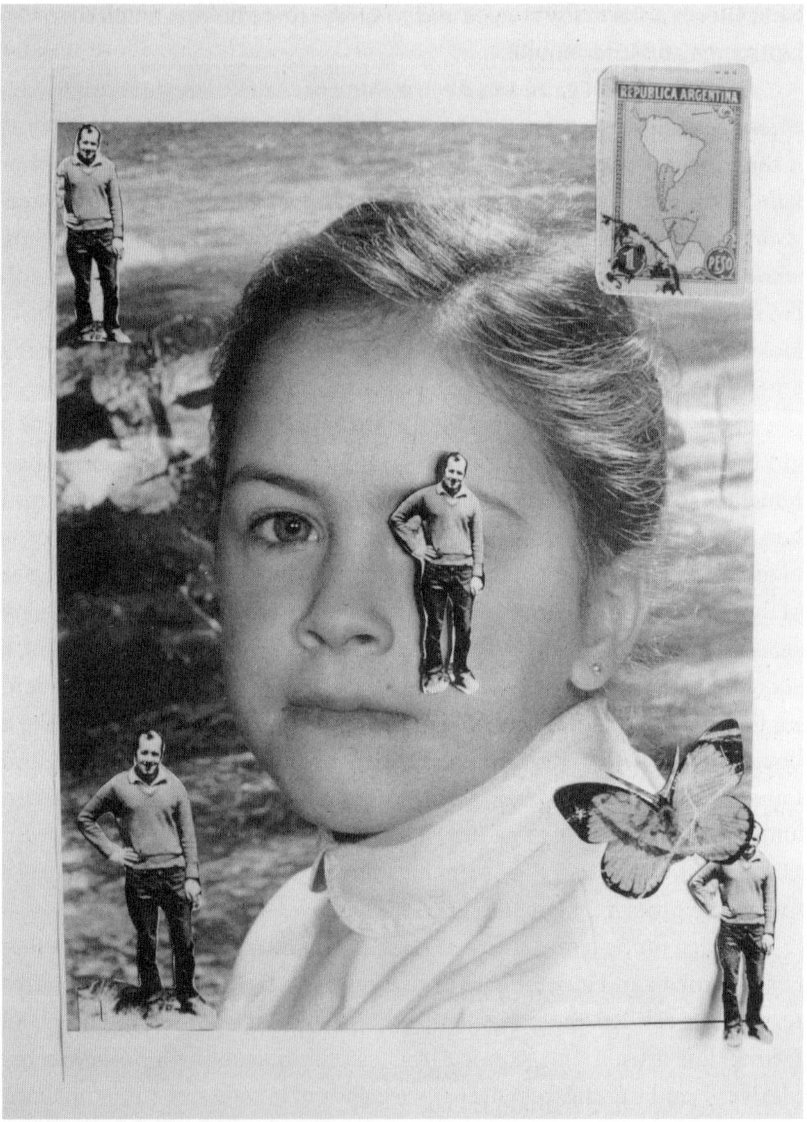

Figure 4.7 Image from *Filiación*.
Source/Author: Lucila Quieto.

overlapping of, and the play with, the familiar. But by bringing together, on the same surface, diverse visual fragments and temporalities, sometimes in conflict with each other, they open up to the fantastic. They offer themselves as impossible landscapes and memories and, in doing so, put forth a riddle.

They offer what documentary photography seems unable to provide: the strangeness and uncanniness of the poetics of fragments. These unique works intersect history and politics by combining pieces of photography. Lucila Quieto, with her unsurpassable skill for finding filiation and kinship in her gaze, invites us in her collages to visit unique sceneries, the prairie of her family history. She has the courage to reuse, reconstruct, overlap, paint, alter and combine family photographs, knowing that, in her re-arranged images, the joints of time will always show, like a scar.

Photographic Landscapes and Political Artefacts

Natural, urban and family landscapes emerge in the photographic artefacts analysed in this chapter, highlighting their historical and political burden. In their book on the representations of massacres throughout history, Burucúa and Kwiatkowski (2014) examine Warburg's concept of *Denkraum*, that space of distance and knowledge between subject and object. In their reflection on the 20th century, the authors put forward the idea that the representational formulas of recent massacres are related to the figure of the *Doppelgänger*, under the guise of silhouettes, masks, replicas, shadows. Ultimately, it is the duplication that will define the representation of massacres, among which figure the disappearances at the hands of the Argentine dictatorship.

Many contemporary photographic works follow the theme of distance, like the cinematographic-identarian play between Albertina Carri and Analía Couceyro in the film *Los Rubios* (Carri 2003), which narrates the disappearance of the director's parents.[17] They are games that have to do with the construction of double identities, like in Orge's photograph that projects López's portrait, in the strategies used by Zout to photograph survivors, in the scaled model made as a double of the bombarded house in Aveta's work, and in the duplications of the faces of family members in Quieto's collages. As if wanting to escape from the repetition of trauma, the landscapes of these photographic memories opt for distance and the duplicating detour of artifice. The potential inaccuracy of these doubles seems to be a necessary element to avoid remaining trapped in the painful past, to be able to show something new.

On the other hand, the singularity so characteristic of photography is carried to the extremes in these memory artefacts and their procedures for reconstructing the past. These are photographic devices that construct their versions of history through cutting and assemblage work. For maybe this is what the photographic image is about: assembling and disassembling, mounting and dismounting, creating devices that, no matter how close to pure artifice, may still preserve that strange and rich root that joins the photograph to the object, and to the world to the past.

Translated by Jorge Salvetti

Notes

1 Earlier versions of parts of this chapter have been published in Spanish in "Pervivencia del 'collage' fotográfico: Paisajes y memorias" (Fortuny 2021b) and "Dos veces Julio: sobre algunas memorias fotográficas del pasado reciente en la Argentina" (Fortuny 2016).

2 I draw here on the ideas of Héctor Schmucler (1996) and Ludmila da Silva Catela (2001), respectively.

3 Photography is highly susceptible to being turned into a political instrument as proven by the extensive political use of photographs in Argentina and Latin America. According to Jorge Ribalta (2004), the problematic autonomy of photography – halfway between visual arts and the archival instrumentality of mass media – turns it into a particularly useful way of developing possible articulations between art and politics. The political potential implicit in each image, where even the framing is political (Didi-Huberman 2008a), is emphasised in and by the works examined here.

4 See the glossary for the symbolic significance of the Ford Falcon and more information about Death Flights.

5 I have written about this tension in Fortuny (2014 and 2021a).

6 See the glossary for the definition of "whitewashing" of the disappeared in the Argentine context.

7 To mention just one example, Mariana Eva Pérez – a writer, researcher and daughter of disappeared parents – explains that it took her years to initiate the lawsuit in the case of the disappearance of her parents and the abduction of her brother. The delay was, partly, due to the recent murders of several witnesses: "I let several years pass by because of fear, among other reasons. Former repressor Héctor Antonio Febres was poisoned in jail, Jorge Julio López disappeared, Silvia Suppo died in obscure circumstances" (Orosz 2021).

8 In this sense, Zout's perspective is akin to that of Paula Luttringer, also a survivor and photographer, whose photographs explore spaces, remnants and testimonies of disappearance. For further reading on Luttringer's photographs, see Fortuny (2014) and Blejmar (2021).

9 In the original Spanish, the gerund is expressed as *apareciendo*, as in appearing. The non-literal translation offered here is used to acknowledge the presence of agency in *making* someone appear.

10 Another photograph in this series is "Making Andrea López's gaze appear": an image, also projected onto trees, of a woman disappeared on 10 February 2004, in Santa Rosa, La Pampa. It is suspected that Andrea was murdered by her husband who sexually exploited her in a human trafficking network.

11 Historically speaking, the silhouette – the drawing and then cutting out of the outline of a face out of a projected shadow – has been one of the precursors of photography, if not technically, then at least conceptually (Freund 2006). Both are representations of the absent person produced through a direct contact with their body: in one case, from the shadow, in the other, by recording the body's light emanations.

12 Other artists who use this technique include Lucila Quieto and Verónica Maggi. For a discussion of their work, see Fortuny (2014).

13 This references one of the slogans and demands of the Mothers of Plaza de Mayo: aparición con vida – which can be translated as: re-appearance with life or re-appearance alive.

14 Piquetero is a member of a street protest aimed at blocking usual activity to bring attention to a particular issue. This form of protest became particularly widespread in Argentina in the 1990s. Travesti is a term widely used in Latin America for people who were assigned male at birth but identify (and often present) as female.

15 Also in homage to López's testimony, Dell'Oro created the website https:// desaparecidoendemocracia.tumblr.com, a sct of images recording several symbolic "appearances" of López's image that emphasise the ongoing relevance of the struggle for his appearance alive.

16 Writer Félix Bruzzone, whose mother was disappeared, alludes to this privation in one of his texts when he describes how the sunlight of Campo de Mayo – where he lives but also where his mother was held captive – gradually fades the only image he has of his mother (Bruzzone 2011).

17 Although in a different register, this is also reminiscent of W. G. Sebald's literary playfulness in *Austerlitz* (2002), where the narrator's voice distances and duplicates itself.

5

Waiting for the Light

Inés Ulanovsky
in conversation with Piotr Cieplak

Inés Ulanovsky is a photographer and writer based in Buenos Aires. Her book of photographs – *Fotos tuyas* [*Your Photos*][1] (2006) – is a visual exploration of the complex, intimate relationships between the relatives of Argentina's disappeared and the surviving images of their loved ones. Relationships that – as Ulanovsky puts it in the following interview – often "lasted much longer than relationships with actual people." *Fotos tuyas* consists of nine stories. Each one is told with between five and six photographs. Handwritten notes from one or more of the surviving relatives of the disappeared begin each section. All the stories conclude with a factual

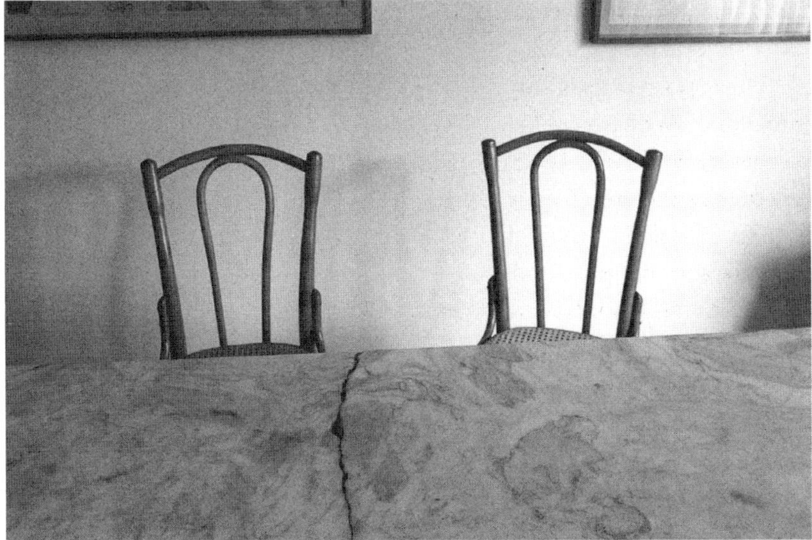

Figure 5.1 Image from *Fotos tuyas.*
Source/Author: Inés Ulanovsky.

account of the kidnapping or murder, usually supplemented with a testimony from a family member.

Ulanovsky shot the project on film and *Fotos tuyas* is full of colour. Even the photographs of old, black-and-white family images are marked by highly contrasted vividness. Ulanovsky recounts that most of the photographs in the collection are the result of long-term observation and waiting for the "organic," natural moment of interaction that she merely captured. But even though Ulanovsky's declared approach is that of recording rather than staging, the collection's nine sets of photographs are bound together by strong aesthetic and thematic threads. The dialogical and the material, tactile play a particularly important role in *Fotos tuyas*. There is a robust sense of dialogue between the past of the family images and the present of their importance to the children, parents and other relatives of the disappeared. This dialogue is sometimes enacted in expected ways: most of Ulanovsky's images feature, in one way or another, the old photographs. But often, it comes from the aesthetic and formal choices, which result in a palpable sense that something is wanted from these old photographs and that, at the same time, they themselves demand something. Ulanovsky has commented on the perceived agency of the people in the photos she saw during protests and marches: "I had the sensation that they weren't dead. That they observed everything from their own photos. That *they* looked at *us*" (Ulanovsky 2006, back cover; emphasis added).

Other types of interactions are also strongly present in *Fotos tuyas*. The individual photographs in each section are discretely powerful on their own but they are also dependent on sequentiality; they work together and rely on one another. They reference each other and act as part of a singular narrative tied so intimately to a specific person or people. Contact as expression of the painful desire for an impossible dialogue is also at the heart of how Ulanovsky's subjects interact with their images. Some cradle photos in their hands; others hold them up to the light, as if they wanted to look through them; to see something beyond the image. Others still do not touch their pictures but stand or lay next to them; like one would next to a person, when posing for a photograph. This rich tapestry of compositional techniques allows Ulanovsky to present the central theme of loss through both presence and absence.

While other Argentine artists such as Julio Pantoja and Lucila Quieto have also employed the technique of photographing family members with the images of their disappeared, *Fotos tuyas* plays a particularly important part in situating the photographs of the disappeared in the domestic setting. A lot is and has been asked of these photographs. And many requests have necessarily been utilitarian: to connect a face to a name; to identify; to find; to individualise; to commemorate. Many of these requests – also necessarily – took place in public: the protests, the rounds of the Mothers and Grandmothers of Plaza de Mayo; the courts; the memory sites. What Ulanovsky shows us is, on the one hand, an emotive continuation of this utilitarian demand in the home and, on the other, a veneration and intimacy of the "contemplative moment in which the relatives look at these photos."

While the photographs in *Fotos tuyas* are full of people, Ulanovsky's other corpus of work discussed here – a series of images taken at the site of the notorious detention and torture centre in Buenos Aires, ESMA (2008) – are completely devoid of human presence, at least seemingly so.[2] Taken with a medium format camera, these images are also full of light and colour, unlike much photography from places of torture and suffering. They capture the ESMA complex before the renovation works that turned it into the memorial museum and headquarters of numerous human rights organisations and institutions that it is today. These are heavy images; heavy with the burden of symbolic associations and the incongruity of the beauty of the colour, light and framing and what is known to have taken place on the site. They at once engage and try to look beyond context through a dogged, determined exploration of the aesthetics of ESMA – from the peeling paint on the walls to a disused swimming pool.

In this interview, Ulanovsky discusses her work but also the relationship between photography and the legacies of the Argentine dictatorship more broadly. Alongside her artistic practice, Ulanovsky brings her experience of working with images related to the disappearance in other contexts, including at the National Memory Archive and the Biographical Archive of the Grandmothers of Plaza de Mayo. In her most recent book, *Las Fotos* [*Photos*], she writes: "I've worked with photos that came from completely different places (from family albums to police records), but shared the same characteristic: history gave them unexpected prominence" (2020, 13). The same can be said of so many photographs of the disappeared that have now circulated in Argentina for almost fifty years.

Piotr Cieplak

Piotr Cieplak: *On the back cover of* Fotos tuyas *you write: "When I was little, the photos of the disappeared held a mysterious attraction for me. Every time I looked at them [the people in the photos] I had the feeling that they weren't dead" (2006). So many Argentine artists making work related to the dictatorship and its legacy have such a strong – direct or indirect – connection to that period. What drives your photographic work?*

Inés Ulanovsky: It started in my childhood. During the dictatorship, my parents and I went into exile in Mexico, but our connection to what was happening in Argentina remained strong. I was very young. There was always this half-mysterious presence around me: Argentina as an idea. At first, I didn't know what Argentina was; what it meant. For me, it manifested itself as certain things, amongst which were the photos of the disappeared. I knew that something bad, something tragic was happening there. When they talked about Argentina, the grown-ups became serious. They would tell us that the bad guys were in Argentina at the moment and that when the bad guys went away, we would be able to return. This idea permanently hovered around our lives. We went to political meetings, always full of flags and photos of the disappeared. I have a photo, taken by my mum, which shows that even back then, in Mexico, there were already people carrying placards.

Once we returned, my mum took me to marches – in December; on 24 March – and to the weekly rounds of the Mothers and Grandmothers of Plaza de Mayo. The photos present there made a very strong impression on me. Since most of the images were from identification documents, the people in them looked straight at the camera. I was fascinated by the idea that this photo, the first one grabbed in a desperate rush, became an icon that would later end up *being* each of the disappeared. There was something serious and something alive in that. It was moving.

When I started taking pictures, I knew I wanted to do something related to the photographs of the disappeared. But I didn't know how. I went to the marches, but I couldn't find a visual way to express what I wanted to say. I kept taking pictures of the photos until I realised that what actually interested me was the link between the relatives of the disappeared and the photos – which often lasted much longer than relationships with actual people. It was a unique bond. I started discovering the differences between these relationships, and between people and

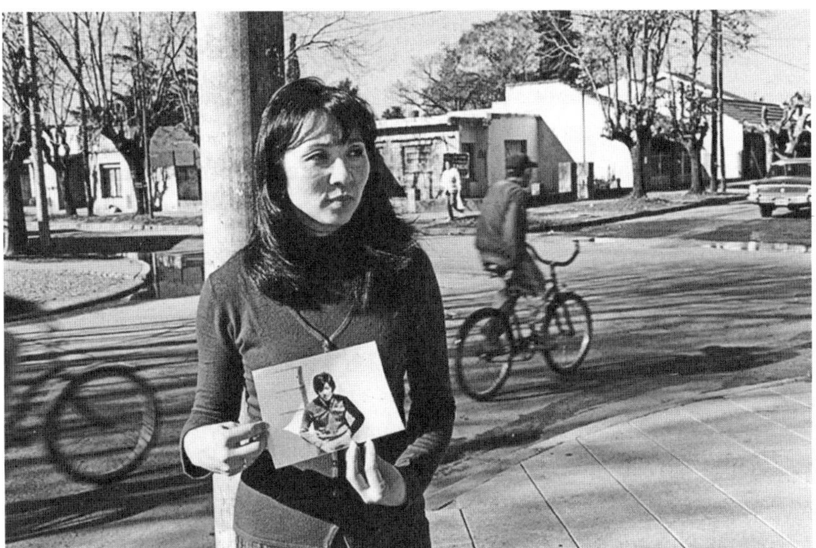

Figure 5.2 Image from *Fotos tuyas.*
Source/Author: Inés Ulanovsky.

their photos: the differences between those who had many photos; those who had only one, sometimes already destroyed; those who managed to recover photos after many years of not having one. I began the work of trying to record these bonds.

A lot of the people featured in *Fotos tuyas* were my friends. In some way, the project also records the fact that I had many relatives of the disappeared around me at the time. One thing led to another. Once I completed two or three stories, people recommended me to other friends. The word got around, and people wanted to participate. I did the project in one year: between 2000 and 2001.

PC: *Photographs can hide things as well as reveal them: class, sexuality, the nature of militancy, details of relationships. The photos of the disappeared in particular have always taken their power, at least partly, from the context in which they circulated. Is this why the accompanying text is so important in* Fotos tuyas?

IU: Yes. After developing the photos, I realised that I needed the relatives themselves to explain the bonds they had with these images. What you can't see in the photos matters. It's not the same if the disappeared was your mum, your aunt, your brother, your husband. This information, this context was something that was missing. I asked my subjects to write something that expressed the uniqueness of each link. I liked the idea of leaving a personal mark, so I asked them to write something by hand – about the photo as well as about the photographed. At the same time, the collection needed something more objective. I asked my father to write these more objective texts at the end of each section.

I accept that it was a decision. A lot of contemporary photography takes the approach of refusing explanation, leaving things unsaid, putting it on the viewer to fill in the gaps. But I don't think that context and information take value and power away from the image. On the contrary, when I understand what that image means and where it comes from, it gains a greater power to move me. Another reason for the presence of the texts was wanting to acknowledge the documentary, evidential value of the photographs, both of the disappeared and my own. What mattered to me was the concreteness of these stories. When did that person disappear? How long have they been missing? How did they disappear? What was the nature of their militancy? A lot of photography related to the concentrationary experience relies on being difficult to decipher. Often, it is out of focus; what I would call "artistic." I'm not particularly interested in this kind of work as I feel it doesn't let me in; it leaves me outside. I need to be able to access the documentary and social sense of record.

Adding voices to the images was also a homage to the contemplative moment in which the relatives look at these photos. Each day, they try to see something new in them because they don't have anything else, no other place to go. The disappeared are not there; it's impossible to ask them a question. So the photo gains this strong, unique value; becomes so loaded. Each time the relatives look at the photos, they try to find and conjure something new. That's why it's such a big deal when a new photo appears somewhere. It's a revolution; a huge joy to find an unexpected new photograph of the disappeared.

PC: *When we talk about photographs of the disappeared, this can mean so many different things: photos from banners and placards, identification documents, family albums. But also, images such as those taken by the police in Córdoba or by Víctor Basterra at ESMA. The uses of these photographs can and have evolved over time. What are the trajectories of*

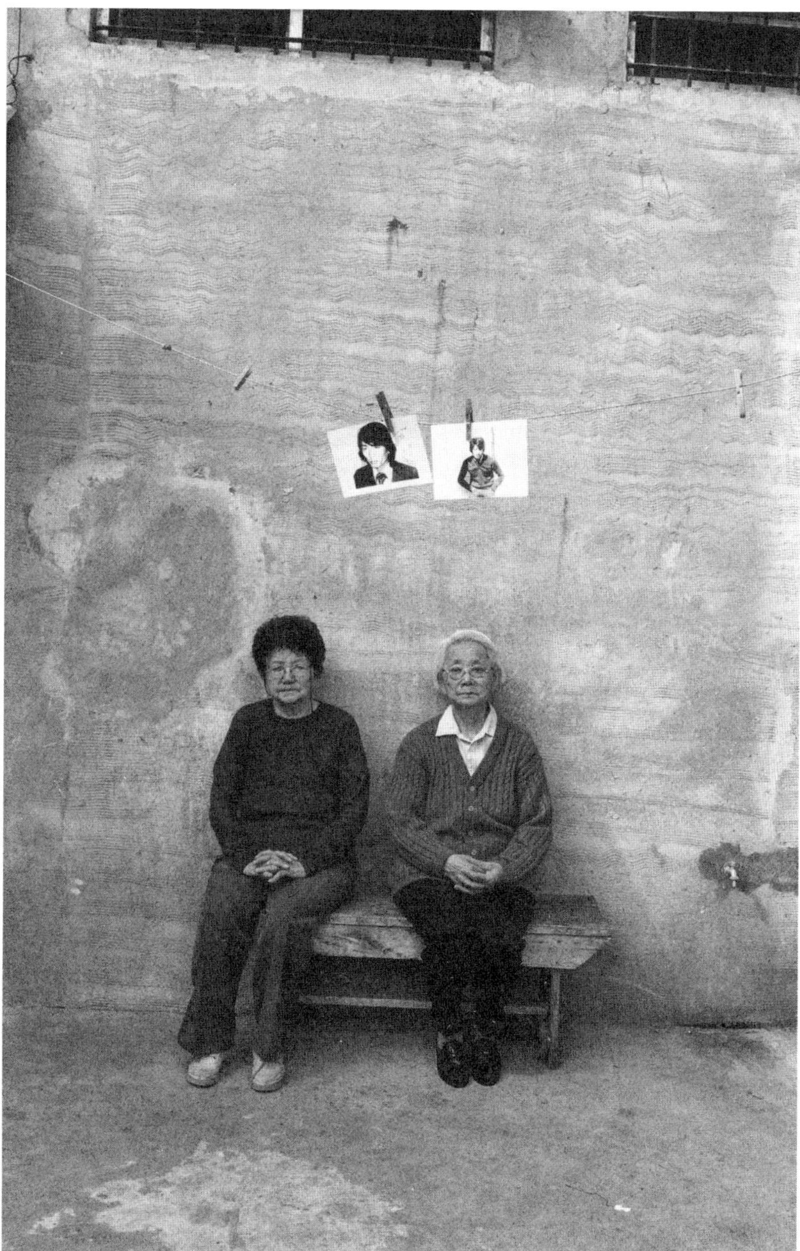

Figure 5.3 Image from *Fotos tuyas.*
Source/Author: Inés Ulanovsky.

these photographs over the decades? Do you think their functions have changed? Do they still have the power they used to have?

IU: Around 2000 and 2001 several artists, photographers, writers and film-makers explored, zoomed in on, the photographs of the disappeared as subjects. By then, these images had become part of Argentine identity, intimately connected to human rights. It seems to me that it was no coincidence that this renewed interest took place at that time; when Argentina was in the grips of a profound crisis.[3] Something emerged then that connected one crisis to the other. People began to wonder about the origins of these various struggles. Political and social background of activism became important in people's minds. At this juncture, the photos of the disappeared moved categories, so to speak. They entered a more artistic field. This essentially documentary material began to be seen through the prism of artistic expression. This fresh perspective and the act of artistic construction gave a new twist to images that initially had emerged to answer the need to make visible the disappearance and continued absence of all these people.

After it became clear that the disappeared were not coming back, the difficult question of justice began to materialise. We are all children of that process and we were all affected, in one way or another, by the dictatorship; whether or not we have disappeared relatives, whether or not we had to seek safety in another country. This isn't finished. Four hundred grandchildren are still missing. That's a lot of people who are denied the knowledge of their true identity – the most basic right. So these photos – and what they mean – keep returning. Like a recurring nightmare. But they also come back because they are part of our history. Because the disappeared are still missing; because they're not here. The presence of these images is not homogeneous. Politics plays a part in it.

PC: *Many images that came to symbolise the dictatorship – such as the photographs from placards and banners – began their existence as images not intended to represent history as such. Mostly, they were private images. What happened made them public. What is the significance of this transition? Do the private roots of the photos contribute to their perceived authenticity?*

IU: It's interesting. You have to remember that initially these photos were what people turned to in order to address a specific emergency – the missing of a person. How else do you do that: show that someone is not there? The photos were sought out in a desperate attempt to make absence visible. What was around? Documents. A picture from a birthday. Some were lovely photos, with beautiful light. Photos that conveyed happiness. It's strange to be able to access these moments of family intimacy; for them to become public. As you say, many of these photos weren't meant for that. The images were family records and became evidence. They say: this person existed. But they also say something else. The people in these photos are alive; often seem happy. So, the photos also say: these people lived; they weren't an invention. They had lives. They had photos of them taken. They smiled. Someone made the effort to find the best light for this picture. It's very moving to then think that this photo becomes evidence. The Mothers resorted as much to the white handkerchief as a way of recognising each other as they did to carrying the best photo they could find so that their child was recognised or, at least, recognisable. In some cases, the photographs were of very poor quality. Sometimes there was only one and that's what had to be used. This is connected to the relationship between social class and photography: who can afford to have images? Some had a singular image and others had hundreds.

Some of the chosen photos had been photocopied many times – it was the technology available at the time. This process resulted in a particular aesthetic, with just the outline of the face eventually visible; almost like an icon and not dissimilar to what happened to Alberto Korda's portrait of Che Guevara. They become akin to a brand; like Coca-Cola. Pop-icons.

It was so powerful to see for the first time the Grandmothers and Mothers with the badges they had made with the photos of their children and, in some cases, children-in-law, grandchildren. In particular, I remember Laura Bonaparte.[4] She was so feisty. Three of her kids and her husband were disappeared; a tremendous tragedy with so many people gone. She went to the marches with all the badges, all the photos of everyone who was missing. It was incredible to see. When one asks: what is photography for? That's the clear answer: this is what it's for.

In some instances, photography was fundamental to complete the circle. Some of the recovered grandchildren were given a photo of their parents, whom they had never seen before, and they were identical. A person with doubts about their identity recovers a photo and it's like magic. In a second, something they lacked all their life is returned to them. This was the case for Horacio Pietragalla Corti.[5] He was one of the found grandchildren and he is identical to his parents. He recognised himself and them in the photo immediately.

But it's not only personal. The photos are also a political tool. They were the sign, the marker of that time; part of our identity. A personal, private document, such as a family photograph, transformed into a social document, by the power of history itself. A photo album no longer belonged only to a certain family, but, in a way, to the country. This transformation from the personal to the social is so powerful. And, then, from the personal to the political. These photos are political objects.

PC: Fotos tuyas *makes extensive use of visual metaphor. It runs through the whole collection but two sets of photos in particular evoke this very strongly. In the first section, you photograph Alicia Gershanik, whose*

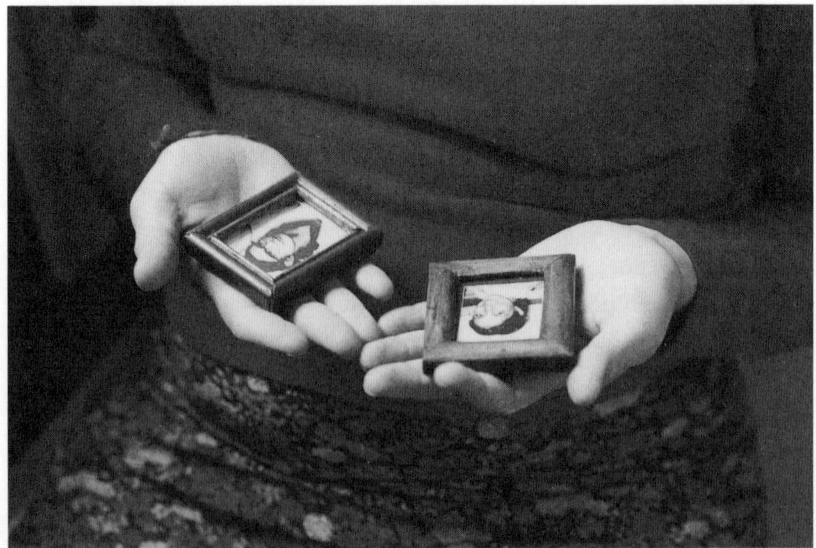

Figure 5.4 Image from *Fotos tuyas.*
Source/Author: Inés Ulanovsky.

brother, Mario Alberto, was murdered in 1975. One of the photographs shows a large marble table with two empty chairs next to it. A crack runs along the width of the table – splitting the top but also, invisibly, separating the two chairs (Figure 5.1). The next photograph is of the same setup, but this time Alicia is sitting on one of the chairs – the other remains empty – and the table is covered in photographs. The images only partially disguise – paper over – the crack. The other photograph I have in mind is in the last section of Fotos tuyas *and shows Julio Eduardo Gushiken's sister, Graciela. She is standing in the street, holding Julio's portrait. Like the photo she holds, Graciela seems frozen in time. Behind her, pass two people on bicycles; on the move; their contours blurred (Figure 5.2).*

IU: The photo of Alicia's table was the first one I took; the first photo on the first roll of film. I put it in the camera while Alicia went to make coffee. And there it was, in front of me, this magical moment. I took the picture and thought: "I'm done here. Done." I realised in that moment that I had to be very attentive not only to the photos themselves but also to their context, to everything that happened around them. It's about being able to look beyond what you imagined you'd be looking for. I didn't set the table up; the metaphor just presented itself to me. If it moved me, there was a good chance that it would also move the viewer. I think each of the stories in the book has a moment like this; what I would call a photographic moment.

The photo of the bike was another one I didn't know I would take. These moments – half-random, fortuitous – just happened and I recorded them. It's one of the reasons why I never photographed my subjects on just one occasion. I went back time and again. And sometimes these moments were difficult to encounter. I couldn't find a way to tell the story in five or six photographs. That's why it all took so long. I kept looking. I would go one day and get one photo and then return a few months later and take another.

PC: *The photographs of the disappeared, generally, tend to be seen as very special and precious remnants of the past. Have you encountered any that had more negative connotations?*

IU: Yes, there is definitely a complexity to these relationships. In my new book – *Las Fotos* (2020) – there are two stories of the relatives of the disappeared who cannot go back to these images. They are interested to know that the photos exist; they're even glad that they exist. But they don't want to look at them because it's too painful. One of the stories in the book is of a man who, after many years, comes across a photo (taken by the Police) of his detained father.[6] Among other things, this story shows that what matters is what kind of photo it is. The photographs that originated from the Police or other security forces are very harsh images – in more than one way. The flash illuminates everything; all the marks. These images tend to have the institutionalised oppression written into their very aesthetic. They show pain and they show fear. So it's no wonder that when one comes across a photo like this, one wants to say: "I don't want to see this picture because it's a very terrible time in my dad's life." You can also see these differences in what people do with the images they have. Some have the images displayed on the walls of their home; sometimes printed on their clothes. And others don't. They have the photos hidden, stored away in a box. Seeing the photos of the disappeared loved ones can be a journey you don't want or are unable to take.

PC: *Fotos tuyas is full of people. But you have also photographed the spaces of the former detention and torture centre in Buenos Aires, ESMA. These images are completely devoid of human presence, at least on the face of it.*

IU: The ESMA images came after *Fotos tuyas*; between 2008 and 2010 when I was working at the National Memory Archive. I started the project as a way of dealing with the anguish of having to go to that place every day.[7] I had to do something constructive with this feeling because I wasn't handling it very well. I was in mourning. My mum had died not long before then. So, in a way, these photos also speak to this personal loss. The empty spaces of ex-ESMA were in conversation with my empty space, left behind by my mother. I was pregnant with my second daughter. I was using a medium format camera and a tripod; very heavy; lugging it around while pregnant. The issue of motherhood within ESMA weighed heavily on my mind. Everything – my own situation and what happened there – felt all mixed up. I struggled to understand what the women there had suffered and what they had gone through.

I focused on taking pictures of empty spaces which seemed to me somewhere between horrific and beautiful. They had very particular light and very particular colours. Back then, ESMA's aesthetics were still very

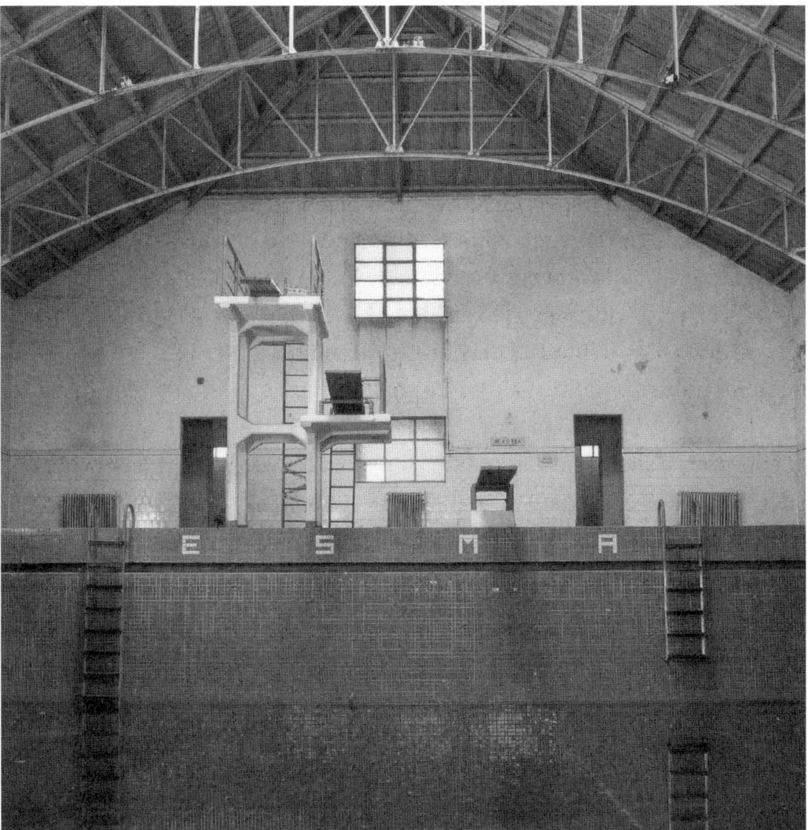

Figure 5.5 Image from the ESMA series.
Source/Author: Inés Ulanovsky.

much of the period when it had been operational, in a manner not dissimilar to how the photos of the disappeared share a particular aesthetic of that period. It's something specific; concrete. This also interested me as a historical record. I was given keys to the various buildings in the complex; seventeen hectares and thirty-five buildings. It's enormous; a small town. It had its own swimming pool, a bakery, a printing press. I'd enter a space, set up my cumbersome camera and wait for the light. These were intense, emotional moments of solitude. And the resulting photos also don't have any people in them.

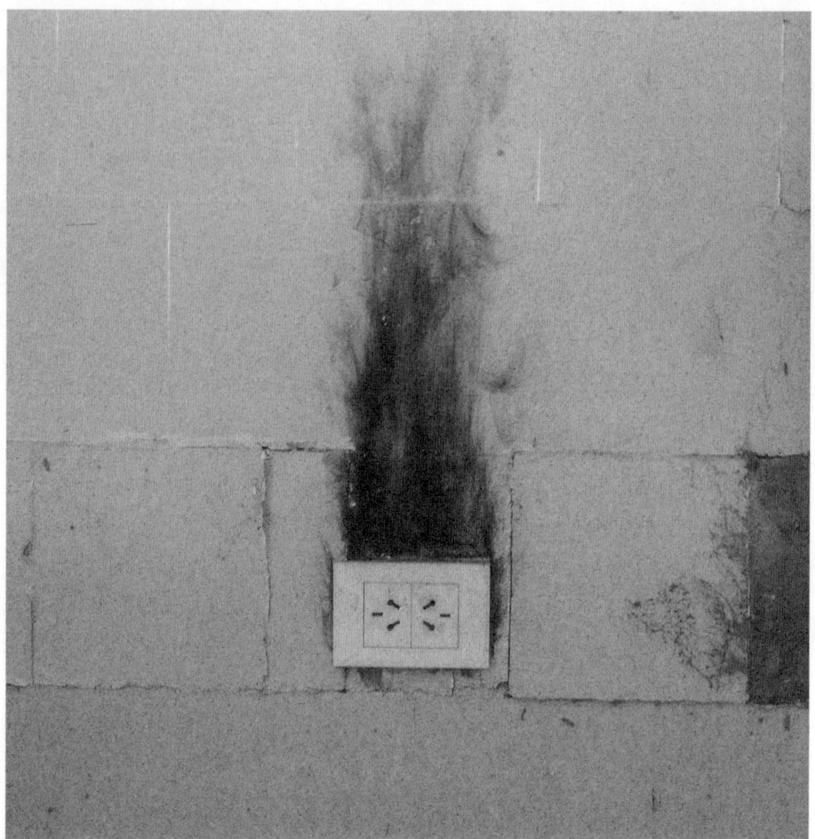

Figure 5.6 Image from the ESMA series.
Source/Author: Inés Ulanovsky.

Looking back at the images, I keep coming back to the light. It is a joyful, luminous light. When one thinks of places like this, it's all black-and-white. So how is it possible to see colour there, and to record it? Waiting for a good light in itself generates a frightening effect. To me, it shows that people lived with total naturalness in these places. And the horror that happened there was part of this normality. I found that there was a very special and very rare colour palette. It felt important to record that before the refurbishment work occurred – far too quickly for my taste – covering much of what that place had been. In the building that houses the museum, they preserved a lot of things. But in the other buildings, walls have been painted over, even murals. All of the things I photographed don't exist anymore.

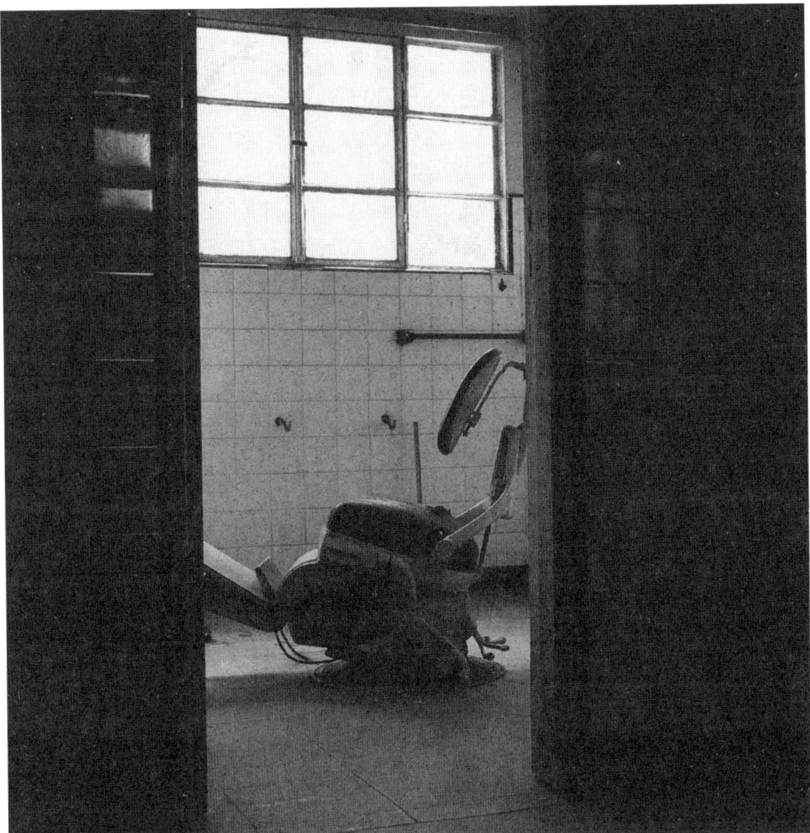

Figure 5.7 Image from the ESMA series.
Source/Author: Inés Ulanovsky.

PC: *There is an evocative feeling of ghostliness, of the mysterious in your ESMA images. But there is also the presence of the symbolic; of the knowledge of what happened there creeping into the images. You photograph the empty and foreboding pool (Figure 5.5). You photograph a plug socket on the wall that has been burned (Figure 5.6). There is also a picture of a medical chair in a building called The Infirmary (Figure 5.7). Unlike many other photos, which are framed from the front, this one is framed from the side; the perspective mediated by several frames. It's as if you and the viewer don't dare to face the situation directly.*

UI: All the images in the collection have that symbolism. The photo of the burned plug socket immediately made me think about la picana.[8] The image of the pool was so powerful to me because of the testimonies of former detainees I had read in which they talk about suddenly being taken for a swim. All these mundane things of this mini-city, with total normality inside it. I kept thinking about the idea of a contained universe, but without morality and with different rules. And when it comes to the photo of the chair, that place was marked by terror. The energy there was frightening, and I was terrified. I sat there for half an hour, waiting for the light. It was full of ghosts.

Buenos Aires/London, 11 March 2021

Translated by Piotr Cieplak

Notes

1 An alternative translation here could be *Photos of You*.

2 Ulanovsky's ESMA photographs can be seen here: https://vimeo.com/49512838

3 In 2001, the culmination of an economic depression and disastrous fiscal policies resulted in widespread civil unrest (Argentinazo) and a period of economic and political instability in Argentina.

4 Laura Bonaparte (1925–2013) was a prominent Argentine human rights activist. Three of her children, two sons-in-law, a daughter-in-law and Bonaparte's husband were disappeared by the Argentine dictatorship. Bonaparte was a leading member of the Mothers of Plaza de Mayo – Founding Line.

5 One of the most publicly well-known and widely publicised cases of "found" disappeared grandchildren. Corti's real identity was restored by the Grandmothers in 2003. Corti is a well-known politician who served as the president of the National Memory Archive between 2015 and 2016 and currently heads Argentina's Human Rights Secretariat.

6 Ulanovsky refers here to the case of Daniel Bibiano; see Ulanovsky (2020, 23–26).

7 The National Memory Archive, alongside many other human rights organisations, has its headquarters on the expansive site of the former ESMA.

8 A torture instrument commonly used in Argentina under the dictatorship, akin to an electric cattle prod.

6

Photography and Disappearance in Argentina: Sacredness and Rituals in the Face of Death

Ludmila da Silva Catela

Looking at photographs, seeking out images of one's childhood, rifling through family albums and examining photos on social media, in exhibitions and urban interventions are just some of the social practices that connect us to photography. Each day, through fortuitous, quotidian or ephemeral events, we construct different representations of the world from what we see and observe. The relationship between the photographic and the gaze shapes us as individuals; parts of our lives are told through images, what we see in them and what and how they *make* us see. Photography generates a link between life and death. It becomes a referent when we lose a loved one and search for their photo so that their face can remain amongst us, or when we reinforce the affective ties with our children by showing them photographs we have gathered to document their trajectories. As Kossoy points out, "we are characters of the photographic experience; for we all keep photographs of our life: *reliquary-images* that preserve our memories crystallised" (2014, 247; emphasis added).

The act of looking raises questions about the relationship between photographs, the memories trapped in them, and the power of familiar images as articulations of the experiences of our past, knotted as they are with our present and future (Sontag 1978; Barthes 2000; Belting 2009; Dubois 2015). The moments recorded and translated by exposure to light are part of our lives and form multiple territories of meaning. Seeing, touching, feeling, suffering, remembering, kissing are just words, but they acquire a different significance when faced with the photographic image and the ways we relate to it.

The frustration is all the stronger because the indexical substitute signifies the absence of the referent, offering itself, qua representation, as a concrete object endowed with real, physical substance (the fetishism of the photographic image derives from this double posture: the photograph is an object that can be touched, framed, collected, enclosed, burned, torn up and embraced, yet it can only show us the untouchable, the inaccessible, a memory, an absence). In photography, therefore, there is never just an image, separate, disjunct, alone in its solitude, haunted by the one, intimate moment it had with a real that has vanished forever. It is this hauntedness, formed by distance in proximity, absence in presence, the imaginary in the real, the virtuality of memory in the effectiveness of a trace, that draws us to photographs and gives them their aura: the unique phenomenon of a distance, however close they may be.

(Dubois 2015, 298)

To photograph is to fix, leave out, appropriate; to "steal the soul" as is sometimes proposed in the indigenous world.[1] To photograph is to capture that which will be lost or merely believe that we are copying the trace of what we refuse to forget. Ultimately, taking a photograph, keeping it, buying it, asking for it, tearing it up, exhibiting it, cutting it, showing it, is a way of establishing a certain relationship with the world.

This chapter analyses the evidential force of the photographs of the disappeared, and the role they play in rituals that accompany mourning processes in Argentina. The corpus of material chosen for analysis, from an ethnographic perspective, stems from my fieldwork in the cities of La Plata, Córdoba, and the villages of Calilegua and Tumbaya in Jujuy province.[2] All these places experienced the disappearance of hundreds of citizens during the period of state terrorism under the most recent Argentine dictatorship (1976–1983). In many ways, this chapter is an itinerary of the relationships between photography and memory that allows for an examination of how images circulate, are appropriated, used, sacralised or banalised in the face of violence and politics. I am particularly interested in opening up a conversation about what people *do* with photographs. What are the images' meanings and the emotions ascribed to them? How do people circulate them to produce multiple connotations in the context of the violence they experienced first-hand or that was inflicted on the bodies of their loved ones? But what is also at stake here is the examination of what other strategies of visual representation are created or invented when photography is not available or cannot be used as the main material object in a ritual. In other words, my aim here is to analyse photography's power and ability both when it is there and when it is not. What ensues is a reading of variations on a single theme, where photography – like a kaleidoscope – projects multiple meanings that guide political action and practice. Consequently, the focus here is on the use and the discarding of photographs of the disappeared; on (re)presentation and forgetting; on the image's centrality and marginality. The questions running through this chapter are based on an inquiry into what type of memory cycles and memory spaces the images of the disappeared complete and occupy.

The two central themes I explore here are, one, the capabilities of the images related to disappearance, and, two, the recourse to other forms of representation when photographs are absent. The first theme is explored through a close look at the sacrality of the images of the disappeared as inscription surfaces for the family's mourning, and at the relationship between photography of disappearance, public space and ephemeral materialities. Here, photographs take on an evidential role – make a truth claim – in the struggle against the impunity of those responsible for the disappearances. The second theme is examined through the analysis of what happens when photographs are not available and how, as a response to this lack, other forms of representation such as silhouettes emerge, especially in the ritual of the Day of the Dead often associated with local memory practices.

Memory and Visual Procedures

Memories, conceived as an act of labour and a procedure, acquire visual forms and manifestations (Jelin 2002). In our daily practices, memories move and gestate in superimposed representations of the past in the present. They overlap timelines and spaces to create new forms with which to populate and inscribe meaning on surfaces, territories and cartographies of recollection. The relationship between photography and memory creates a powerful, well-established link.[3] Images allow not only the *representation* of otherness but also a *reflection*, *analysis* and *understanding* of other worlds and realities. In the specific case of the photographs of the disappeared in Argentina, and particularly in the context of violence, it is impossible to ignore the images' potency and legitimacy. One thinks of each time a photograph – throughout its material life – might have served to account for the existence of a variety of cultural contexts, to preserve identities, to promote the struggle for truth and to become a powerful tool for making visible what had been previously suppressed and concealed. Faced with these multiple uses, the question arises about the photographs' symbolic potential and their power to counter violence and other forms of erasure. How does a piece of paper, stamped with an image, transform into a document of truth or a relic that must be kept and preserved? From the family album to the political rally, what processes and actions endow an image with sacredness, truth and power in the context of violence? Memory processes sediment and generate concrete practices out of photography's capacity to translate, enunciate, show and fix the remains and traces of the past in the present. Photography allows us to play with multiple timelines, to go back to different pasts and construct the present with new meanings; to project messages towards the future while preserving parts of the past.

The ethnographic approach to this body of material centres on photography's ability to signify space with the power to reveal the hidden and shed light on extreme situations. This approach allows for the analysis of the intersections between memory and the visual, between the public and the private, between the sacred and the profane.[4]

Working with photographs made, used, handled and treasured by those who must account for the acts of violence committed on their bodies or on the bodies of their loved ones invites questions about the alterities pierced by that which remains captured in an image. All photographs are anchored to a vision of the world and try to explain that world through, more or less, delimited means. As Dubois rightly points out, "[p]hotography (as a practice) is not 'the photographic' (as a category of thought). It is an important distinction that must always be kept in mind" (2015, 17). By its very nature as a document, photography refers us to the past, but it speaks to us from the present. While in the strict technical sense photography fixes what it shows on paper or in digital memory, relegating it to the past, this is not the case when it comes to interpretation. Viewers confer a photograph with a new meaning each time they look at it, through their own cultural experience, their political values, or the sacredness with which the photograph has been preserved, exhibited, used or forgotten. It is in this sense that photography and memory enter a complex interrelation. The image functions as an aide for the recollection, when the moment captured in the photograph was lived by the person who looks at it, and as a vehicle of memory when that moment is reconstructed from the present of communal identities made up by both those who lived that experience and those who did not. Photography can thus act as a "witness." There is no memory without images, or as Andreas Huyssen puts it, there is no knowledge without the possibility of seeing, even if images cannot give a complete account of what happened (2000, 116). They are just fragments, remnants, "instants of truth" (Didi-Huberman 2008c, 31).[5] Those instants endow photography with the power of enunciation and evidence.

Sacred Photographs of Grief and Mourning

"Look, look at their picture... they were so beautiful," Eulogia "Rita" Garnica says as we start the interview in which she relates the moments preceding and following the disappearance of her two sons: Miguel Ángel (23) and Domingo Horacio (20), abducted on 20 July 1976, in Calilegua (Garnica 2002, personal communication). Sat at the table where the photos of her children are displayed, Rita tells me of her quest to find out what happened to her sons' bodies, but also of the horrible experience of her own kidnapping and detention. As we chat through the hot Jujuy siesta, her gaze keeps returning to the photographs whenever she needs to reaffirm the fight she had been waging for years so that her sons' disappearance would not remain unpunished.[6] Those two framed faces stand there like small reservoirs of affection that allow Rita to look at them now and again, to touch and kiss them so as to be able to endure those unbearable absences.

As an almost obligatory ritual, Rita and every single one of the people I interacted with in Calilegua, preserve the photographs of their disappeared children, siblings and comrades, as a form of continuous battle, as a space of affection and as a locus of political action. Each of those photographs marks the immortal representation of a human being who was denied all humanity. When there is no body that can be buried or occupy a material space of mourning, as is often the case when it comes to disappearance, the photographic image becomes an essential presence. For the relatives of the disappeared, each image is both a gesture and a rebellion: a gesture of attachment and memory; an act of rebellion against the very notion of disappearance.

Each photograph represents a history, a trajectory, a struggle and a multitude of recollections. Myriad memories are attached to its material forms and aesthetics. Each family chooses a particular format: some are small 4x4-centimetre photographs, others are large photos stuck onto a placard; some are protected within a picture frame, others pinned to a piece of clothing or hanging around one's neck in a locket; some are part of a collage on a wall full of photographs or political posters; some are in a family album or in a notebook; some are adorned with a drawing; some are accompanied with flowers or candles. In the faces shown in these photos reside and unfold the stories that are enunciated as marks of memory, and, as they flow, they break the silences and reveal what the state wanted to conceal. Disappearance comes apart and breaks into pieces in these photographs, which signal the existence of human beings whose life was repeatedly negated.

In all my fieldwork – in La Plata, Córdoba and Jujuy – photographs were the intermediaries in the dialogue with my subjects; small objects charged with symbolic energy and the ability to make those absent present.[7] The evolution of those images showed, in each encounter, that it was necessary to "look at" those faces in order to understand and compensate for their absence; that the gesture of looking created a *commitment* to *completing* those unanswered deaths, those still unpunished disappearances. But the photographs – sometimes the only images of these people – were also treasured like sacred objects, for they allowed, and still do, the possibility of a dialogue, a transmission; the only thing their families have to keep their memory alive; the proof of the existence of that particular human being. Conceived in this way, a photograph becomes both a space of recognition and of mourning; of remembrance *and* of identification.

For instance, Gloria, the sister of Rosalino Ríos, and Rosalía, the daughter of Elias Toconás – both men disappeared in Tumbaya in 1977 – use photographs as a place of inscription and a link to the memory of their disappeared loved ones. During an interview, I ask Gloria how she remembers her brother, given that there is no grave she can visit or lay flowers on. She considers this for a few seconds and then answers that she remembers her brother because he is present in every corner of the house. But she adds that the only photograph the family has of him is the most important thing. "That's how I remember him, with a photograph. We had only one photo, because people didn't take so many photographs back then, so we had only one picture, his small identity card photograph" (Ríos 2003, personal communication). Similarly, Rosalía tells me that she has scarce memories of her father, as she was only two at the time of his disappearance. Once again photographs emerge as a central element in the way recollections are woven. Rosalía remembers an image that is very important for her: "I have a photograph of my father, my mother and me [...] they are having me baptised. I have that photograph but that's all, [apart from] a photograph of my father in his military service uniform that I use for the placard" (Toconás 2004, personal communication).

As can be seen here, photographs function as an anchor for the possibility of reconstructing family identities but also as a medium for transmission over time, as surfaces onto which a sense of belonging can be projected when a more direct recollection or reconstruction is not available. With this ability, these small pieces of paper begin to acquire both a sacred and a religious power: religious inasmuch as they constitute an inscription space for specific rituals. It is in front of the photo that one talks to the disappeared, tells them stories, asks them for protection and remembers them. Candles are lit, prayers said, certain dates commemorated; in other words, acts of intimacy and affection performed within the home. The photograph of the disappeared loved one thus becomes a representation that exceeds the imaginary relationship and transforms itself into the *illusion of a presence*, right where disappearance created an absence (Kossoy 2014).

This *illusion*, in turn, creates a sacredness that alters the technical, utilitarian, record-like quality of photographs. A sacredness that envelops them in a unique aura that emanates from the fact that they must not be lost, they must be multiplied and used in all possible spaces and chains of affection, created to ensure that they are passed on and transmitted to future generations. Consequently, the images pass on from mothers to their children and grandchildren as small, precious treasures that transmit energy and protection. Many siblings of the disappeared, after their mother's death, carry the photographs and thus convey the legacy of the struggle and memory. The photographs of the disappeared brothers and sisters are inherited just like the white headscarves. But unlike the headscarves, which retain another type of sacredness and are rarely worn as they were by the Mothers of Plaza de Mayo, photographs continue to be worn around people's necks, pinned on their chests or taken to the marches on the same placards the Mothers used to carry around the Plaza in the 1970s.[8] For instance, during the 2004 march to commemorate the Ledesma Blackout, I witnessed two brothers marching with the photographs of their disappeared brother pinned on their chests.[9] These photographs had originally been used and carried by their mother and they inherited them as relics to be treasured and venerated. Time had worn the images out, the faces had become blurred and faded, but the importance of this act rested not in the photographs' quality but in the legacy of the struggle they transmitted. The act of carrying the photographs now involved not only the disappeared sibling but also the mother that had fought to recover him. In some banners carried by the "next generation" it is also possible to see the transmission process in the form of the overlapping of photographs. For instance, during the same march, the placard in memory of Leandro Córdoba, detained-disappeared on 20 July 1976, was paired with a colour photograph of his dead parents, superimposing two recollections now carried by Leandro's sister (Figure 6.1). In addition, she also bore on her chest the image of the denunciation of her brothers' disappearance accompanied by two small ID photographs that her now dead mother had carried on her body for years.

This past preserved in the image is taken up again and again in each evocation of the loved one whose body remains disappeared. Those remnants and fragments of the past accompany the emotions that did not and cannot remain materially stamped on the photograph but that dwell in the memories of each family member. From there stems the importance of the preservation and maintenance of these portraits, of their propagation, reproduction and transmission. What each person does with them, gradually invests and endows them with symbolic power, transforms them into sacred objects requiring religious rituals (lighting candles, laying flowers, praying, conversing, wearing them on one's chest, taking them on a pilgrimage) in order to maintain their symbolic power.

As in any other relationship in the realm of the sacred, time and space are essential to understanding the processes that accompany it. While in

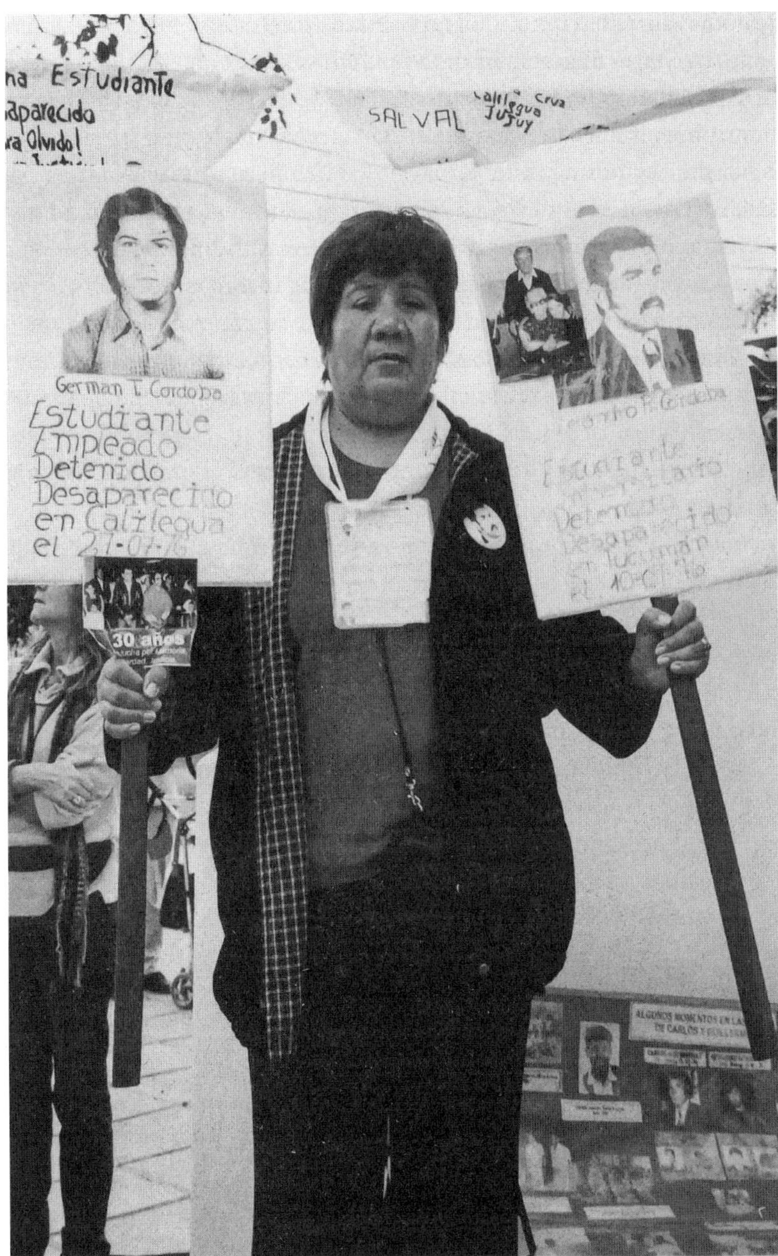

Figure 6.1 Germán and Leandro Córdoba's sister carries placards and denunciations originally used by her mother, Jujuy.
Source/Author: Ludmila da Silva Catela.

the domestic milieu the photographs have a temporal continuity, this continuity becomes fragmented in the public sphere, once the photographs are exposed to the commemorative calendar that regulates public events. There, photographs are used at particular moments and in specific situations, while acquiring ritual forms very different to their use in the home (da Silva Catela 2009). Ethnographically speaking, it is possible to discern at least two different types of ritual practices with the images of disappeared in the public space. One is the carrying of the photograph on one's own body, itself an extension of one's home, thus preserving and taking care of the photograph through one's own corporality. In general, these are the same images as those that occupy a central space in the domestic sphere; their sacredness preserved by the fact that they are not shared with others. The second type of practice concerns photographs that are shared in the public space, as placards and photocopies that can be used in a march, stuck on a wall, used collectively or printed on a banner. In this case, the collective use prevails and photographs are carried by those who join or support the cause by marching or taking part in the commemoration. Family members "lose" or hand over the possession of the image, which then becomes collectivised but without losing its power. This second category shows that photographs have acquired the capacity to represent and symbolise the disappearance. But at the same time, as they are endlessly reproduced through photocopying or other interventions, such as stencilling, once the ritual is over, they are left out in the open, as it were, and exposed to the elements that can affect them both physically and politically, once this ephemeral, time-limited cycle is over. They may break, get damaged or eventually disappear altogether.

Photographs, Remnants and Biographies

While a photograph of a disappeared person within the domestic space performs the role of a memory aide and maintains the link between the dead and the living, once an image enters the public space and comes out of the sacred refuge of the home, it acquires other meanings and uses. The photographs on placards, banners and as objects displayed in anniversaries and commemorations gain the power of denunciation. As mentioned earlier, the circulation and use of the photographs of the disappeared in public spaces tends to occur on fixed dates in the memory calendar – 24 March on the national level and on other specific dates locally – and necessitates an additional layer of analysis of the ritual surrounding the images. I am particularly interested here in what happens with the photographs used in memorial commemorations once the event is over. After playing such a crucial role in a march or a ceremony, where do the photographs end up? Does someone gather and collect them and, if so, who? In my fieldwork I have witnessed images being thrown away and images that have been vandalised in deliberate acts of violence against them. Most of the time, however, the photographs are respected, left where they were placed, like sacred objects.[10]

During the 2020 Covid19 pandemic, there were no mass gatherings or events in museums or memory sites that usually accompany the big march to mark 24 March. Instead, commemorations were held at a local level and mostly took place in the courtyards of private houses. Under the slogan "we plant memories, we reap rights," small acts multiplied here and there, centred around planting trees and being in direct contact with the earth. The local, fragmented nature of these activities offered a glimpse into what is often diluted in the mass rituals of 24 March. Perhaps like never before, we were able to observe how memory is preserved in the spaces we live in, in our street, in our neighbourhood, in our town. A few days after 24 March, I went out to walk around the memory places in Unquillo-Córdoba, where I live. New trees had been planted near the public library, with white handkerchiefs hanging from their branches. Several houses were adorned with slogans or, again, white handkerchiefs hanging on the doors. The artists' collective Memoria de Unquillo had stuck posters in several places, recalling the violent crimes carried out by the military dictatorship.[11] I strolled through the Memory Park, located at the entrance to the town. This green space, situated on a hillock, is marked and adorned with sculptures by local artists; trees have been planted in memory of the disappeared. For several years, a long line of photographs had also been displayed here, attached to a black cloth bearing an inscription with the slogan, *Never Again*, and stencils of the white headscarf, the symbol of the Mothers of Plaza de Mayo. When I arrived in 2020, I was surprised that the photographs were not displayed in their usual place. I walked on and eventually came upon the images, or rather fragments of them, arranged on the ground. I had to bend down to be able to read the small biographies (which accompany each face) that lay there, all broken up into pieces, and put back together like a jigsaw puzzle. In some, the whole face was visible, in others some parts were missing and the identity data included on the originals was incomplete (Figure 6.2).[12] As I went through them one by one, I couldn't help imagining the municipal employee laboriously sorting out all those stories, placing them on the ground, as though in a mourning ritual or a funeral rite, refusing to throw them away, even though they couldn't be used again in a commemorative act. I reflected on the sacredness of each of those images, on their materiality and on the fate that awaited them. And there, again, what struck me was the power that each of those images had to tell the lives of the disappeared, as well as the need for their presence as individual traces of collective memory. There lay the *stories* of Unquillo's disappeared that are reborn each year, gathered from individual fragments, images and biographies used to produce new political meanings and communal affect.

Putting pieces together, overlaying stories, recognising traces, getting to know the moments and fragments of someone else's life: all these actions imply the work of construction and reconstruction. All those fragmented images that now lay on the grass and the dirt sparked other enunciations. The biographies that had been interrupted, shattered by disappearance and were now once again fragmented because of the tearing of the images. If a biography entails the narrative of someone's life, what function do images that "simply cannot be thrown away" perform? What role do *visual biographies* play in the memory process related to situations of violence?

Visual biographies, and the spaces of enunciation they can open, mark a baseline from which to embark on a journey of learning about the lives they touch upon. This baseline, which allows the articulation of multiple viewpoints, functions as a prism that refracts those lives into myriad perspectives. But it also sheds light on what is being – and can be – told, and on what is silenced or forgotten. Consequently, it elucidates the tensions between objectivity and subjectivity, between history and memory of those lives (Archuf 2002). Perceived in this manner, a visual biography is a fictional representation of a life. It is a representation in the sense that it symbolically condenses what that life was, and it is fictional in the sense that, like any construction, it selects, assembles and puts together events

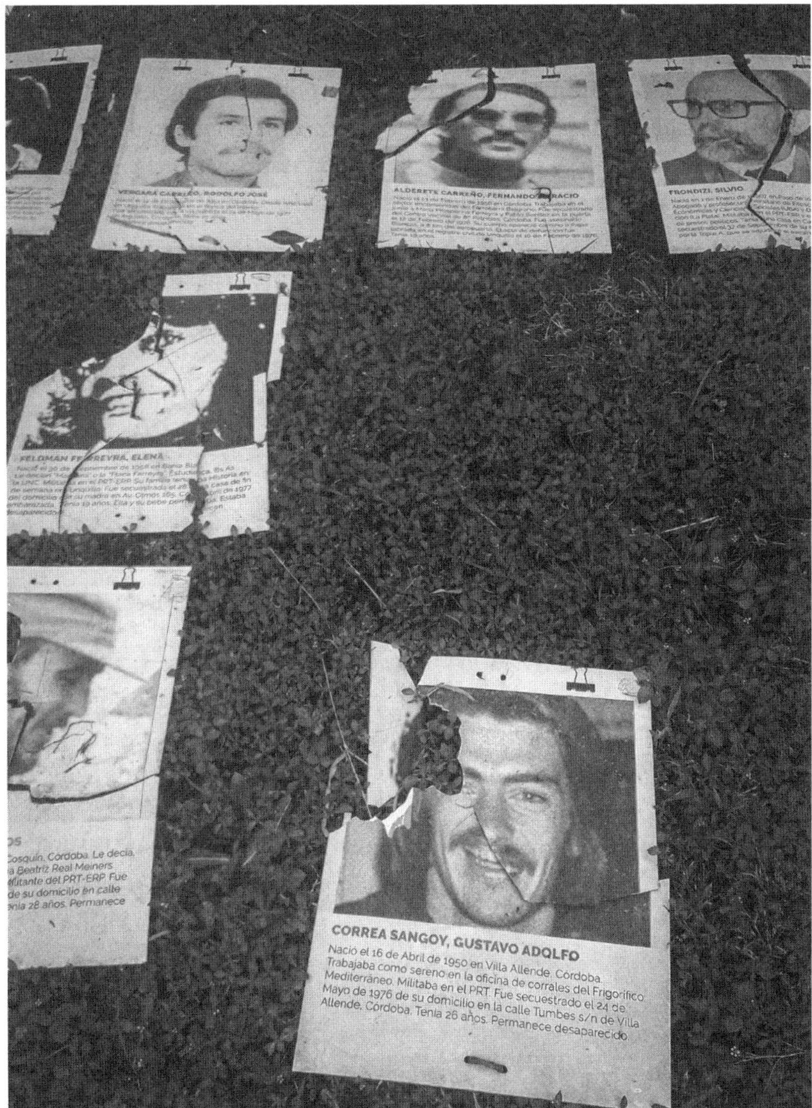

Figure 6.2 Fragments of photographs in the Unquillo Memory Park, 2020.
Source/Author: Ludmila da Silva Catela.

in order to tell a story, highlighting certain aspects of that life, and, inevitably, omitting others. However, two elements of the photographs of the disappeared conceived as visual biographies remain as indexical signposts. One is the name, often included on the photos that circulate publicly, that becomes "the visible affirmation of the identity of the bearer across time and space, the basis for the unity of one's successive manifestations, and for the socially accepted possibilities of integrating these manifestations" (Bourdieu 2003, 413). The other is the face.[13] In the total loss of identity that one suffers through disappearance, these elements sustain the memory of a person. They are the founding elements that allow us to reconstruct lives, search for stories, unravel the past. Photographs, as visual biographies, with their fluidity and constant movement, come time and again to feed narratives, stories, texts, lists, artistic objects, research work, virtual platforms, videos and so on. On the other hand, every biography – and especially one constructed from the photographic image of a disappeared person – and its production, circulation and appropriation, can be conceived as a *life archive*.[14] As such, it gains a symbolic and almost religious power. But to perceive them as archives also means it is impossible to discard them as rubbish once they've served their commemorative purpose. Neither does this, however, imply constant preservation. But there is a reluctance that comes from the symbolism of the act of deliberately throwing them away. Instead, they may be simply left where they are, for the elements to do their work of destruction, as time does to dead bodies, or as a metaphor for disappearance itself. In other words, these photographs persist as traces of memory; acts of memorial resistance that refuse to be erased or discarded but which are not immune to the passage of time.[15]

If, as Sontag (1978) says, images of suffering can anesthetise us, and their multiplication and repetition can transform them into something that does not appear real to the viewer, then perhaps it is precisely in this act of deconstruction and metamorphosis, which occurs when we are faced with familiar images not in their usual form, that we perceive their real power to signify, their sacredness. It is then that they display the truth of disappearance, and that person, that face, that printed name become something whole.

Bodies, Silhouettes, Photographs

Visual biographies of the disappeared are not limited to photographs. Rather, they should be thought of as a symbolic system made up of different elements (photographs, handkerchiefs, flowers, rounds of the Plaza, commemoration ceremonies, anniversaries) that constitutes and institutes the representation of disappearance and its referential (in)capacity. As mentioned earlier, photographs are not always available, and even if they are, they are not always used. In these cases, other frameworks accompany the biographies and express their visuality. I'd like to focus here on one device in particular: the silhouettes. Since the return of democracy in 1983, silhouettes occupied – and continue to do so – a central place as a form of visual representation of the disappeared. Used in public spaces, they employ a minimal referent to produce maximum significance. They establish a liminal point of transition between those who are present and those who are absent, between the body and its trace, between life and disappearance. Unlike the photographs of the disappeared, which transitioned from the domestic to the public, the silhouettes emerged in the public space. They became visible in the 1980s as a result of an artistic and political intervention called Siluetazo, which took place, predominantly, in Argentina's major cities (Longoni and Bruzzone 2008). It was both an action and a ritual:

Siluetazo – as this particular action and two similar ones that followed it, in December 1983 and March 1984, became known – marks one of those exceptional moments in history when an artistic initiative coincides with the demands of a social movement, and takes shape thanks to the impetus of a crowd. It involved the participation of hundreds of demonstrators who, in a huge makeshift workshop set up in the open air and which lasted till midnight, painted and lent their own bodies for the outlines of the silhouettes, and then stuck them on walls, monuments and trees, despite the strong police presence.

(Longoni and Bruzzone 2008, 8)

It is interesting to note that the central point of this action lies in placing one's body right where the body of the disappeared is missing. Therefore, the tracing of the outline, the silhouette, marks a re-appearance. It makes the absent body, or its outline, present in the public space. This is also reminiscent of the forensic practice of drawing a chalk outline of a dead body at a crime scene. The double reference to the visibility of a body that is no longer there functions as a sign within a system comprehensible to those who come upon a silhouette in the street, either painted on a wall or held up on a placard. Like the black-and-white photographs of the disappeared, the silhouettes constitute an effective representational mode that is frequently augmented with other data, such as names, dates and other recognisable symbols that indicate that such a representation alludes to the body of a person disappeared during state terrorism. Quite often, silhouettes end up replacing photographs when the latter are not available or when it is necessary to leave permanent marks in significant places, such as the sites where CDCs operated.

During a research visit to the Guerrero CDC in Jujuy, I noticed, for instance, that the small photocopies with the faces of the disappeared – which originated from photographs – have faded as a result of the passing of time and exposure to the elements.[16] Their deterioration drew my attention in the same way the photographic fragments at the Unquillo Memory Park did. Because of the work of time, these left-behind images became a testimony in their own right. A testimony to the rituals that had occurred in that place – traces of commemorative actions and justice claims – like ghostly presences that refused to let the ceremonies, and the disappeared, be forgotten.

As one arrives at the Guerrero CDC, before reaching the entrance, one must walk down a concrete platform. For years, this long path had only been marked by patches of grass growing out of the cracks and crevices in the cement. Nothing indicated that this was the entrance to a place of memory. Later, the first markers appeared – a monolith created by Jujuy human rights organisations and a sign put in place by the Ministry of Justice and Human Rights (in 2016) – indicating that this is indeed a site of historical significance. Human rights organisations and neighbours' associations constantly organise and hold acts and commemorations, marches and protests there. While the former CDC hasn't been yet reclaimed as an official memory site, the entire area surrounding it is dotted and signposted with markers that record different interventions: silhouettes, graffiti depicting the faces of the genocidaires, remnants of photographs and wreaths used in the Day of the Dead rituals, inscriptions signalling important dates.[17] These are rituals that organise, surround, invade and declare that memory lives on, leaving behind a trail of visual traces.

Sketched on the asphalt are the silhouettes that also permanently display the names of each one of the disappeared who were held in this CDC (Figure 6.3). The silhouettes here fulfil a function similar to that performed by photographs elsewhere; they're here to attest to the presence,

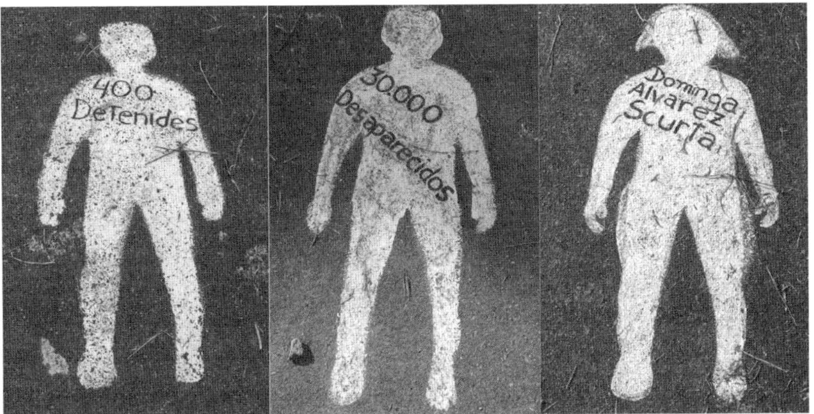

Figure 6.3 Silhouettes at the entrance to the former Guerrero CDC.
Source/Author: Ludmila da Silva Catela.

to bear witness to the bodies that remain absent but had an association with this particular site. They mark a path that cannot be walked without asking questions. The silhouettes act as shadows that recover those missing bodies, but also as a reflection of our own social shadow, the one that disappearance cast over the whole country. They act as vessels holding disappearance, as well as a medium for visual biographies, used both as a referent and a symbol. The silhouettes sketched at the CDC also appear on the streets of the city of Jujuy during 24 March commemorations.

For instance, as can be seen in Figure 6.4, a silhouette is attached to a lamp post and doubles as a support for the photographs of the disappeared. It is an object that, in its handcrafted materiality, reminds us of the silhouettes we used to cut out as children to represent our family. Here, it confronts us with death and violence. What can be observed are bodies turned into objects that, in turn, represent bodies as symbols of the quest for justice. "The figures of death and the dead are present in an immediate correspondence with their living projections" (van Alphen 2015, 203). Conceived in this way, the silhouettes graphically show the breadth and impact of disappearance on a local scale. Painted on the asphalt, they make us look down; supporting collective identities with the faces of the disappeared, they question us in the hustle and bustle of cities; painted on walls as graffiti, they make us stop and reflect. They emerge here and there, depicting the horror of disappearance and the restlessness of those missing bodies.

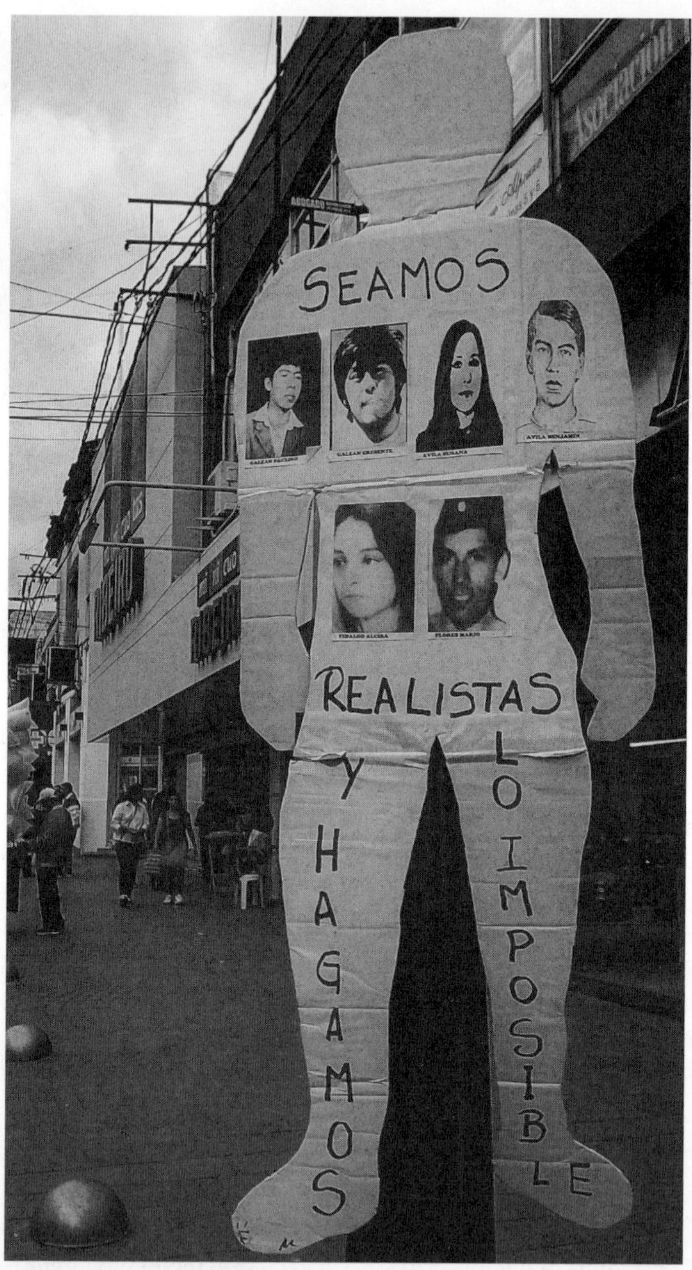

Figure 6.4 Silhouettes in the city of Jujuy.
Source/Author: Ludmila da Silva Catela.

"Souls that Need to Return..."

While a representational shift takes place in the transition from photographs to silhouettes, disappearance is maintained throughout in the form of a trace. Around that trace both sacred rituals, related to the past, and current struggles gestate. But when it comes to the practices that have stemmed from the use of photographs (present and absent), one in particular brings into focus the way disappearance is conceived and related to death. Interestingly, here the photographs of the disappeared may or may not be present – they are not required for the ritual to be performed – because the object of the ritual is the soul. The actual image of the disappeared is not essential because, on many occasions, the people carrying out the ritual are not relatives but members of the community, who do not necessarily need to individualise the disappeared. I am referring specifically to the Ritual of the Dead that takes place every 2 November, a tradition of religious syncretism between ancestral indigenous practices and Catholicism. The reason to consider this practice is precisely the fact that photography has played such a predominant role in Argentine commemoration, and yet there exist other forms of representation that descend from long ancestral memories and which, although they lack the means of photographic representation, present alternative ways of symbolising the dead and their souls. This specific ritual is performed around a table with objects made of bread and offerings to the dead that reference their tastes: sweets, drinks, food, flowers and candles.

Guerrero and its community never forgot what they had gone through during the dictatorship. They could not erase from their memory the violence of the CDC, located right in the heart of the town, amongst the houses of its inhabitants. Those who were murdered there still haunt the community, the members of which often do not know with any certainty who the victims were, what they did, and, perhaps most importantly of all, where their bodies rest. This particular uncertainty is connected to the fact that the disappeared that passed through this CDC did not come from the Guerrero community itself. They were transferred there – after their abduction – from other villages and towns in Jujuy.

Chela, who was a little girl during the years of the dictatorship and saw what happened at Guerrero's CDC, regularly opens her house for the ritual of the Day of the Dead. Re-signifying its origin, she "receives" the souls of Guerrero's disappeared. She recounts:

Souls need to return somewhere. I always wondered where the disappeared went back to, if anyone was waiting for them [...] I felt their souls wandering about around here. So, one day I said to myself: I'll receive them in my house. They are going to like it, because I've been told they helped others and were very solidary [...] and besides, my grandmothers taught me that one has to be generous to the dead, so I'm glad to receive them in my house, just as I receive my father's soul.

(Chela 2019, personal communication)

If generosity is an act of affection, solidarity is a political gesture.[18] The two come together in the ritual for the Day of the Dead in Guerrero. Generosity, affection, solidarity and politics coalesce in this ancient practice of the Andean world that welcomes the souls of those who are no longer on this earth. The question the community asks itself is: what do the dead need? The question is not addressed at memory politics but at the dead themselves, who need to be remembered, time and again, every year, every day. These are memories that flow, that offer affection so that recollection does not petrify and die out.

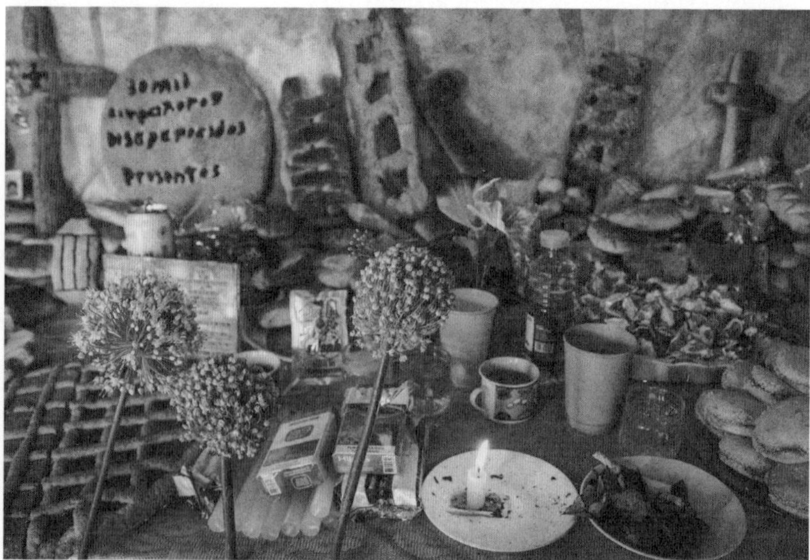

Figure 6.5 The Day of the Dead ritual at Guerrero's former CDC.
Source/Author: Ludmila da Silva Catela.

The ritual comprises the preparation of food and sweets; candles are lit; paper flowers made; drinks offered; and bread ladders are placed for the dead to "climb down." The food is shared at a large colourful table. The ritual, thus, constitutes a symbolic system of materialities, particular aesthetics and ways of thinking about memory and visuality different to those normally associated with the commemoration of the disappeared in Argentina. The ceremony culminates with the participants walking to Guerrero's CDC and passing through each of the silhouettes on the way, with the names of the disappeared written in the outlines. This pilgrimage, too, is accompanied with the offer of drinks, food, cigarettes, and conversation. It is a moment of communion at a site of horror reconfigured by the strength and power of local memory-making. A site of horror now full of colour, flowers, objects and food to remember and honour the dead.

Each bread figurine prepared for the day offers and references a surface of meaning that creates a bond with the dead. There are white headscarves that commemorate the memory aides created by the Mothers of Plaza de Mayo; bread pencils that recall young, disappeared students; a large round loaf with the number "30,000" in homage to each of the disappeared. These particular manifestations of the materiality and visuality of memory establish a specific religious ritual to face the past. They receive the souls of the disappeared but also return a sense of community to the people who choose to remember the disappeared through the expression of affective bonds that rely so strongly on the collective rather than the individual; bonds that reference the common good. Although photographs, where available, accompany the ritual as reinforcements and a way of making the disappeared of that CDC present in the ceremony, they are neither central nor indispensable. The role of the main material object here is assigned to the bread figurines.

Ancestral memory practices that bring the memory of the disappeared and dead to the present are not guided by a strict manual, a protocol or a set of fixed rules. What there is instead is a traditional ritual, now re-signified to widen the sphere of affection to include the disappeared whose souls still haunt Guerrero's former CDC. Men, women, children and young people all participate, watch and share. Here, the body is part of that memory practice. One has to bend down, light candles, speak to the disappeared. There is no obligation. Everyone participates in the ritual as and if they want to. The table is set, the loaves of bread arranged. Homage is paid with sweets, food, drinks that the dead find to their taste. The dead are expected, waited for. They are celebrated with a meal to which they are invited. Then, at the CDC, the offerings are arranged once again and each participant has an affective interaction with their dead and the memory of the disappeared. There are talks, flowers, drinks. It is a political assemblage based on solidarity with the disappeared and the generosity of the world of the living. Whereas the still, grey signpost marks the site of the former CDC with a motionless memory, in this ritual, local memories throb with life, re-signifying this particular space.

Conclusion

Throughout this chapter, I attempted to draw a map that situates some of the forms of circulation and appropriation, sacralisation and/or banalisation of the photographs related to disappearance. The analysis draws on materials gathered in a decade of research, allowing us to observe variations in the use of these images; their passage from the private to the public sphere; the transformation of religious rituals into political practices; the appropriation of memorial activities around the silhouettes; the use of the photographs of the disappeared carried on the bodies of, first, their mothers and, then, their siblings and children. The focus on the materiality of memory that is transmitted through photographs allowed me to shed some light on other strategies of visual representation employed in the public sphere not only by the blood relatives of the disappeared but also by friends, neighbours, comrades or political militants.

On this map of practices, it is possible to see how the disappeared re-appear and are reborn in images, photographs, silhouettes, objects. This does not mean that they are necessarily present in each photograph, but they appear in and out of them. Each image brings with it, like in a hall of mirrors, reflections and refractions of lives that are no more. The photographs are present in each home and with each mother; in each Plaza and on each march; in rituals that inaugurate the memory cycle every year. Disappearance is an unbearable absence; its visuality has been constructed over the years as a way of accommodating its representations and creating a material space for the expression of emotions in the absence of a grave or a tomb. Belting, referring to the relationship between image and death, offers an insight into the interaction between visuality and disappearance that seems particularly pertinent here:

The dead will always be absent, and death [is] an unbearable absence that one fills with the image in order to render it bearable. For this reason, humans have banished their dead, which are nowhere, to a chosen site (the grave) whilst at the same time giving them, in the image, an immortal body: a symbolic body, by which they are re-socialised while their mortal body dissolves into nothing.

(2009, 179)

Those "symbolic" bodies carried, as in a reliquary or shrine, on the bodies of the mothers and siblings, contained or drawn in a silhouette, shaped into bread loaves, fragmented in torn photographs, both trace and blur the notion of disappearance. In a way, photographs come to replace the bodies. Bodies turn into photographs and silhouettes, with rituals to commemorate the arrival of their souls.

Photographs and rituals have fixed the bodies, their gestures and gazes, in the context of disappearance. Each photograph carries in itself and brings to light the truth about the human beings who had been negated by the state. Their bodies represented in silhouettes, sometimes anonymously, as well as people carrying the images of the disappeared, evoke, time and again, the demand for justice. And the rituals, acts of inscription and transmission of memory, reinforce the power of evocation and solidarity.

Perceived this way, photographs, visual biographies and memory practices create backgrounds and settings where truth and justice are symbolically administered in a constant dialogue between the past and present. Each photograph of a disappeared person is in itself a struggle for memory. They mustn't be lost or abandoned, for, should those photographic documents disappear, those represented in them would die again. Hence their sacredness, the care they receive, their constant reproduction in domestic and public spaces. Each photograph, as an exercise of memory, must be kept and cared for as a relic to be preserved for generations. It is in the photographs that the power of evocation and political action of remembrance lies.

Translated by Jorge Salvetti

Notes

1 Masotta writes that "the notion of 'soul' responds to the Judeo-Christian tradition," as does "the fear of losing it and the demoniacal implications such loss would entail." He also acknowledges that "the theft of the soul sounds more like a White interpretation of the indigenous resistance to entering the power apparatus that the portrait imposes. It is possible to detect in it the traces of the old European legend of Faust's bargain with the devil in exchange for his soul, as well as the more recent echo of Schlemihl's story. In America that pact was transformed into a theft" (2012, 9). Also, see Frič and Fricová (2012).

2 The fieldwork in La Plata was conducted between 1996 and 1999 as part of my doctoral research, later published in *No habrá flores en la tumba del pasado* [*There Will Be No Flowers on the Grave of the Past*] (2001). The fieldwork in Jujuy was conducted between 2000 and 2006, and then between 2017 and 2019. In Córdoba, I held the post of the director of the Provincial Memory Archive (2006–2015) and, since 2019, I have coordinated the Nucleus for Studies in Life and Death (PIP-CONICET grant 2021–2023).

3 See, for instance, Berger (1972), Didi-Huberman (2008c), Feld (2010b), Blejmar, Fortuny and García (2013), Castillo Troncoso (2017) and Jelin (2021).

4 I have previously written about disappearance as a space where mourning acquires new modes of meaning, inasmuch as it generates social processes in the face of death: without graves, without bodies, without the possibility of materialising death (da Silva Catela 2001).

5 Didi-Huberman applies the idea of "instants of truth" to reflect on the images of the Holocaust, drawing on Hannah Arendt's writing on Auschwitz: "Lacking the truth, [we] will however, find *instants of truth*, and those instants are in fact all we have to give us some order to this chaos of horror" (Arendt 1966, 257–258, cited in Didi-Huberman 2008c, 31; original emphasis).

6 Eulogia "Rita" Garnica died on 14 June 2017, without having managed to recover her disappeared children's remains.

7 It is necessary to note here that there are differences in the role photographs play in each family in relation to the quantity of images present in each home, be that due to the differences of social class or other reasons. The more urban, middle-class the family, the greater the number of available images. This is particularly visible in Jujuy where images are scarce and those that exist, in most cases, come from identity documents or from specific contexts such as mandatory military service.

8 For further discussion of the Mothers of Plaza de Mayo's strategies for ensuring their disappeared children's visibility through the wearing of the symbolic white headscarves and the use of photographs, see: da Silva Catela (2001), Longoni and Bruzzone (2008), Jelin (2009, 2021) and Gamarnik (this volume).

9 The Ledesma Blackout was organised and carried out by the dictatorship. A series of intentional blackouts at the Libertador General San Martín power plant between 20 and 27 July 1976, was used to kidnap and detain around 400 people in the Ledesma region of Jujuy.

10 During my directorship of the Provincial Memory Archive in Córdoba, photos of the disappeared were hung every Thursday in Pasaje Santa Catalina. With the passing of time and their exposure to the elements, the photos, originally copied onto vinyl, started to

wear out and break. New copies were made to replace them. The "old" worn-out photographs were never thrown away; for years they were put into boxes and kept there. The impossibility of desecrating them is linked to the power of representation and the affect they contain beyond the usefulness of the material on which they are printed. It did not cross our minds to throw them away. Even if they could not be used again, they contained in their materiality a political and affective heritage that could not be discarded.

11 Memoria de Unquillo is a human rights organisation in Sierras Chicas, Córdoba.

12 The photographs had been taken down from their usual place of display because they had deteriorated over time.

13 When the image of the face is not available, its symbolic representation, such as the silhouette, can also fulfil this function.

14 In my previous work (da Silva Catela 2001), I wrote about the memory aides that take the form of short biographical notes, often accompanied by a photo, that have been published daily in the *Pagina 12* newspaper ever since the 1980s. Generally, they appear on the birthday of the disappeared person. In some ways, they are analogous to obituaries, but they do not announce someone's death. Rather, they "update" the disappearance as a cycle that cannot be completed.

15 Natalia Fortuny (2013) writes about memory's erasures as well as its persistence. She asks, metaphorically, how long does it take for memory to be erased?

16 For a history of the Guerrero CDC, see Garcés (2019).

17 As part of state policy in Argentina, former CDCs are either marked as memory places or officially transformed into memory sites open to the public. There are currently thirty-seven memory sites; the rest of the former CDCs have only been signposted. This is the case with the Guerrero CDC, which bears a series of signs but formally belongs to a trade union and is currently used as a recreational space for its members.

18 It is important here to highlight the significance of working with collective emotions and gestures, often ignored by the social sciences or regarded as minor, superficial or essayistic topics. Anthropology has made a considerable effort to acknowledge the expression of sentiments and feelings as a sphere of production of social meanings. It is crucial to consider what affective, emotional communities generate in their environments by looking at their practices in terms of solidarity, generosity, affect, love, etc. This allows us to understand, from a symbolic perspective, the evaluation and hierarchy of the emotions themselves, the ways in which they are expressed, and, in particular, the nature of the bonds between the people expressing the emotions and their objects, including the affective modes they presuppose, e.g. to defend, to value, to tolerate or to reject (Elias 1998; Le Breton 1999; Mauss 2009; Passerini 2011; Rosenwein 2011).

7

An Impossible Scene: Towards an Ethnography
of the (In)Visible in the Memories of the
Survivors of La Perla

Mariana Tello Weiss

It's a photograph of its time; a sepia snapshot from the 1970s. The white border – with "Jul. 77" printed on it – frames a scene of a family posing on a pavement, with their backs against a brick wall (Figure 7.1). Fourteen people; children and adults. The adults have strange expressions on their faces, as though they're forcing themselves to smile; their lips hardly curved and their eyes looking intently at the camera. Every family photograph is governed by the fulfilment of its social, ritual and ceremonial functions (Bourdieu 2003). But in this picture, something seems out of place. Something unsettles the viewer.

The photo was taken in Bell Ville in July 1977, and it shows the family of Ana Iliovich.[1] Ana herself appears in every single one of a sizable number of photographs, of which only two remain in her possession (Figures 7.1 and 7.2). In each surviving photo, one can detect different inflections of the grammar of the same familial arrangement, but they are difficult to spot at first. In one of the images (Figure 7.1), for instance, Ana looks at the camera, while leaning on her father's arm. In the other (Figure 7.2), she's holding her nephew. But in both, Ana's gaze is fixed on some distant point beyond the camera, and she is clearly finding it difficult to smile. Her expression seems to convey sadness or resignation. It's true that the reason for the family gathering is important; but it is definitely not a happy one. In these photos, Ana is twenty-one. Over a year earlier – on 15 May 1976 – she was kidnapped and taken to a clandestine detention centre (CDC) known as La Perla.[2] These photographs capture the first occasion on which she was allowed to reunite with her family after having been disappeared for fourteen months.[3]

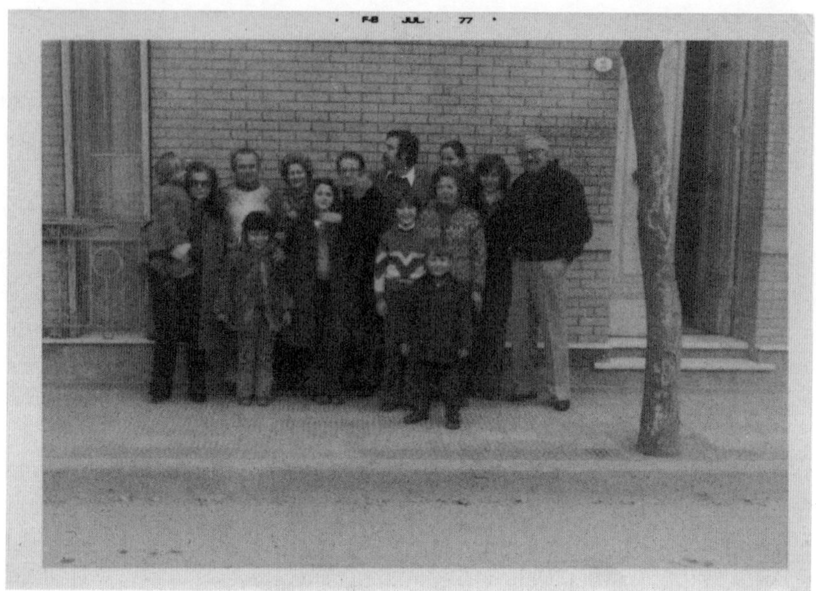

Figure 7.1 The Iliovich family, Bell Ville, 1977.
Source: Ana Iliovich/Mariana Tello Weiss.

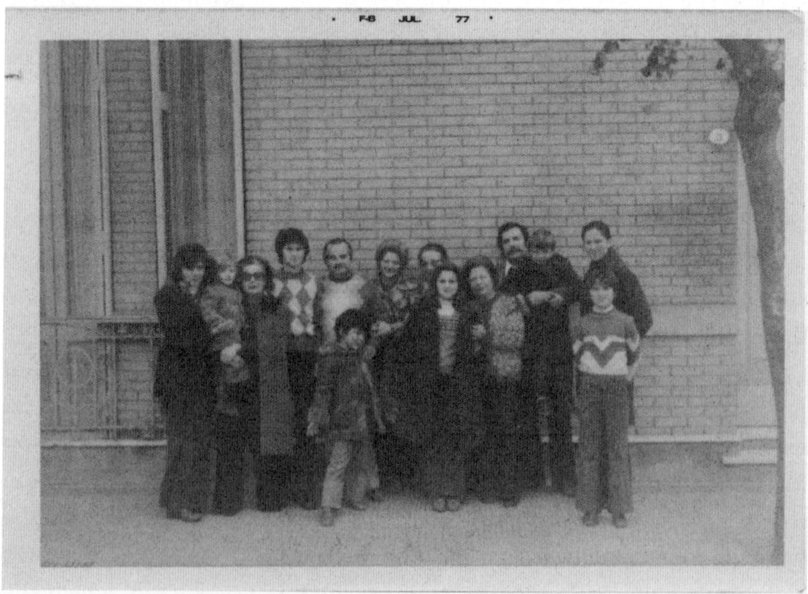

Figure 7.2 The Iliovich family, Bell Ville, 1977.
Source: Ana Iliovich/Mariana Tello Weiss.

The 1976 coup in Argentina was followed by the implementation of a systematic method of annihilation of the "internal enemy" (Pontoriero 2016). Some 30,000 people are estimated to have been disappeared during this period. We know today that they were kidnapped and confined to CDCs, where they were tortured and subjected to countless torments. The great majority suffered a dire fate: they were murdered, and their bodies disposed of in total secrecy. However, a small number survived and returned to society.

This chapter is part of a wider research project in which I analyse, from an anthropological perspective, the strategies that the survivors of CDCs employ to reconstruct and suture their devastated sense of self and their shattered worlds. This analysis includes the process of *managing wounded identities*; wounded both by the *concentrationary experience* and the stigma implicit in the act of re-appearing, of returning from a place from which many never came back (Pollak 2006). My particular focus here is on the use of images to accompany or document the survivors' memories. My case studies are the photographs of Ana Iliovich, who survived La Perla, taken at the moment of her re-appearance. These photographs – later published in *El Silencio: Postales de La Perla* [*The Silence: Postcards from La Perla*] (Iliovich 2017) – exemplify a practice that occurred among other survivors once their repressors started allowing them to contact their families: that of taking pictures of themselves as a way of proving they were alive.

In this chapter, I am guided by the following questions: what role do these photographs play in the survivors' memories? How crucial can photographic practices become at the moment of one's re-appearance? What value do these photos acquire as documents? What ways of looking at and understanding the *limit situation* do they offer to the viewer? At the same time, given the strong visual connotation implicit in the term disappearance, this chapter also seeks to contribute to the understanding of how the *distribution of the sensible* operated – and still operates – in relation to the last Argentine dictatorship (Ránciere 2013). Consequently, I ask what this type of visuality enables us to conclude about the ways of remembering that period; and about their relevance within the broader visibility regimes and memory practices (Jelin 2021).

The relationship between images and disappearance has been extensively studied in the literature devoted to repression in Argentina.

These studies focus, on the one hand, on the use of the photographs of the disappeared as instruments of public protest and commemoration (da Silva Catela 2009; Longoni 2010a), and, on the other hand, on photographs within the context of family and social grieving and mourning processes (da Silva Catela 2001; Triquell 2013; Fortuny 2014; Blejmar 2016; Cieplak 2020; Jelin 2021). Yet another body of work centres on the images portraying spaces related to disappearance (Crenzel 2009), and the photographs produced in them (da Silva Catela 2012; Longoni and García 2013; Feld 2014b; Magrin 2015). Only within the latter, a certain interest in the images of survivors emerged. Generally, however, photographs of survivors in Argentina have received much less attention than the photos of the disappeared who never came back. If, as Ránciere states, the *distribution of the sensible* constitutes "the system of a priori forms determining what presents itself to sensory experience" (2013, 8), then the scarcity of survivors' images in the public space reflects the structural invisibility they have suffered ever since the return of democracy. One of the reasons for this arguable invisibility is the stigma of survival itself. According to da Silva Catela (2001), survivors carry a double stigma related to: one, having sown violence in the country in the first place; and two, continuing to carry the story of a horror hardly anyone wants to hear. The stigma that specifically weighs on those released from CDCs is also inscribed within *the imaginary of treason* (Longoni 2007; Tello 2014). Consequently, many survivors have only appeared in public when they were called to testify in court.

It is only recently that images involving survivors started to acquire some significance as a medium of remembrance and, consequently, as an object of study.[4] These seemingly ordinary photographs have an extraordinary potential when it comes to examining the relationship between images and re-appearance – rather than disappearance, which has dominated the work in the field thus far. I consider them as paradoxical images – objects that channel the evocation of a likewise paradoxical experience. They enable a consideration of how the *distribution of the sensible* was organised at the time, of how this distribution is reinterpreted in recollecting that past, and the challenges this poses for the ways of facing and interpreting these images.

(Dis)appearing

In the visual narratives of the family – whose archetypal material manifestation is the family photo album – photographs usually portray rites of passage, mostly happy moments. Births, school ceremonies, marriages; only these special landmarks tend to gather together the extended family; only then are photographs deemed necessary. Rituals reaffirm the group's cohesion, photographs immortalise it. The grammar of those images repeats itself almost identically from one family to another (Triquell 2012). The photographs analysed here could be of any family in the mid-1970s in Argentina. The women's huge glasses, their voluminous or straightened hairdos, the sheepskin jackets; all those style traits function as markers of the times. One can tell in what period the photo was taken, even without the date printed on the border of the image. But in this case, the presence of this date is much more than a mere mechanical mark used by the photography studio. It demands to be reinterpreted in relation to the visual content of the photograph itself: the co-presence of the bodies fixed by the image at that particular place and time. The date explains the unsettled look of the people in the photo – a look that also unsettles the viewer – which can only be revealed with the unveiling of the simulacrum the image contains. In this case, the unveiling also includes what is outside of the frame; what's been left out of the picture. There is someone in this photograph who could have been dead, who was virtually dead, and, nevertheless, is there, standing with her family. Under the innocent guise of an ordinary family picture, this photograph is nothing less than a proof of life.

Ana remained disappeared for over a year. Her family had no news of her throughout that period. She was one of the few prisoners chosen to survive. As such, she became part of a mechanism of "monitored freedom." The people put in this situation by their oppressors were first allowed to contact, and then to visit, their families. Ana Iliovich's family photographs analysed here are the first record, a casual ambiguous trace of a winding and tortuous process of re-appearance. The process had started months before, when the repressors allowed her to write a letter to her family:

When they told me to write a letter to my family, that functioned as a source of hope and it's difficult to explain what it meant [...] to think that *my folks were going to have news from me, that they were going to know I was not dead, that I could start thinking of them and of myself again [...] until that moment I was dead [...] to resume contact with them was like allowing myself to think myself alive.*

Then I wrote the letter. It went through many twists and turns because someone [...] took it to my father [...] and then something very devious followed, because my father had to publish an ad in the paper saying he had received it.

From that moment on, a very strange process started – with no clear rules – where one of them [the repressors] took me to the house of a fellow prisoner [and] from there I rang my parents and that was my first contact with them [...] *My folks hadn't the faintest idea what had become of me, nothing [...] all they knew was that I had stopped being around.*

(Iliovich 2012, personal communication; emphases added)

Ana's words demonstrate that neither the disappearance nor the re-appearance were a fixed event in her life. While the kidnapping had a precise date in her memory, Ana had begun to disappear from her community long before then, due to the clandestine life most of the militants were forced to lead back then. From the moment she started to lead an underground existence, her parents hadn't "the faintest idea" where she was living or what she did, except for occasional contact which ceased once she was kidnapped. At some point, they just stopped having news from or about her and had no way of knowing what had become of her. They were only aware of her absence, of the fact that she had stopped "being around." This explains why her re-appearance touched them so very deeply:

When they received the letter, it was all very intense for them [...] a new phase opened, a ray of hope [...] After that phone call [...], they [the repressors] told me to arrange a meeting with my folks and [...] they [Ana's parents] came all the way from my town to my grandmother's, who lived in Córdoba [...] We talked all night long [...] we cried a lot [...] That was the first meeting with my folks [...] I remember telling my mum that they were killing people and my mum told me 'that's not possible, that cannot be [...] you're wrong, Ana, it cannot be;' *even a year and a half after* [Ana's disappearance] *it seemed unimaginable* [...] I think that the next time, that must've been a month later, they allowed me to go to my town.

(Iliovich 2012, personal communication; emphases added)

Ana's words shed light on the complex relationship between the outside world and the "concentration camp," a space that was experienced only by those who inhabited it, inmates and perpetrators. Others had only a partial glimpse of what was happening. People witnessed the kidnappings;

they saw the prisoners inside cars – although they didn't know that's what the "passengers" really were.[5] After these fleeting sightings, once a person disappeared, nobody knew for certain what happened. People preferred not to see. "Knowing little meant living long," pointed out a neighbour of the San Vicente Cemetery in Córdoba in a 2007 film *Señor Presidente* (Arraya and Monti), as he recalled being a silent witness to the clandestine burials. The families of those who re-appeared – temporarily released from the CDCs – listened to the dreadful accounts but often found them too horrific to believe. The magnitude and brutality of the extermination, without the ability to see it with one's own eyes, was difficult to imagine.

After that first meeting with her parents, the repressors of La Perla permitted Ana to visit her family periodically. However, this did not mean that she had been freed. After each visit, they would collect her or she had to make her way back to the "concentration camp" on her own. This situation lasted for a year and a half.

When I first started working with the survivors of La Perla, it was hard to comprehend the precise moment of their "exit" from the camp. They referred to a period when they would be allowed to have "days out" – a time when the practice of taking pictures of themselves occurred. While the kidnapping appeared as a fixed event that presented itself in their memory in a distinct manner, most survivors were unable to recollect at what precise moment they had started to come out, let alone when exactly they had begun to feel freed. This was particularly the case for survivors who, like Ana, were never "whitewashed."[6] In some cases, coming out of La Perla implied being transferred to a regular prison or to another CDC. In other cases, the prisoners were allowed to live in their homes, under an arrangement which, although it situated them out of La Perla, wasn't felt by many as a liberation, due to the constant harassment, which included their families, enacted by the repressors. Thus, liberation and survival weren't experienced as clear, distinct moments – and much less so as definitive ones – by those subject to a period of "monitored freedom." Instead, they were experienced as a vague, paradoxical and often maddening form of existence. In many survivors' recollections, the objective aspects of the situation – being out of the CDC and having a certain amount of ambulatory freedom – often appear disconnected from their subjective experience that fluctuates *between* a death sentence and the hope of survival; *between* a death space and life spaces (Taussig 2002). This paradoxical experience, and what it meant for the families of the detainees, explains why – at least in the case of the survivors of La Perla – no one ever tried to escape. Whenever the repressors released or allowed some prisoners to go to their homes, they always kept other prisoners as "hostages," who would pay the price for anyone on the outside who'd try to escape.

Those subject to "monitored freedom" faced other challenges, too. The repressors often interacted with the prisoners' families: they entered their homes, expected to be served and thanked for "returning" loved ones to their families. Consequently, the prisoners' relatives started to suffer the same harassment as the prisoners themselves. In a way, they became subject to the power of the "camp" and its perverse relationships. Through this, the "camp" succeeded in spreading its power beyond its physical borders, beyond what was immediately visible.[7] It is important to note that the passage from confined captivity to "monitored freedom" was devoid of the presence of any official documentation to attest to it. What role, then, did photographic images assume in that context?

In *On Photography*, Susan Sontag points out that "to photograph is to appropriate the thing photographed. It means putting oneself into a certain relation to the world that feels like knowledge – and, therefore, like power" (1978, 16). In the context of the capture of prisoners by disappearing them – an invisibilising force – the act of photographing the re-appeared acquires a crucial significance as an act of resistance and re-insertion into society (Calveiro 2001). To take photographs of the disappeared within their invisibility denotes an important degree of agency on the part of those who photographed them.

In conversations with Ana, the period of "monitored freedom" is a recurrent subject because it represents a particularly *ominous, uncanny moment* (Freud 1992). Despite the period's indistinct character, certain acts of resistance emerged, which would, gradually and eventually, allow Ana to reconstruct her shattered world and devastated subjectivity. Ana's period of "monitored freedom" was marked by a drive – both hers and her family's – to document that experience.

One of those acts of resistance concerned the documentation and inscription of the identity of those who shared the *death space* with her: the killers, but, above all, Ana's fellow victims (Taussig 2002). During that period, Ana smuggled out the names of prisoners extracted from the lists she was forced to transcribe for La Perla's bureaucracy. She began by memorising ten names at a time, then, she started to jot them down on slips of paper she took with her when she visited her family. The names were then meticulously transcribed into a notebook she left in a safe in Bell Ville.[8]

The lists of names were undoubtedly the first act of recovery of Ana's humanity; an inscription that stabilised, materialised and conferred existence not only to the disappearance of others, but also her own.[9] It was also in the specific context of these transitional moments – when survivors were still, or might have been still, disappeared – that photographs suddenly acquired their profound significance as documents. Instigated by their loved ones, those images represent the will to re-inscribe the disappeared into the world of the living; into the family environment; into the domain of the visible. These images also acted as a guarantee, a certification. By capturing the referent – that body in the here and now – they stabilised the re-appearance.

After the return of democracy in 1983, the account of these transitional experiences adopted the paradigmatic form of judicial testimony. Throughout the last forty years, survivors have testified on numerous occasions. But the enunciation context the judicial testimony required of their statement was mainly focused on facts, persons, cases and very little, or not at all, on their identity as witnesses (Pollak 2006). Often, this type of testimony restricted the *biographical space* to the period of their life which was invested with general interest, and to the detriment of more subjective or personal questions (Arfuch 2008). This manner of constructing testimony prompts questions about the temporal limit of the experience, and its paradoxes, both in objective and subjective terms. How can one account for an experience that – in a sense – never ceases? It's only recently – and thanks to a court case in which they participated as victims[10] – that La Perla's survivors have been able to speak about their own experience, not only while they were still captive, but also after they left the CDC. This was accompanied by a subjective shift in which other types of testimonial writing emerged, such as the "introductions" the survivors were able to add to their judicial testimonies (Tello 2017). Parallel to these processes, other autobiographical texts were composed, which modified the locus of enunciation, expanded the space of the sayable, enabled alternative aesthetics, as is the case with Ana's book, *El Silencio.*

"An Impossible Scene"

Ana opted for one of the family photographs her parents took in July 1977 for the cover of *El Silencio* (Figure 7.3). The picture emerges from under a layer of torn paper. During an interview, Ana chose to answer my questions about the photo by reading the following passages from the book:

A few days ago, Alice Herz-Sommer, a Terezin survivor, died peacefully, conscious and smiling, at the age of 110. Music saved her then as well as later in life. I've seen the film they made about her life; *there is an impossible scene.* The children, prisoners of the camp, all dressed and made up as if for a school party, singing in a choir, and some women prisoners and guards watching them, like an audience. Almost none of them survived.

Those eyes, those little faces, are aware of the absurdity of it all, dressed up sadness is more perverse, more maddening than the distinct territory of prison. That picture, too, is the real horror I've been trying to express ever since I started writing.

(Iliovich 2012, personal communication; emphasis added)

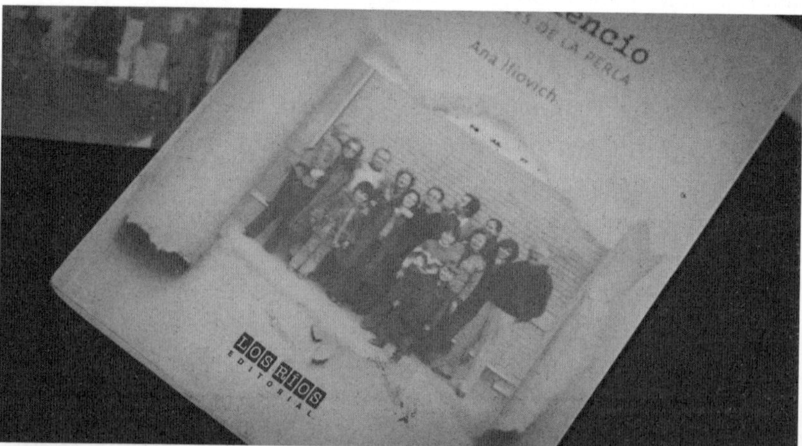

Figure 7.3 Cover of *El Silencio: Postales de la Perla.*
Source: a still from *(Dis)Appear* (2023). Courtesy of Piotr Cieplak.

Later, Ana referenced another "impossible scene":

My folks took many pictures of me to prove I had been there. I was alive. To see those faces trying to smile. The grief and fear that bubble underneath are easily read. *Another impossible scene*, not in Terezin in 1943, but in Bell Ville, in the winter of 1977.

(Iliovich 2012, personal communication; emphases added)

This desire "to prove" that she "had been there," that Ana was "alive," follows the trajectory of existence, record and death outlined by Barthes in which that which is photographed:

is the target, the referent, a kind of little simulacrum, any *eidolon* emitted by the object, which I should like to call the Spectrum of the Photograph, because this word retains, through its root, a relation to "spectacle" and adds to it that rather terrible thing which is there in every photograph: the return of the dead.

(2000, 9)[11]

The space-time coordinates that converge in the photograph, its capacity to capture a living referent, turn it into an "impossible scene." When we talked about this image, Ana pointed out that:

... this picture is what I'm trying to describe: the horror, the horror of the camp, and the picture as a staging of that horror [...] where the absurdity of the situation can be seen. [...] I was in my town, but I had to go back to the camp [...] I was part of the camp, I never stopped being in La Perla, even though I was in Bell Ville [...] For me that picture [...] summarises so many things.

(Iliovich 2020, personal communication)

What Ana's parents tried to capture, authenticate and solidify in those images was her existence, blurred fourteen months earlier. They tried to capture this existence in the face of the death that threatened it. It was a deliberate, desperate strategy, promoted above all by Ana's mother: "My mum insisted firmly that we should go out to take pictures of ourselves [...] She feared that they would kill me. She had no confidence in the fact that they would let me live" (Iliovich 2020, personal communication). Life and death as ontological categories, burst asunder by the experience of disappearance, were brought together in what Ana's mother did as the instigator of these photographs. She captured a scene in which she could prove that her daughter was alive, in Bell Ville, in July 1977. Those pictures were a document that could certify that her body existed, every time Ana had to go back to the "concentration camp."

"I never stopped being in La Perla, even though I was in Bell Ville." Once we know this, the constellation of disturbing signs that prick us – the half smiles, Ana's vacant gaze, the numerous relatives present – starts to make sense. The photographs capture a paradox; a scene that was, in Ana's own words, "impossible" because it captured a split, a *bilocation*.[12] She hadn't stopped being in the "camp" and the "camp" was everywhere she went; including in the family home. Expressed in subjective, emotional terms, what resonates in these images is Freud's (1992) concept of the *uncanny*, both in the recurring figure of the *double*, and in his definition of it as the familiar that has become strange.

The disturbing feeling that these photographs irradiate derives from the overlapping of physical, affective and moral spaces that once were clearly separated – "dressed up sadness is more perverse, more maddening than the distinct territory of prison." They signal the sudden emergence of a *death space* at the heart of ordinary, everyday life (Taussig 2002). All those planes *overdetermine* one another in the images (Didi-Huberman 2008b). The situations they capture are part of the simulacrum, the "staging" before a world that ignores – or denies – the disappearance, because acknowledging it has the potential of being dangerous, of contaminating all those who encounter it.[13]

The making of the photographs was in many ways a conscious, affective act. It utilised the paradox to constitute a document. But as well as being documents, the photographs are also a testimony, in whose microscopic clues – folds that both reveal and hide – we can decipher what cannot be seen in the pictures themselves. Triquell argues that "photography becomes a testimony – of an experience – and a document – a proof of truth – which limits the universe of the unreal to a smaller space in relation to the content of its referent, establishing, from the social contract of the verisimilitude of the record, a more reliable construction of one's own history" (2012, 50). Didi-Huberman points out that:

managing a disappearance [...] means inventing, organising the logical and visual marks of that disappearance. However, these marks necessarily form – morphologically – 'folds' (in the words of Gilles Deleuze) or 'catastrophes' (in the words of René Thom) [...] they are above all subtle games of the limit, between the open and the closed, the visible and the invisible, the here and the beyond, the thing captured and the thing that captures, the front and the inside.

(Didi-Huberman 2015, 186)

So far, I have tried to account for what these photographs of Ana and her family sought to achieve at the moment of their taking, "for the present of this experience, for the memory it evoked, and for the future it promised" (Didi-Huberman 2008b, 32). I have focused on the photographs' most stable characteristics: placing the body in this place, on the date printed on the white border. All of these elements designate the photographs as documents, proofs, reassurances. But disappeared bodies that appear in photographs belong to an unstable ontology, and, consequently, the photographs that capture them are also unstable objects which require a particular type of gaze. What layers of visibility open-up and overlap when we look at these images? What, in the act of looking, invites us to remember the group of signs set within a frame but dislocated by the paradox which exceeds them? What pricks us in photographs such as these?

We are not dealing here with a mere illustration. The importance these images acquired as a *visual testimony* was the result of Ana's deliberate choice:

When I started to think the book was possible, [...] I always thought that the photograph had to be on the cover. I never hesitated [...] I [imagined] half of the photograph should be the family in Bell Ville and half, the photograph of the children in Terezin. When I saw that video of Terezin where the children are playing an opera in the middle of the concentration camp somehow that seemed to me the most [...] terrible [...] synthesis [...] of the absolute loss of humanity. And I felt [...] that this was in Terezin, this was in Bell Ville, but the situation, in terms of the horror, was the same. I would go back to La Perla and on the following day they could kill me.

(Iliovich 2020, personal communication)

No official photographs of the period of internment existed – this is to say, the kind of photographs that could be seen to function as official documents. Paradoxically, what gives these family photographs the possibility of becoming documents is precisely the fact that they're family photographs, able to pass unnoticed by those incapable of deciphering their "staging," their status as a simulacrum. But to be perceived in this new sense by a wider public, the family photos had to undergo a series of transformations and displacements, and become subject to narrative acts.

Ana's choice to use the photograph on the cover of the book constitutes a displacement from the private to the public sphere and, later, a relocation into the context of a much more universal tragedy. The original project was conceived as an assemblage, as a kind of collage with the image of another "impossible scene": in the Terezin concentration camp during World War II. This assemblage situates the Argentine tragedy within another; one that functions as the paradigm for imagining the camps and the total denial of humanity to those who inhabited them.

The idea of using assemblage to inscribe the family photograph into the public sphere did not end up on the book cover. The designer proposed another form of presentation which centred not on comparison but on the singularity of this simultaneously veiled and unveiled object. The family photograph emerges as if from under a torn wrapping-paper. This results in a stratified view which the reader is only able to access after digging deeper, after removing a layer, and where – by Ana's request – they can also date the object of this discovery: the date of the taking of the photo printed on the white border, the sign which condenses the paradox.

Ana uses the family photographs to accompany two of the many "postcards" that constitute the narrative of *El Silencio*. The postcards take the form of brief texts in which Ana's memories of La Perla are situated between different presents, and upon which the past supervenes throughout her life. In this first-person account, Ana's experience is intertwined with that of others who have been affected by it: her family, her fellow militants and prisoners, and others who did not exist yet, such as her children. The passages function as real postcards in that they are brief situations, sometimes arid, and extremely moving. Through the postcards, the reader witnesses Ana's unfathomable experience and its multiple reverberations across different times and spaces of Ana's life.[14] The only visual images of that experience are the paradoxical images, the family photos, which offer another way of seeing and imagining, one which, without abandoning the logic of testimony and proof, moves away from the literality required of them.

These family photographs, like a different type of postcard, require another way of seeing and understanding, another *ethics of the gaze*

(Longoni and García 2013) when it comes to looking at images of repression. Due to their inconspicuousness as documents, they raise multiple questions about the visibility of oppression, or rather, about the sensitive and ethical tools of the gaze from which to catch a glimpse of those simulacra, those paradoxes.

As Pollak (2006) points out, if there is something the concentrationary experience destroys, it is the mutual understanding of the world. Nothing is what it seems. Paradox and restlessness can be – as Didi-Huberman (2008b) has aptly remarked – an excellent starting point for questioning what is dislocated from the common understanding of images. But such a way of looking requires previous training in the detection of the nuances between the visible and the invisible, especially in the face of the need for a simulacrum as a condition for the very possibility of the record existing in the first place.

The Familiar and the Strange

In her analysis of Christian Boltanski's *Photo Album of Family D* (1991), Leonor Arfuch (2002) explores the work from the perspective of the unsettling feeling it arouses in her. What unsettles Arfuch in *Photo Album of Family D* – a series of photographs of a French family, dating from the post-war period, all set in a symmetrical mosaic – is the disarrangement of the individual pieces, which do not respect the lineal story one would expect from a family album. What's also disconcerting for Arfuch are the shadows, those ghostly traces which from the context of those photographs appear to sneak into the image that's fixed in them. Something dark reverberates in the work, and also something dead. The atmosphere of the times captured in those photographs seems to turn the scenes portrayed into something which, despite its seeming banality, cannot be seen without the feeling of restlessness.

Like Boltanski's installation, Ana's family photographs are part of a series that remained in the family's house after her parents died. Ana recounts that her folks "had some albums, and some photographs [...] that had come loose [and] were in boxes" (Iliovich 2020, personal communication). When the parents passed away, Ana distributed the images among her brothers. Triquell writes that the family album "preserve[s] and give[s] testimony of the life of a family group" (2012, 51–52). These family portraits, taken during the period of "monitored freedom," represent a disruption to the usual function of such images outlined by Triquell. Firstly, all the photos in the series are almost identical. Secondly, the signs that signal the importance of the event which had gathered the extended family also disrupt: people do not appear to be dressed up for the occasion, and, although they seem to be relieved, they don't look happy. So the photographs of that first visit to Bell Ville constitute – within the family album which can be understood as an archival record – an independent, separate series, composed of numerous images with minute, almost negligible differences between them; a trait that somehow gives them an unsettling character. So many almost identical photographs is a rarity in family albums – especially at a time when taking pictures implied the use of film – and can only be explained in the light of Ana's mother's desire to take many pictures to have a proof that Ana was alive. But by the same logic, the photographs not only document, but also reassemble the dismembered family, reuniting its members through an event in which they all become part of the "staging," and thereby, also part of that paradox of being simultaneously inside and outside the "camp." This reassembling then allows for memory work to take place, for reinterpretations and revelations to emerge, which, in turn, enable one not only to reflect on the subjectivity devastated by the experience of the "camp", but also on its reconstruction on individual, community and family levels: a re-assemblage of which the photographs constitute a central part.[15]

During one of my interviews with Ana, we started the ritual of looking at photographs. After unravelling the significance of the paradox, other layers of meaning began to emerge. They had to do not so much with what appeared in the photos, but with the familiar quality that they seemed to pierce. While looking at the photographs, the gaze tries to decipher the passing of time entangled in the bodies and their gestures, but also in the clothes which, in this case, hint at Ana's attempt at reassembling herself in her own right, as well as in relation to others present in the image:

It's something I always talk about […] my mother with that *intuition* of taking me to buy clothes. Nice Clothes. As though she had known that my body was completely dismantled and, so, it was as if with those clothes she helped me buy and […] choose […] *she helped me assemble those pieces of my body with those nice clothes she bought me.* I remember perfectly the two sweaters she bought me, beautiful ones that I wore when I went to Bell Ville. And a pair of trousers. [When I arrived in Bell Ville I wore] La Perla's clothes, clothes they brought from the houses. They threw them around just like that, they distributed them among us. Those were the clothes they made us wear.

(Iliovich 2020, personal communication; emphases added)

Once Ana relates them to the memories of her own body, the signs of the time, such as clothing, suddenly take on an entirely different dimension. When someone was kidnapped, they were stripped of all their personal effects. If the kidnapping happened at one's home, the kidnappers ransacked the house and carried away the kidnappee's belongings, many of which were then taken to La Perla.[16] Once the captives arrived at the CDC, they were completely undressed and taken in for torture sessions. They were subsequently forced to wear somebody else's clothes; the clothes of former detainees, now dead. Clothes, as a second skin, are part of the *corporal hexis* (Bourdieu 1986), they give shape to our own image, both for ourselves and for others, and, therefore, the act of stripping someone of their clothes constitutes an alienation ritual, the first step in a long process of de-subjectification.

In the context of captivity, recovering a piece of one's own clothing – a personal effect – constituted a triumph over de-subjectification. In the traumatic path of coming back to, so to speak, the world of the living, the change of clothing was not a minor thing. Years later, Ana felt that at that moment her parents rebuilt her. Ana's mother, in particular, helped her reconstruct a wholesome body, perceived as dismantled and "in pieces" up until then. Having nice clothes of her own, clothes she had chosen, meant starting to recover the agency taken away by the passage through La Perla. Wearing new clothes allowed Ana to re-found herself as a person, to take the "camp" – if not out of herself – out of her body; to cleanse herself of its death emanations which, like skin or a scab, covered her body.

Ana writes that, through these actions, her mother put her back into the womb and delivered her again (Iliovich 2017, 24). The birth metaphor eloquently reflects that rite of passage which endows one with existence, which incorporates a biological being into a social environment. With the maternal rituals – buying a new set of clothes, holding social meetings, taking pictures, making food – Ana was slowly "reborn." Through the scrutiny of these photographs for the *folds* of meaning, emerges, for Ana, a memory that attempts to surround the ineffable; to disambiguate the paradox so that we – who only approach that experience through our listening – may *understand.*

From something as ordinary as a family photograph, Ana's gaze punctures us. It returns to be reinterpreted, to confer new meanings on this "impossible scene." These photographs fix the paradox which, in turn, is projected out of the image, towards a society where the *distribution of the sensible* was manipulated to generate terror. Thus, by lifting the veils cast over the image, by making others see what is hidden beneath them, Ana manages to communicate the paradoxical, much of which would otherwise remain invisible to the uninformed eye.

Towards an Ethnography of the (In)visible

As mentioned at the beginning of this chapter, survivors in Argentina have been almost invisible publicly in the four decades since their liberation. The invisibility – reflected in the scarcity of public, and often private, photographic records – can be traced to situations prior to the moment of disappearance. Firstly, what needs to be accounted for is the secrecy in which the militancy of the 1970s developed, particularly within the framework of the clandestine military political organisations. Ana recounts:

In the days of the militancy, we practically didn't take any pictures of ourselves, so I have almost no photographs of that time, except for some family pictures that my folks took of me when I went there to visit my friends [...] In the camp, [...] they didn't take any pictures of me. I think they took one snapshot [...] so that I could have a [fake] ID and could move round.

(Iliovich 2020, personal communication)

Secrecy was a characteristic which permeated those times. Many militant survivors recall altering their appearance in order to evade persecution (Tello 2008). It was in that context that organisations recommended their members not to take pictures of themselves for security reasons. The few photographs that were taken in that time where accidental records of public acts or meetings with friends or family, who were oblivious to the dangers of photographic practice in this context. Photos taken within the organisational frameworks were intended to be used in fake identity documents. When militants were captured and ended up in a CDC, they were disappeared, that is, invisibilised. They did not stop existing but came out of the realm of the visible in relation to the rest of society. In many CDCs, photographic operations were carried out to book the prisoners. In La Perla, however, no such practices took place, which meant that for those imprisoned there, that period of their lives constituted a time without images. This situation lasted until survivors started to be taken out of the "camp." It was at that precise moment that photographs began to play an important role in relation to the existence of these individuals. It was in this context that photographs took on a completely different value: what had previously represented a potential threat, a power in the hands of the repressors, was now regarded as a visual document that proved, both in a sensorial and official sense, their existence.

Throughout this chapter, I have sought to account for that *liminal* period represented by the "monitored freedom" of the disappeared, both in structural and visual terms. It is in this context that photographs, such as those taken by Ana's family, became crucial as a mode of giving substance and visibility to an existence still threatened by disappearance. This is further evidenced by the phrases employed by other survivors to accompany the moments in which they tried to explain this complex experience in interviews I conducted over the years. "Taking pictures of myself was the first thing I did during monitored freedom." "That was the first photograph of me after all those years." "Look, this is when we were allowed to go see our family, we are by the riverside, but I look like an Auschwitz prisoner." The memories of that period find in those photographs a way of approaching the paradoxical *folds* between the visible and the invisible. It is in the simultaneous *there* and *then* (Edwards 2001) of these ordinary photographs and the here and now of memory work that their seemingly harmless and trivial signs are surpassed to allow "the paradox [to] flower" (Oviedo Funes in Didi-Huberman 2008b, 14). The images themselves, as well as the accounts of the experiences registered in them, suddenly demand the expansion of the frame in order to confront the act of staging in which nothing is what it seems.

Ana Iliovich calls these images "impossible scene[s]." The impossibility refers to the paradox of a bilocalised experience, of an ontology devastated by the camp experience. But how much of this impossibility is visible to us? Those photographs are paradoxical objects, anachronisms that, precisely because of their "inaccuracy," are capable of setting in motion a dynamic process of memory work. As such, they have the power to encourage an oblique gaze at those *liminal territories* of social life, the "concentration camps" (Turner 1990).

On the other hand, Ana's accounts, and her unique reflections about these photographs, involve more general topics related to the *distribution of the sensible* that permeate that experience: the tension between clandestinity and photography, between photography and disappearance. Tensions that may shed some light on how the *distribution of the sensible* and the subsequent performative power of visibility and invisibility operated both in the Argentine state's criminal actions and in the strategies of resistance developed against them. In other words, on photography as a practice which, between the there and then of those who captured the scene and the here and now of those who observe it, allows us to scrutinise the invisible.

We need – as Longoni and García (2013) point out – a *new ethics of the gaze* which, by placing our ways of seeing between the *folds* captured in the images, may allow us to hear them as though they were the marks of a visual silence; a kind of gaze, perhaps, that may do justice to those instable images in their correspondence with a referent. Or, in Andrés Tello's words, a *disjunction* between:

a way of speaking and seeing which goes beyond the concatenations limited to the empirical, immediate corroborations of words and things which might induce us to believe that one always speaks about what is seen or sees that which is spoken about, when in reality there exits an interstice between both dimensions – covered and reorganised in each variation – that gives rise to a different historical formation.

(2016, 46)

In order to gain an insight into the *distribution of the sensible* generated by and around state violence in Argentina, we need first to develop a critical questioning of the sensorial regimes and the ways in which we understand those photographs that captured everyday life scenes as fragments of an enormous "staging." Any attempt at deciphering these images confronts us with the impossible, invites us to accept epistemological, ethical and emotional challenges that go beyond the evidential. Meeting these challenges, I believe, amounts to a transformation that requires an ethnographic approach to those documents and the ways we see them. An approach that might allow us to come out of the frame of what these images show us, in order to apply our attention to their materiality, their localisation, their circulation and erosion. In other words, to the meaning these photographs acquire in the lives of those connected to them; and to the images' potential to bring the past to the present. It is their ramifications, their silences, which allow us to look with fresh eyes at the invisible fragments of that past each time they appear.

Translated by Jorge Salvetti

Notes

1 Bell Ville is a town located some 200 km from the city of Córdoba.

2 La Perla was a CDC that operated from 24 March 1976 to the end of 1978. It was located within the grounds and under the command of the III Army Corps in a rural area 12 km from the city of Córdoba. Between 2,200 and 2,500 victims passed through La Perla and only around 200 survived. Only a few detainees have been identified, the rest remain disappeared.

3 In this chapter, I use quotation marks to indicate terms used and expressed by the people directly affected by the violence and italics to express my own, analytical categories. "Disappearance" is an exception here. It very much belongs to the first group of terms (those used by survivors) but it also functions as a recognisable analytical term. It is, in fact, a euphemism, since people - materially speaking - did not disappear, but were hidden or taken.

4 Survivors rarely include images in their testimonial writing. There are a few exceptions, such as the inclusion of sketches employed to illustrate the situations described in testimonies, the well-known photographs that Víctor Basterra took in ESMA and which were published together with his testimony (Longoni and García 2013; Feld 2014a, 2014b), and the ID photograph which Carlos Pussetto, a survivor of La Perla, included at the beginning of his testimony. In the last fifteen years, some biographical texts dealing with disappearance included photographs of the authors (e.g. Robles 2010). In her book, Teresa "Tina" Meschiati (2019), a survivor of La Perla, used images - not always photographs - to illustrate parts of the story. Photographs of survivors have also recently entered commemorative spaces in exhibitions - usually shown in the act of testifying during the Trials of the Juntas - or in ceremonies and tributes at the time of their death.

5 Prisoners were often taken out of CDCs and put in cars as decoys or to lure other suspects to be arrested.

6 See the glossary for the meaning of "whitewashed" in this specific context.

7 Many survivors began to feel truly free only after going into exile. For those who remained in the country, this harassment continued for years. This explains why the subjective experience of their re-emergence is so closely linked to the act of putting an end to impunity.

8　Ana handed that notebook with names to the National Commission on the Disappearances of Persons (CoNaDeP). The lists of names also played an important part in her later judicial testimonies.

9　In the majority of testimonial writing from the late 1970s and early 1980s, one's own experience tended to be recounted in order to substantiate a *testimonial authority* (Tello 2015). What each survivor suffered remained largely inaudible, vis-à-vis the massacre to which they were acting as witnesses.

10　The case is known as the Acosta Case, in which twenty-one repressors were prosecuted for the crimes of unlawful deprivation of liberty and torture with aggravation committed against 139 survivors.

11　It is important to note here the meaning of *eidolon* as understood by the ancient Greeks: as a ghostly or phantom-like double of the human form.

12　Physical laws dictate that an object, a person in this case, cannot be in two places at the same time. However, the possibility of naming this splitting or division – even if relegating it to the realm of the paranormal, supernatural or divine – proves that this phenomenon, although incompatible with the common laws of time and space, has always existed as an experience.

13　As mentioned earlier, when family members encountered the kidnappers, they often attracted the repressors' attention. Thus, the reincorporation of the survivors into the ordinary world was a long, maddening process. The common, general pretext used to justify the absence and then the return of the survivors, was that of travel. Another survivor told me that, when she re-appeared, her mother organised a party. When the survivor expressed her intention to tell the truth, the mother responded: "as far as the guests are concerned, you were in Miami."

14　The postcard emerged at the turn of the 18th century as an alternative to letters. Postcards, as a format, have several interesting features in the context of what is at stake in this chapter. Firstly, they are not a completely private means of communication, as they are not enclosed in an envelope and can be read by whomever handles them. Secondly, they tend to display an image on the front, while reserving a small space on the back for a brief message. They are usually bought as souvenirs acquired at different stages of a trip and sent to those who have remained home. All these characteristics are reflected in the texts in *El Silencio*.

15　For a further discussion of the ways in which subjectivity of inmates is affected by the concentrationary experience, see Calveiro (2001) and Pollak (2006).

16　In addition to objects of value, other items commonly seized in those raids were family albums. The photographs were then incorporated into intelligence records and served to identify other potential victims. The seizure of photographs meant the loss of an important part of many families' visual history and bestowed another layer of invisibility on the victims.

8

What Appears and What Still Shines Through

Ana Longoni

I

Julio Pantoja, a photographer from Tucumán, made a well-known statement in which he declared that the most passionate conversations about photography he has are with the sons and daughters of the people disappeared during Argentina's most recent military dictatorship (Pantoja 2021). Many children of the disappeared, very young and sometimes not yet born at the time of their parents' kidnapping, came to know their mothers and fathers – and have continued to connect with them over the years – through, often scarce, photographs.

These old, tattered, treasured and caressed images are, in many cases, the few remaining material traces of those forced disappearances, those abruptly interrupted lives, torn from us, for the most part, without any knowledge as to their final destination, without certainty, without a grave. This nebula that surrounds the disappeared and those they left behind was, and sometimes still is, a means to spread the terror instilled in Argentine society by the sinister and repressive pattern of the forced disappearance of 30,000 people in nearly 500 clandestine detention and extermination centres (CDCs) around the country (Calveiro 2001).

But the photos – and their multiple, intimate and public uses – are also a clear sign of persistence, another way for the disappeared to continue being amongst us, demanding a place, compelling personal and collective memory practices. Like a Chinese puzzle box, many of the photographic projects that address disappearance are often photographs *of* photographs, photographs *with* photographs. And it is in this invocation of the absent that photography is able to evidence the disturbing dimension of the spectrality of these faces. Faces that demand not to be forgotten. As Luis García points out:

> They [the disappeared] do not return alive, but they return as photos, that is, these photos begin to speak not so much, or at least not only, of the *previous* life of the disappeared, but of their later life, of their *posthumous life*, of their *survival*, of their re-appearance: they testify not only to something that was, but to something that will return and is always returning. These photos can be thought of not only as an *index* of what was, nor as a relic of what will no longer be, but also, and above all, as a *material support for what returns* [...] A future anterior.
>
> (2013, 134; original emphasis)

I want to situate the closing chapter of this collection at the intersection of the insistence and, simultaneously, the fragility of the photographs of the disappeared. For a concrete example of this, mentioned in Natalia Fortuny's chapter, let us zoom in on the moment the writer Félix Bruzzone notices that the portrait of his disappeared mother, which he keeps on his desk where he can look at it daily, is gradually fading because of the sunlight that sneaks through the window of his new house. Bruzzone subsequently realises that his new home is very close to Campo de Mayo, the military compound which housed the CDC through which his mother is known to have passed (Bruzzone 2011). The fading photograph is precisely that remnant, capable of summoning a dimension of the presence of absence that does not cease, remains latent and unresolved – always at risk of disappearing again.

II

This book explores the central condition of photography as a multifaceted artefact of both personal and collective memory of disappearance, a document proving an existence denied by state terrorism and an invocation, a ritual of mourning. *Familiar Faces* offers a meeting of voices, perspectives and case studies, explored by researchers who have been working for decades on the intersection between photography and the memory of Argentina's most recent dictatorship. The contributors – researchers, curators, photographers and human rights activists alike – address a series of precise dimensions and specific case studies that make up a revealing mosaic, as articulate as it is polyphonic. While all the approaches present in the volume reflect on the relationship between photography and disappearance, they do so from different angles, asking different questions: from photography as a creative resource in the human rights movement, as an artefact of social memory, as a glimpse into the lives of survivors, to photography as a language of art.

Cora Gamarnik's chapter painstakingly traces the detail of how the photographs of the Mothers of Plaza de Mayo began circulating in local and international media and became key in making the Mothers, as well as the wider human rights movement and its demands, visible to the world. Being photographed is seen here as a survival tactic in the face of concentrationary terror. Natalia Fortuny's chapter delves into the photographic landscapes, used by a group of contemporary artists to evoke traumatic experience: natural landscapes in which the absent appear, trembling; artificial landscapes that construct fictions in order to throw reality into sharp relief; familial landscapes that propose the impossible task of completing an irremediably truncated family album, full of holes.

In conversation with Piotr Cieplak, the photographer Inés Ulanovsky reflects on the importance of biographical coordinates in the unfolding of her photographic project based on the uses that family members make of the photographs of the disappeared. In the interview, Ulanovsky returns to her childhood in exile and the impact that the faces she saw in the photographs had on her at human rights marches. While Ulanovsky defends the "documentary and social sense of record," she does not fail to consider the affective dimension of the bond that family members establish with the photos, the ghostly presences that live in them.

Ludmila da Silva Catela's contribution retraces her pioneering work on photographs and disappearance in Argentina, and especially the intersection between their ritual and political dimensions (da Silva Catela 2001). Da Silva Catela zooms in on the use of photographs of the disappeared in northern Argentina. Particularly poignant is her recounting of the interaction with Rita, the mother of two young people disappeared in Calilegua (Jujuy): "photographs were the intermediaries in the dialogue with my subjects; small objects charged with symbolic energy and the ability to make those absent present." The photograph features here as a substitute for the place of mourning, the grave that does not exist, somewhere to leave flowers, remember and mourn. A ritual in the domestic sphere that treasures the possibility of its public, collective and street use, when those same photos become banners or posters.

The rituals described by da Silva Catela resonate with other funerary practices related to the absent body, in which photography is a participant. Amongst them is the ceremony performed by Mariana Corral on All Souls' Day, when she chooses a "borrowed" tomb in the Flores cemetery, during the popular celebration of the Bolivian community that inhabits that area of Buenos Aires, to honour Manuel Corral, her missing father. As part of the ritual, she shares fragments of letters, photos and pieces of bread shaped like jaguars and other animals that inhabit the missionary jungle, where the father disappeared.[1]

The consideration and analysis of these rituals is not only pertinent to Argentina but also to other parts of the continent. For instance, Ileana Dieguez's book, *Cuerpos sin duelo* [*Bodies Without Mourning*] (2016) investigates funerary practices on the banks of the Magdalena River in Colombia. In particular, the burying of anonymous bodies of unknown victims in graves that later receive the names of the disappeared people from that community. This practice raises questions of the transience or collectivisation of the unresolved mourning of so many. Renaming is one of the "funeral imaginaries" of unresolved mourning in the face of violent death or disappearance, marked by the impossibility of the farewell rite (Dieguez 2016, 283). Of particular relevance here is Dieguez's analysis of the portraits by Gabriel Posada, "Magdalenas en el Cauca" – large canvases painted with the faces of the women of the massacred population of Trujillo bearing the photographs of their disappeared, thrown into the river on fragile cane rafts that are dragged by the same current into which so many bodies have been dropped by paramilitary violence in the region.

III

There exists an often-repeated claim that there are no photographs of the systematic programme of disappearing people carried out by the most recent Argentine dictatorship. But these images do in fact exist and, in some cases, have been publicly available from soon after the dictatorial regime collapsed. These are not photographs of the *before* or *after*, but images of the *during*, that unthinkable, unfathomable time.

Most of these images attest to the existence of a well-oiled, bureaucratic machine of the repressive apparatus that routinely recorded everything, including its clandestine and illegal acts. The repressors resorted to photography not only to book the disappeared (as if they were regular prisoners, legally detained), but also to record the monitoring of suspects, build media campaigns and falsify documentation useful in intelligence operations and criminal acts. At the same time, the relative lack of circulation, or perhaps visibility, of such photographs attests to the stigmas bestowed on the disappeared who re-appeared alive. Although some images were presented in judicial instances very early on (as is the case with the photos taken in ESMA by Víctor Basterra), the social conditions of their legibility have been, at least initially, diminished or undermined.[2]

Mariana Tello Weiss's chapter delves into a very different kind of photographs taken *during* the dictatorship. What at first could be perceived as a conventional record of a family gathering turns out to be an "impossible scene": an unprecedented image in which Ana Iliovich, a young woman who was held in a CDC called La Perla, in Córdoba, is seen posing next to her entire family, including her younger brother who, in the photo, is just a boy. The image in question was taken *during* Ana's disappearance, fourteen months after she was kidnapped.

The seeming "normality" of the photographed situation (as if nothing strange was happening there) conceals the sinister procedures that enabled that encounter and the ways in which photography could become an act of resistance within the matrix of disappearance. Taking that photo of Ana Iliovich with her family during one of the visits she was allowed to make under surveillance – as part of her supposed "rehabilitation process" – meant constituting an incontestable proof of life, when Ana's existence (alongside thousands of others) was denied by the authorities. Just like the Mothers of Plaza de Mayo, the re-appeared disappeared also wanted to make themselves seen, to open up a slit that enabled the prospect of survival or, at least, of providing a reliable testimony of their own condition. The photo was a way of documenting that one was alive.

In dialogue with Piotr Cieplak, María Eleonora Cristina reflects on the different creative tactics that – with considerable freedom and risk – have been deployed at the Provincial Memory Archive (APM), which operates in the former headquarters of D2, a CDC, a few metres from Córdoba's City Hall.

In particular, Cristina elaborates on the APM's team responses to the appearance of the so-called Register of "Extremists" – a tip of the iceberg when it comes to confirming the existence of the archive of terror that the repressive apparatus continued to routinely produce during the dictatorship. Composed of no fewer than 132,000 negatives, this discovery constitutes the largest photographic collection of dictatorial repression to date. The photographs are being (re)stored at the APM, investigated, supplied to the courts as proof of disappearance and returned to the photographed (if they are alive) or their families.[3]

These negatives show so much more than the typical front-and-profile booking photographs of the detainees, accompanied by their identification number. In addition to seeing the faces (often beaten, emaciated, injured), which evidence who passed through the CDC, it is possible to glimpse the surrounding environment. An involuntary peek outside of the frame: the hands handcuffed behind the back of the photographed person; the repressor, in control of the scene and with a comb in his hand which he has just used to tidy up a detainee's hair; the recently removed blindfold, ready to cover the eyes again as soon as the photo is taken; the presence of other prisoners, waiting for their turn to be searched, their hoods still on.

IV

The title of the book, *Familiar Faces*, suggests a polysemic game. On the one hand, the affective and filial bond that unites the disappeared with those who carry their photographs on their bodies and in the streets *is* familiar. On the other hand, these are faces that resonate with – *seem familiar* to – all of us, even though we often do not know exactly to whom they belong – ignorant of their names and specific biographies. The familiar, then, speaks of the love that unites the sought and the seeker, and also of the profuse dissemination of the presence of absence in social memory.

The image on the cover of this book explores this double dimension: the *punctum* is situated in the photo of a smiling young woman, with her gaze turned upwards – surely chosen from the family album, a repertoire of happy moments from an interrupted life. Converted into a banner, the image is carried by a crowd that marches with their gaze forward, its gesture serious and focused. Two crossed looks and two temporalities are combined in this captured moment: the time stopped by the disappearance and the tireless time of the search.

In these "familiar faces" exists a way of composing strange family portraits. As counterpoints to the family portrait of the dictator Videla (he, his wife and their children going to mass on a Sunday) – part of the propaganda of the "Western and Christian" values of the united and "well-constituted" family – emerge other family portraits, constructed from the irreparable lack and absence. Families devastated, amputated and, at the same time, reconfigured. I'm reminded of the photo Eduardo Gil took at a human rights demonstration at the end of the dictatorship, in 1983: a Mother of Plaza de Mayo, with her son's image on a placard, takes a break from the march and looks at the camera (Figure 8.1). The photographer knew nothing about her, but he captured the loving gesture that unites the person on the placard and the person who carries it. Many years later, during the exhibition *El siluetazo*, which Gil organised at the Memory Park in Buenos Aires, someone from the city of Zárate recognised Beba Galeano and her son Julio, who had disappeared in that city in 1977, in the photo. Subsequently, Gil was sent a photograph of Gretel, Julio's daughter, a little baby when her father was kidnapped (and she and her mother took refuge in Catamarca, in northern Argentina). Gretel wrote to Gil, telling him that for years she had searched for a photo where her grandmother, a founder of the Mothers of Plaza de Mayo, appeared alongside her father. Thanks to this random chain of events, she had finally found the image, thus filling a gap in her family album.

The same lack, the same absence, have been the driving force behind Lucila Quieto's *Arqueología de la ausencia* [*Archaeology of Absence*] (2011) (Figure 8.2). Quieto is one of the founders of H.I.J.O.S., an organisation that has been bringing together the children of the disappeared since the mid-1990s. In 2001, she began devising a way to produce the missing photo in her family album (no photo existed of Quieto with her father, who'd disappeared four months before she was born) and turned it into a collective procedure, accompanying other children in that construction.

The process is simple and it does not disguise its own artifice: the subject chooses a beloved photo of the disappeared father or mother, which is

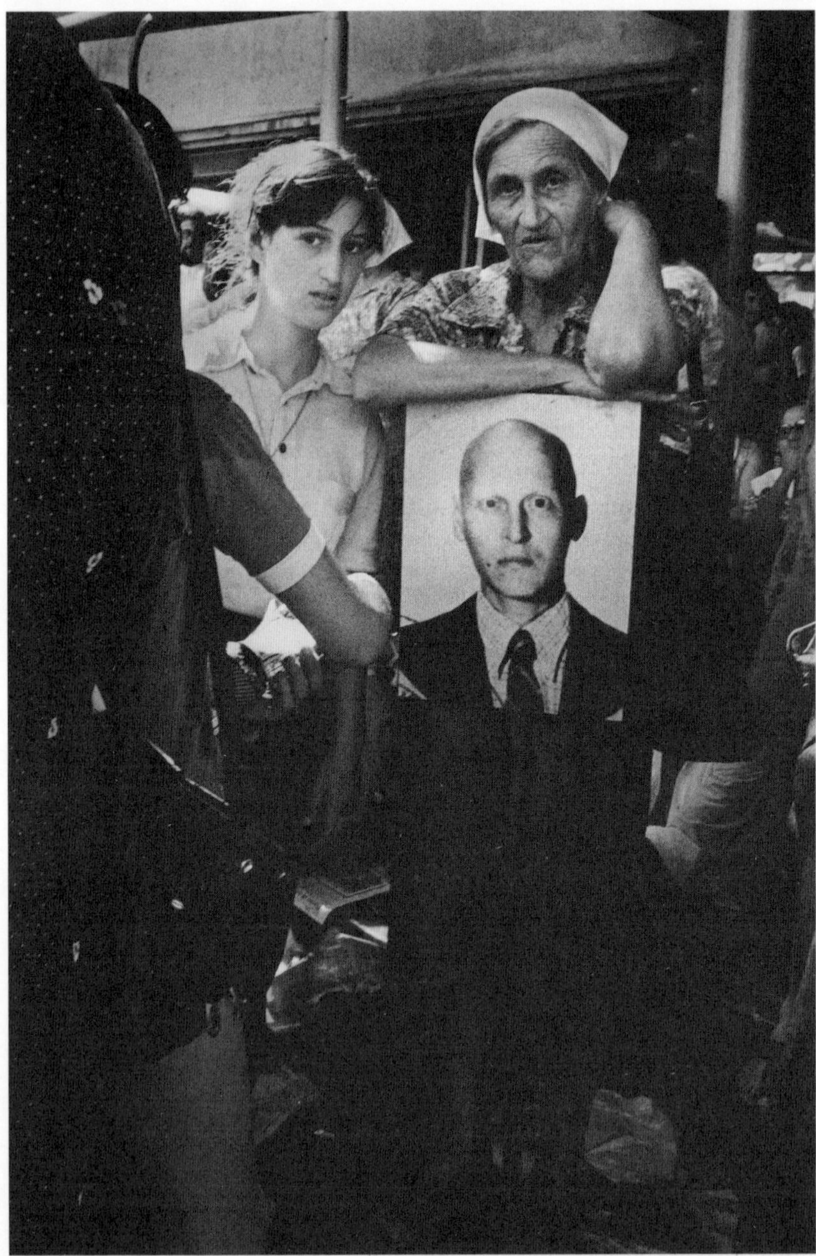

Figure 8.1 "Three looks." The 2nd March of Resistance, Buenos Aires, 9 and 10 December 1982.
Source/Author: Eduardo Gil.

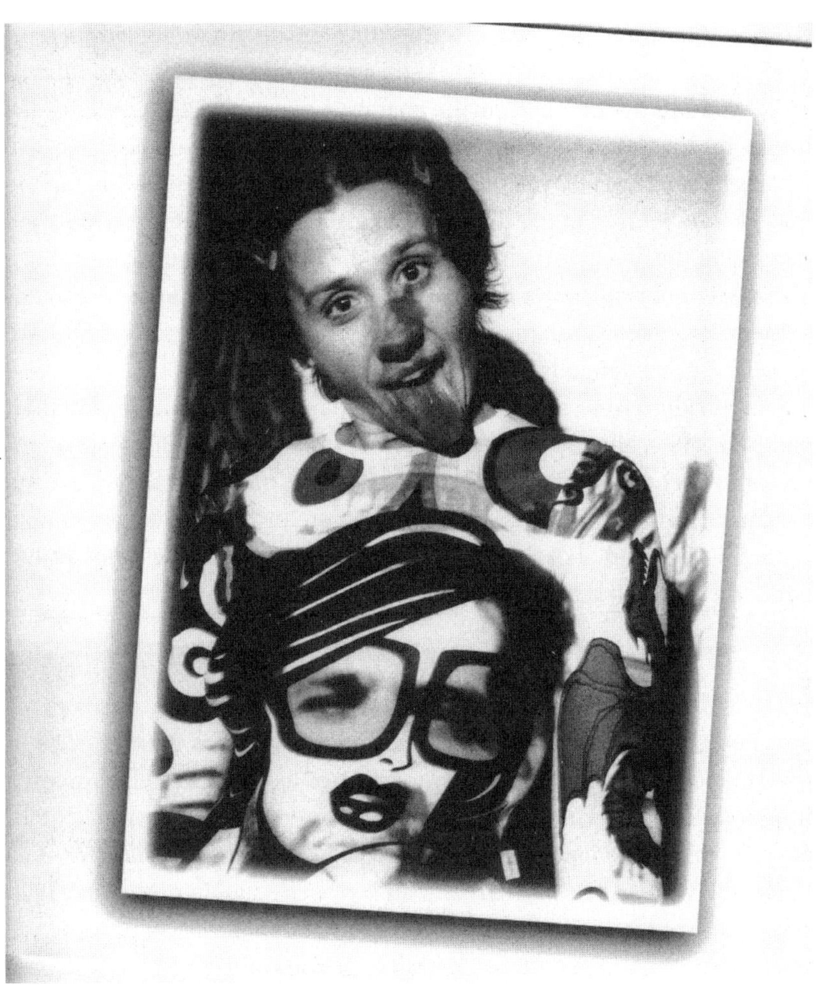

Figure 8.2 Image from *Arqueología de la ausencia*.
Source/Author: Lucila Quieto.

then projected on a wall. The child slips into that scene, and Quieto photographs that encounter. The result is an irruption of an impossible time; a previously denied moment (a hug, a conversation, contact) between fathers/mothers and children. The tense of this encounter is neither the past nor the present, but a *third time* (which does not hide the fictitious, constructed condition of the process).

Something uncanny happens when one looks at these "forced encounters" that occur in each of the stories that constitute *Arqueología de la ausencia*. Perhaps this comes from the alteration of temporality, which results in the parents and the children appearing to be the same age. Because what is laid bare here is the stark, critical and often stormy moment in the lives of the children of the disappeared: the moment when they become older than the age that their parents will be at forever. The faces produce a strange phantasmagoria that emerges from their juxtaposition and co-existence. Suddenly, the presence of the disappeared seems less blurred, somehow more defined than that of their children's.

In this *third time*, gazes can cross, the parents can coincide with their children, often already fathers or mothers themselves, who lend themselves to orchestrate the meeting, offering the body, the bare skin, the tongue, as surfaces onto which the images are projected, like ephemeral tattoos, indelible marks. Smiling. Playing. Because memory is not always pain, sometimes it is a shelter and a refuge.

V

This book overflows and goes beyond itself. Not only is it an exercise in thinking about photography, but – as part of its collective elaboration – it provokes and produces another type of intervention, a complicit alliance: an artist-photographer (Gabriel Orge) together with a survivor of La Perla who writes (Ana Iliovich) and an activist/researcher (Mariana Tello Weiss), travel with Piotr Cieplak to the town of Bell Ville to provoke the reappearance of the memories of what happened and of what was denied. The trigger for this journey? The photo that Tello Weiss explores in her chapter. Without knowing it, Mariana and Piotr stay in what had been the home of the Iliovich family, which today functions as a small hotel. The result of this trip (in addition to this book) is a film, *(Dis)Appear* (Cieplak 2023), that takes as its point of departure a search for another possible approach to disappearance and photography, making room for "a *new ethics of the gaze* which, by placing our ways of seeing between the *folds* captured in the images, may allow us to hear them as though they were the marks of a visual silence," as Tello Weiss writes in her chapter.[4] To open a gap so that we can see what appears, what still shines through; to wager that which was denied can be revealed and unveiled, with all its complexity and its infinite shades of grey.

As I am writing this, in front of a fire burning in the cold heights of the Popocatépetl volcano, in Mexico, arrives the sad news of the death of Hebe de Bonafini, a historical figure and point of reference of the Association of the Mothers of Plaza de Mayo, a bastion of the struggle of the human rights movement. With her long ninety-four years of life, her death should not surprise us, and yet it comes with a sense of being orphaned that is felt by many of us. We will miss her tenacity, her courage and her political incorrectness. Her volcanic, uncontrollable passion that seemed forever on the verge of bursting; just like the land I currently tread on. On many occasions, we disagreed with her positions and outbursts, and yet we have grown up nourished on her persistence, her disruptive, stubborn, unyielding presence. It will be difficult to reconfigure the political scene without her wayward ways.

Translated by Piotr Cieplak

Notes

1 Also, see Hacher (2012).

2 For more on this, see: Longoni and García (2013); Feld (2014a); Longoni (2022).

3 For more on this, see Magrin (2012).

4 (*Dis)Appear* is a film about the relationship between photography and the legacies of the most recent dictatorship in Argentina, with Ana Iliovich and Gabriel Orge as the protagonists. In conversation, Cieplak relayed that during the shoot in the town of Bell Ville, the production team stayed in a hotel that was once the Iliovich family home. Cieplak and the production team had no idea that had been the case. This is one of several coincidences or synchronicities that occurred during the production, reported by Cieplak.

Contributors

Piotr Cieplak is an academic, author and award-winning filmmaker. He is an Associate Professor in the Department of Creative and Critical Practice in the School of Media, Arts and Humanities, University of Sussex. Piotr has published extensively on the relationship between violence, memory, politics of representation and photography in the Global South. He is the author of *Death, Image, Memory: the genocide in Rwanda and its aftermath in photography and documentary film* (2017). He has also directed two feature documentaries about the relationship between photography and memory: *The Faces We Lost* (2017) – in the context of the 1994 genocide against the Tutsi in Rwanda – and *(Dis)Appear* (2023) – in the context of Argentina's civic-military dictatorship (1976–1983).

María Eleonora Cristina is the Director of the Provincial Memory Archive and the Ex-D2 Memory Site, a former clandestine torture and detention centre in Córdoba, Argentina. She holds a diploma in Document and Archive Management from the Provincial University of Córdoba. She is an active member of H.I.J.O.S. and is part of the research project: "Anthropology of politics and experiences of violence in Argentina."

Ludmila da Silva Catela is a Professor of Anthropology at the national universities of Córdoba and La Plata. She is a member of the National Council of Scientific and Technological Research (CONICET) and the Institute of Anthropology (Córdoba). She was the founding director of the Provincial Memory Archive in Córdoba and the director of the Museum of Anthropology, National University of Córdoba. She has published widely on violence, limit situations, photography and memory. Amongst others, her books include: *No habrá flores en la tumba del pasado. La experiencia de reconstrucción del mundo de los familiares de desaparecidos* (2001) and, with Elizabeth Jelin and Augstina Triquell, *¿Qué hacemos con las cosas del pasado? Materialidades, memorias y lugares* (2022).

Natalia Fortuny is a writer, poet and a Lecturer in Latin American Visual Arts and Photography at the University of Buenos Aires. She's also a member of the National Council of Scientific and Technological Research

(CONICET). From 2016, she has coordinated FoCo, a research group in contemporary photography, arts and politics at the Instituto Gino Germani (University of Buenos Aires). She is the author of *Memorias Fotografícas: imagen y dictadura en la fotografía argentina contemporánea* (2014) and *Arder con lo real. Fotografía contemporánea entre la historia y lo político* (2021a). Fortuny was the director of two recent research projects: "Photographic devices: document, art and politics in Argentina post-2001" (PICT 2018) and "Problems in contemporary photography: between social memories and operational images" (Ubacyt 2018/2019).

Cora Gamarnik is a Senior Lecturer in Didactics of Communication at the Faculty of Social Sciences, University of Buenos Aires, and a researcher at the National Council of Scientific and Technological Research (CONICET). She coordinates the Area of Photography Studies at the University of Buenos Aires. She's the co-director of the Ubacyt project: "Dialectical images. Art, culture, communication and politics from the last dictatorship to the present." She has published widely in academic and trade journals and is the author of *El fotoperiodismo en Argentina. De Siete Días Ilustrados a la Agencia Sigla* (2020).

Ana Longoni is a writer, researcher and curator. She is a Professor at the University of Buenos Aires and a researcher at the National Council of Scientific and Technological Research (CONICET). She was formerly the Director of Public Activities at Museo Nacional Centro de Arte Reina Sofía in Madrid. She is the author of *Del Di Tella a Tucumán Arde* (2000), *La Chira* (2003), *Árboles* (2006), *Traiciones* (2007), *El siluetazo* (2008), *El deseo nace del derrumbe* (2011), *Vanguardia y revolución* (2014), *Tercer Oido* (2021), *Parir/Partir* (2022), and numerous articles and other publications. She has been a key proponent of the Conceptualisms of the South Network since its founding in 2007.

Mariana Tello Weiss is the former president of the National Memory Archive in Buenos Aires and teaches at the University of Córdoba. She's also a researcher at the National Council of Scientific and Technological Research (CONICET). Tello Weiss is an anthropologist who, since 2001, has specialised in the anthropology of memory, violence and socio-political conflicts in Argentina and Spain, and has published widely on these subjects. Tello Weiss held multiple academic appointments in the

Americas and Europe. She was also the director of the research project: "Ethnographic perspectives on the memories of repression and political violence in the recent past: bodies, identities and territories" (SeCyT 2018–2022).

Inés Ulanovsky is a photographer and writer. She is the author of *Fotos tuyas* (2006), *Algunas madres también se mueren* (2010) and *Las Fotos* (2020). She holds an MA in creative writing from UNTREF and works at the Museum of Books and Language.

Bibliography

Agamben, Giorgio. 2000. *Lo que queda de Auschwitz. El archivo y el testigo. Homo sacer III*. Valencia: Pre-textos.

Agamben, Giorgio. 2007. *Profanations*. Translated by Jeff Fort. New York: Zone Books.

Amado, Ana. 2009. *La imagen justa. Cine argentino y política (1980–2007)*. Buenos Aires: Colihue.

Aprea, Gustavo. 2008. *Cine y política en Argentina. Continuidades y discontinuidades en 25 años de democracia*. Buenos Aires: UNGS y Biblioteca Nacional.

Arfuch, Leonor. 2002. *El Espacio biográfico. Dilemas de la subjetividad contemporánea*. México: Fondo de Cultura Económica.

Arfuch, Leonor. 2008. *Critica cultural entre política y poética*. Buenos Aires: Fondo de Cultura Económica.

Arnold-de Simine, Silke. 2018. "Dislocating Memory: Family Photographs in Story-Centred Museums." In *Picturing the Family: Media, Narrative, Memory*, edited by Silke Arnold-de Simine and Joanne Leal, 189–212. London: Bloomsbury.

Aveta, Hugo. 2015. *Espacios sustraibles*. Buenos Aires: Ediciones Larivière.

Aveta, Hugo. 2016. "Visión del arte." Photographic series. *Bola De Nieve*. Buenos Aires. Available at www.boladenieve.org.ar/node/589.

Azoulay, Ariella. 2008. *The Civil Contract of Photography*. New York: Zone Books.

Barthes, Roland. 2000. *Camera Lucida: Reflections on Photography*. Translated by Richard Howard. London: Vintage.

Batchen, Geoffrey. 1997. *Burning with Desire*. Cambridge, MA: Massachusetts Institute of Technology.

Bazin, Andre. 1967. *What is Cinema?* Translated by Hugh Gray. Berkley and Los Angeles: University of California Press.

Bell, Vikki. 2014. *The Art of Post-Dictatorship: Ethics and Aesthetics in Transitional Argentina*. Abingdon: Routledge.

Bellour, Raymond. 2009. *Entre imágenes. Foto. Cine. Video*. Buenos Aires: Colihue.

Belting, Hans. 2009. *Antropología de la imagen*. Buenos Aires: Katz editores.

Berger, John. 1972. *Ways of Seeing*. New York: Viking Press.

Bettini, Gabriela. 2003. "Recuerdos inventados." Photographic series.

Bianco, Ana. 2007. "La foto de Omar Torres." *Humano Buenos Aires*. May 8.

Blejmar, Jordana. 2013. "La Argentina en pedazos: Los collages fotográficos de Lucila Quieto." In *Instantáneas de la memoria. Fotografía y dictadura en Argentina y América Latina*, edited by Jordana Blejmar, Natalia Fortuny and Luis Ignacio García, 173–193. Buenos Aires: Libraria.

Blejmar, Jordana. 2016. *Playful Memories: The Autofictional Turn in Post-Dictatorship Argentina*. Basingstoke: Palgrave Macmillan.

Blejmar, Jordana. 2021. "La corteza de la historia en las imágenes espectrales de Paula Luttringer." *Atlas, revista de fotografía e imagen*. Santiago de Chile, June 21.

Blejmar, Jordana, Natalia Fortuny and Luis Ignacio García, eds. 2013. *Instantáneas de la memoria. Fotografía y dictadura en Argentina y América Latina*. Buenos Aires: Libraria.

Boime, Albert. 1991. *The Magisterial Gaze. Manifest Destiny and the American Landscape Painting, c. 1830–1865*. Washington: Smithsonian Institution Press.

Boltanski, Christian. 1991. "L'album photographique de la famille de B." 105 s/w photographs in metal frame. Berlin and Palma de Mallorca: Kewenig Gallerie.

Bonaldi, Pablo Daniel. 2006. "Hijos de desaparecidos: entre la construcción de la política y la construcción de la memoria." In *El pasado en el futuro: los movimientos juveniles*, edited by Elizabeth Jelin and Daniel Sempol, 143–184. Madrid and Buenos Aires: Siglo Veintiuno Editores.

Bossini, Manuel. 2018. "Adriana Lestido: Se ve con todo el cuerpo. La cámara es lo de menos." *La Santa Crítica*. May 18.

Bourdieu, Pierre. 1986. "Notas provisionales sobre la percepción social del cuerpo." In *Materiales de Sociología*, edited by Fernando Álvarez Uria and Julia Varela, 183–194. Barcelona: La Piqueta.

Bourdieu, Pierre. 2003. *Un Arte Medio. Ensayo sobre los usos sociales de la fotografía*. Barcelona: Editorial Gustavo Gili.

Bousquet, Jean-Pierre. 1983. *Las Locas de la Plaza de Mayo*. Buenos Aires: El Cid Editor.

Bredekamp, Horst. 2014. "Acto de imagen: tradición, horizonte, filosofía." In *Estudios visuales: La epistemología de la visualidad en la era de la globalización*, edited by José Luis Brea, 41–58. Madrid: Akal.

Brodsky, Marcelo, ed. 1997. *Buena memoria*. Buenos Aires: La Marca.

Brodsky, Marcelo. 2005. *Memoria en construcción. El debate sobre la ESMA*. Buenos Aires: La Marca Editora.

Bruzzone, Felix. 2011. "Milpalabras." In *Otra Parte* 24, Spring 2011.

Bullentini, Ailín. 2010. "Lucila Quieto: 'Siempre estoy reconstruyendo la historia que me generó.'" *Agencia NAN*. July 9.

Burucúa José Emilio and Nicolás Kwiatkowski. 2014. "Cómo sucedieron estas cosas." *Representar masacres y genocidios*. Buenos Aires: Katz Editores.

Bustamante-Brauning, Sebastian. 2022. "[Re]appearances Online: Photography, Mourning and New Media Ecologies for Representing the Southern Cone's Disappeared on Two Digital Memory Platforms." *Photographies* 15(3), 381–403.

Calveiro, Pilar. 2001. *Poder y desaparición: los campos de concentración en Argentina*. Buenos Aires: Ediciones Colihue.

Campt, Tina, M. 2012. *Image Matters: Archive, Photography and the African Diaspora in Europe*. Durham and London: Duke University Press.

Campt, Tina, M. 2017. *Listening to Images*. Durham and London: Duke University Press.

Caparrós, Martín. 1997. "Apariciones." In *Buena memoria*, edited by Marcelo Brodsky. Buenos Aires: La Marca Editora.

Castillo Troncoso, Alberto. 2017. *Fotografía y memoria. Conversaciones con Eduardo Longoni*. México: Fondo de Cultura Económica.

Centenera, Mar. 2022. "Abuelas de Plaza de Mayo recuperan al nieto 131: 'Nos da esperanza para encontrar a los que faltan.'" *El País*. Madrid, December 23.

Cerolini, Pablo and Alejandro Reynoso, eds. 2006. *En negro y blanco. Fotografías del Cordobazo al Juicio a las Juntas*. Buenos Aires: ARGRA.

Chela. 2019. Personal communication with Ludmila da Silva Catela. Guerrero, Jujuy.

Cieplak, Piotr. 2020. "Private Archives, Public Deaths in Rwanda and Argentina: Conversations with Claver Irakoze and Ludmila da Silva Catela." *Wasafiri* 35(4), 6–14.

Córdoba Provincial Memory Archive. 2012. *Instantes de verdad. Fotografías del Registro Extremistas del D2*. Exhibition brochure. Córdoba.

Cortés Rocca, Paola. 2011. *El Tiempo de la máquina. Retratos, paisajes y otras imágenes de la nación*. Buenos Aires: Colihue.

Cortiñas, Nora. 2009. Personal communication with Cora Gamarnik. Buenos Aires.

Crenzel, Emilio. 2008. "Argentina's National Commission on the Disappearance of Persons: Contributions to Transitional Justice." *International Journal of Transitional Justice* 2(2), 173–191.

Crenzel, Emilio. 2009. "Las fotografías del Nunca Más: Verdad y prueba jurídica de las desapariciones." In *El pasado que miramos. Memoria e imagen ante la historia reciente*, edited by Claudia Feld and Jessica Stites Mor, 281–314. Buenos Aires: Paidós.

Crenzel, Emilio. 2012. *The Memory of the Argentina Disappearances: The Political History of Nunca Más*. New York: Routledge.

da Silva Catela, Ludmila. 2001. *No habrá flores en la tumba del pasado. La experiencia de reconstrucción del mundo de los familiares de desaparecidos*. La Plata: Ediciones Al Margen.

da Silva Catela, Ludmila. 2009. "Lo invisible revelado. El uso de fotografías como (re)presentación de la desaparición de personas en la Argentina." In *El pasado que miramos: memoria e imagen ante la historia reciente*, edited by Claudia Feld and Jessica Stites More, 337–362. Buenos Aires: Paidós Comunicación.

da Silva Catela, Ludmila. 2010. "Hacer visible lo clandestino. Fotografía y video frente a la experiencia concentracionaria." In *Fotografía e identidad: captura por la cámara, devolución por la memoria*, edited by Elizabeth Jelin, Ludmila da Silva Catela and Mariana Giordano, 85–103. Buenos Aires: Nueva Trilce.

da Silva Catela, Ludmila. 2012. "Re-velar el horror. Fotografía, archivos y memoria frente a la desaparición de personas." In *Memorias, historia y derechos humanos*, edited by Isabel Piper Shafir and Belén Rojas, 157–173. Santiago de Chile: Universidad de Chile.

Daanen, Bram. 2021. "Fútbol, dictadura y derechos humanos. El Mundial de Fútbol de 1978 y la solidaridad neerlandesa con Argentina." MA diss. Universidad de Salamanca.

de Bonafini, Hebe, 1988. "Historia de las Madres de Plaza de Mayo." Liber/Arte Conference, Buenos Aires, July 6.

del Cerro, Camilo. 2005. "El viaje de Papá." *Centro de Medios Independientes*. Buenos Aires, December 3.

Deleuze, Gilles and Félix Guattari. 1987. *A Thousand Plateaus: Capitalism and Schizophrenia*. Translated by Brian Massumi. Minneapolis: University of Minnesota Press.

Dell'Oro, Gerardo. 2011. *Imágenes en la memoria*. Buenos Aires: La Luminosa.

Di Marco, Graciela. 2006. "Entrevista a Hebe de Bonafini, Asociación Madres de Plaza de Mayo." Universidad Nacional de San Martín. Available at www.unsam.edu.ar/escuelas/humanidades/centros/cedehu/material/(36)%20Entrevista%20Bonafini.pdf

Díaz, Gabriel. 2016. "Flores en la ESMA." Photographic series. Available at www.diazgabriel.com/floresenlaesma

Didi-Huberman, Georges. 2008a. "La Emoción No Dice Yo." In *Alfredo Jaar: La Política De Las Imágenes*, edited by Georges Didi-Huberman, Jacques Rancière and Griselda Pollock, 177–187. Santiago de Chile: Metales Pesados.

Didi-Huberman, Georges. 2008b. *Ante el tiempo. Historia el arte y anacronismo de las imágenes*. Translated and introduced by Oscar Antonio Oviedo Funes. Buenos Aires: Adriana Hidalgo Editora.

Didi-Huberman, Georges. 2008c. *Images in Spite of All: Four Photographs from Auschwitz*. Translated by Shane B. Lillis. Chicago: University of Chicago Press.

Didi-Huberman, Georges. 2013. *Cuando las imágenes tocan lo real*. Madrid: Abada Editores.

Didi-Huberman, Georges. 2015. *Fasmas. Ensayos sobre la aparición 1.* Translated by Julián Mateo Ballorca. Cantabria: Contracampo Libros.

Dieguez, Ileana. 2016. *Cuerpos sin duelo: iconografías y teatralidades del dolor.* Córdoba: Documenta/Escénicas.

Dubois, Philippe. 2015. *El Acto fotográfico y otros ensayos.* Buenos Aires: La Marca Editorial.

Edwards, Elizabeth. 2001. "Photography and the Performance of History." *Visual History* 21, 15–29.

Edwards, Elizabeth and Janice Hart. 2004. "Introduction: Photographs as Objects." In *Photographs Objects Histories: On the Materiality of Images*, edited by Elizabeth Edwards and Janice Hart, 1–15. New York and Abingdon: Routledge.

Elias, Norbet. 1998. *La Civilización de los padres y otros ensayos.* Bogotá: Grupo Editorial Norma.

Feierstein, Daniel. 2011. *El Genocidio como práctica social: Entre el nazismo y la experiencia argentina.* Buenos Aires: Fondo Cultura Económica.

Feitlowitz, Marguerite. 2011. *A Lexicon of Terror: Argentina and the Legacies of Torture.* Oxford: Oxford University Press.

Feld, Claudia, and Jessica Stites Mor, eds. 2009. *El pasado que miramos. Memoria e imagen ante la historia reciente.* Buenos Aires: Paidós.

Feld, Claudia. 2010a. "Imagen, memoria y desaparición: Una reflexión sobre los diversos soportes audiovisuales de la memoria." *Atheleia* 1(1), 1–16.

Feld, Claudia. 2010b. "Imágenes de la memoria." In *Fotografiando memorias. Huellas Latinoamericanas*, edited by Sebastian Russo and Daniela Zampiert, 26–36. Buenos Aires: AECID.

Feld, Claudia. 2014a. "¿Hacer visible la desaparición? Las fotografías de detenidos-desaparecidos de la ESMA en el testimonio de Víctor Basterra." *Revista Interdisciplinaria de Estudios sobre Memoria Clepsidra* 1, 28–51.

Feld, Claudia. 2014b. "Fotografía, desaparición y memoria: fotos tomadas en la ESMA durante su funcionamiento como centro clandestino de detención." *Nuevo Mundo Mundos Nuevos.* Available at https://doi.org/10.4000/nuevomundo.66939

Feld, Claudia. 2015. "Imagen y testimonio frente a la desaparición forzada de personas en la Argentina de la transición." *Kamtchatka* 6.

Feld, Claudia. 2016. "Constructing Memory Through Television in Argentina." *Latin American Perspectives* 43(5), 29–44.

Feld, Claudia, and Jessica Stites Mor. 2009. "Introducción. Imagen y memoria: apuntes para una exploración." In *El pasado que miramos. Memoria e imagen ante la historia reciente*, edited by Claudia Feld and Jessica Stites Mor, 25–44. Buenos Aires: Paidós.

Filc, Judith. 1997. *Entre el parentesco y la política. Familia y dictadura, 1976–1983*. Buenos Aires: Biblos.

Fortuny, Natalia. 2013. "Palabras Fotográficas." In *Instantáneas de la memoria. Fotografía y dictadura en Argentina y América Latina*, edited by Jordana Blejmar, Natalia Fortuny and Luis Ignacio García, 133–156. Buenos Aires: Libraria.

Fortuny, Natalia. 2014. *Memorias Fotografícas: imagen y dictadura en la fotografía argentina contemporánea*. Buenos Aires: La Luminosa.

Fortuny, Natalia. 2016. "Dos veces Julio: sobre algunas memorias fotográficas del pasado reciente en la Argentina." *Kamchatka* 6(3), 765–783.

Fortuny, Natalia. 2021a. *Arder con lo real. Fotografía contemporánea entre la historia y lo político*. Buenos Aires: Ediciones ArtexArte.

Fortuny, Natalia. 2021b. "Pervivencia del 'collage' fotográfico: paisajes y memorias." *Lur* 3, 1–12.

Freud, Sigmund. 1992. *Obras Completas. Tomo XII*. Buenos Aires: Amorrortu.

Freund, Gisèle. 2006. *La Fotografía como documento social*. Barcelona: Gustavo Gili.

Frič, Pavel and Yvonna Fricová. 2012. "Guido Boggiani, fotógrafo." In *Boggiani y el Chaco. Una aventura del Siglo XIX. Fotografías de la colección Frič*, 9–27. Buenos Aires: Museo de Arte Hispanoamericano Isaac Fernández Blanco.

Gamarnik, Cora. 2013. "Imágenes contra la dictadura: la historia de la primera muestra de periodismo gráfico argentino durante la dictadura." In *Instantáneas de la memoria. Fotografía y dictadura en Argentina y América Latina*, edited by Jordána Blejmar, Natalia Fortuny and Luis Ignacio García, 69–92. Buenos Aires: Libraria.

Gamarnik, Cora. 2020. *El fotoperiodismo en Argentina. De Siete Días Ilustrados a la Agencia Sigla*. Buenos Aires: Ediciones ArtexArte.

Gamarnik, Cora. 2021. "Límites y paradojas de una fotografía de prensa: análisis de una foto de Madres de Plaza de Mayo durante la dictadura militar en Argentina." *Revista científica de cine y fotografía Fotocinema* 22, 197–220.

Garcés, Mariana. 2019. "Entre materialidades y memorias. Una aproximación a las narrativas locales en el ex CCD en Guerrero." Jornadas FHCE, November 3 and 4. Jujuy, Argentina. Available at www.jornadas.fhuce.edu.uy/

García, Daniel. 2009. Personal communication with Cora Gamarnik. Buenos Aires.

García, Daniel. 2016. "Meter las patas en el charco." *Revista Anfibia*. March 23.

García, Luis Ignacio. 2013. "Espectros: fotografía y derechos humanos en la Argentina." *La Cebra: Papel Máquina* 8, 131–147.

Garnica, Eulogia. 2002. Personal communication with Ludmila da Silva Catela. Libertador General San Martín, Jujuy.

Germano, Gustavo. 2006. "Ausencias Argentina." Photographic series. Available at www.gustavogermano.com/porfolio-2/

Ginzberg Victoria and Luciana Bertoia. 2020. "Los archivos de la SIDE de la dictadura: el informe sobre las Madres de Plaza de Mayo." *Página 12*. December 13.

Giuffra, María. 2005. Los niños del Proceso [The Children of the Process]. Series of paintings and drawings. Available at www.mariagiuffra.com.ar/pintura-ninos-proceso.html

Gomez, Roberto. 2001. "A 25 años del golpe, la fotografía de prensa en la dictadura." *Round table at III Jornadas de Fotografía y Sociedad*, University of Buenos Aires.

González Cezer, Marcos. 2020. "Van der Putten y su entrevista a las Madres: El Mundial 78 nos sirvió para contar qué pasaba." *Agencia de Noticias Télam*. June 1.

Gorini, Ulises. 2006. *La rebelión de las Madres. Historia de las Madres de Plaza de Mayo, Tomo I (1976-1983)*. Buenos Aires: Grupo Editorial Norma.

Grant, Catherine. 2003. "Still Moving Images: Photographs of the Disappeared in Films about the 'Dirty War' in Argentina." In *Phototextualities: Intersections of Photography and Narrative*, edited by Alex Hughes and Andrea Noble, 63–88. Albuquerque: University of New Mexico Press.

Gutiérrez, Fernando. 1997. *Treintamil*. Buenos Aires: La Marca.

Hacher, Sebastián. 2012. *Cómo enterrar a un padre desaparecido*. Buenos Aires: Marea.

Hall, Stuart. 2000. "Cultural Identity and Cinematic Representation." In *Film and Theory: an anthology*, edited by Robert Stam and Toby Miller, 704–714. Oxford: Blackwell Publishing Ltd.

Hirsch, Marianne. 1997. *Family Frames: Photography, Narrative and Postmemory*. Cambridge, MA and London: Harvard University Press.

Huyssen, Andreas. 2000. *Seduzidos pela memória*. Rio de Janeiro: Aeroplano Editora.

Huyssen, Andreas. 2009. "Prólogo. Medios y memoria." In *El pasado que miramos: memoria e imagen ante la historia reciente*, edited by Claudia Feld and Jessica Stites Mor. 15–24. Buenos Aires: Paidós.

Iliovich, Ana. 2012. Personal communication with Mariana Tello Weiss. Córdoba.

Iliovich, Ana. 2017. *El Silencio: Postales de La Perla*. Córdoba: Los Ríos Editorial.

Iliovich, Ana. 2020. Personal communication with Mariana Tello Weiss. Córdoba.

Jelin, Elizabeth. 2002. *Los Trabajos de la Memoria*. Buenos Aires: Silgo XXI Editores.

Jelin, Elizabeth. 2009. "Rosas trasplantadas y el mito de Eldorado. Travesías en el tiempo, en el espacio, en la imagen y en el silencio." *Revista Del Museo De Antropología* 2(1), 75–86.

Jelin, Elizabeth. 2021. *The Struggle for the Past: How We Construct Social Memories*. Translated by Wendy Gesselin. Oxford and New York: Berghahn Books.

Jelin, Elizabeth and Susana Kaufman. 2002. "Layers of Memory: Twenty Years After in Argentina." In *Genocide, Collective Violence, and Popular Memory: The Politics of Remembrance in the Twentieth Century*, edited by David E. Lorey and William H. Beezley, 31–52. Wilmington: Scholarly Resources Inc.

Kahora, Billy and Zoe Norridge. 2020. "What Is Seen and What Is Said." *Wasafiri* 35(4), 1–3.

Kaiser, Susana. 2020. "Writing and Reading Memories at a Buenos Aires Memorial Site: The Ex-Esma." *History and Memory* 32(1), 69–99.

Kossoy, Boris. 2014. *Lo Efímero y lo perpetuo en la imagen fotográfica*. Madrid: Cuadernos Arte Cátedra.

Le Breton, David. 1999. *Las Pasiones ordinarias. Antropología de las emociones*. Buenos Aires: Ediciones Nueva Visión.

Lessa, Francesca. 2022. *The Condor Trials: Transnational Repression and Human Rights in South America*. Yale: Yale University Press.

Levi, Primo. 2006. *Trilogía de Auschwitz*. México City: Océano.

Longoni, Ana. 2007. *Traiciones. La figura del traidor en los relatos acerca de los sobrevivientes de la represión*. Buenos Aires: Norma Editorial.

Longoni, Ana. 2010a. "Photographs and Silhouettes: Visual Politics in Argentina." *Afterall*, 25 Autumn/Winter, 1–10.

Longoni, Ana. 2010b. "Todos somos López. Activismo artístico en torno a la segunda desaparición de Jorge Julio López." *Cuadernos del INADI*, April. Available at http:// cuadernos.inadi.gov.ar/

Longoni, Ana. 2013. "El partícipe, el testigo, el artista: sobre la serie "El siluetazo" de Eduardo Gil." *Escritores Del Mundo*. November 16.

Longoni, Ana. 2015. "9 años sin López de Hugo Vidal." Presentation at *Arte en el Germani* Seminar Series. University of Buenos Aires, October.

Longoni, Ana. 2020. "Pañuelos: de cómo las Madres se volvieron feministas y las feministas encontraron Madres." In *Tiempos Incompletos*, edited by Teresa Ochoa de Zabalegui, 68–88. Madrid: Carta(s) Museo Nacional Reina Sofía.

Longoni, Ana. 2022. "Fotos reaparecidas." In *Reapariciones. La fotografía en deuda con su pasado*, edited by Carles Guerra, 84–119. Madrid: Fundación Mapfre.

Longoni, Ana and Gustavo Bruzzone. 2008. "Introducción." In *El Siluetazo,* edited by Ana Longoni and Gustavo Bruzzone, 7–58. Buenos Aires: Adriana Hidalgo Editora.

Longoni, Ana and Luis García. 2013. "Imágenes invisibles: Acerca de las fotos de desaparecidos." In *Instantáneas de la memoria. Fotografía y dictadura en Argentina y América Latina*, edited by Jordana Blejmar, Natalia Fortuny and Luis Ignacio García, 24–44. Buenos Aires: Libraria.

Luttringer, Paula. 1995. "El matadero." Photographic series. Available at www.camaraoscura.com.ar/portfolio.php?portfolio=67

Luttringer, Paula. 2012. "El lamento de los muros. Cosas desenterradas." Photographic exhibition. Buenos Aires, Centro Cultural Haroldo Conti, March 27–July 1. Exhibition catalogue available at https://issuu.com/ccmharoldoconti/docs/paulaluttringer_issuu

Magrin, Natalia. 2012. "Imágenes de veridicción. Acerca de las fotografías tomadas a hombres y mujeres en el centro clandestino de detención del Departamento de Informaciones de la Policía de la provincia de Córdoba (D2)." *Atheleia* 2(4), 1–10.

Magrin, Natalia. 2015. "Fotografías tomadas en Centros Clandestinos de Detención Tortura y Exterminio. Acerca del encuentro con imágenes de detenidos, secuestrados, desaparecidos en el Departamento de Informaciones de la Policía de la Provincia Córdoba." *Nuevo Mundo Mundos Nuevos*. Available at https://doi.org/10.4000/nuevomundo.68018

Maguire, Geoffrey. 2017. *The Politics of Postmemory: Violence and Victimhood in Contemporary Argentine Culture*. Basingstoke: Palgrave Macmillan.

Manusia, Mario. 2011. Personal communication with Cora Gamarnik. Buenos Aires.

Marder, Michael. 2020. "¿Cuál es el significado del pensamiento vegetal?" *Cuadernos Materialistas: Vegetalidad* 5, 38–51.

Martelloti, Miguel and Rosito, Enrique. 2021. Personal communication with Cora Gamarnik. Buenos Aires.

Masotta, Carlos. 2012. "La colección de sombras Fotografías Siglos XIX-XXI." In *Memoria visual e imaginarios. Fotografías de pueblos originarios. Siglos XIX-XXI,* edited by Margarita Alvarado and Carla Möller, 20–25. Santiago de Chile: Ediciones Pehuén.

Mauss, Marcel. 2009. *Ensayo sobre el don. Forma y función del intercambio en las sociedades arcaicas*. Buenos Aires: Katz Editores.

Máximo, Matías. 2014. "Lucila Quieto: la fotógrafa de la ausencia." *Infojus Noticias*. May 2.

Máximo, Matías. 2015. "López y la ex-Esma en los Premios Nacionales de Fotografía." *Infojus noticias*. June 4.

McSherry, Patrice, J. 2005. *Predatory States: Operation Condor and Covert War in Latin America*. Lanham, Boulder, New York, Toronto and Plymouth: Rowman & Littlefield Publishers, Inc.

Melicchio, Pablo. 2019. *El Lado Norita de la vida*. Buenos Aires: Marea.

Meschiati, Teresa. 2019. *¿Viste, cumpa? Rompimos la tranquera*. Buenos Aires: Mates de Barrio.

Meyer, Adriana. 2008. "La memoria de las imágenes." *Página 12*. April 28.

Molas, Verónica. 2013. "Belleza en el drama." *La Voz*. November 20.

Moreno Andrés, Jorge. 2019. *El Duelo revelado. La vida social de las fotografías familiares de las víctimas del franquismo*. Madrid: CSIC.

Orge, Gabriel. 2012. "El Paisaje crítico." Photographic series. Available at www.boladenieve.org.ar/artista/189/orge-gabriel

Orge, Gabriel. 2014–15. "Apareciendo." Photographic series. Available at www.boladenieve.org.ar/artista/189/orge-gabriel

Orosz, Demian. 2021. "La autora de *Diario de una princesa montonera*: Me gusta desautorizar el lugar sagrado desde el cual se habla." *La Voz*. May 9.

Pantoja, Julio. 2021. "Los hijos. Tucumán veinte años después." *YouTube*. January 5. Available at www.youtube.com/watch?v=7oEWPJXBxhs

Paredes, Jorge. 2018. "Las Madres de Plaza de Mayo y el mundial 78." *Pressenza*. June 10.

Passerini, Luisa. 2011. *A memória entre política e emcao*. Sao Paulo: Letra e Voz.

Perez, Mariana Eva. 2021. *Diario de una princesa montonera*. Buenos Aires: Planeta.

Pollak, Michael. 2006. *Memoria, olvido, silencio. La producción social de identidades frente a situaciones límite*. La Plata: Ediciones Al Margen.

Pontoriero, Esteban. 2016. "De la Guerra (contrainsurgente): la formación de la doctrina antisubversiva del Ejército argentino (1955–1976)." In *Represión estatal y violencia paraestatal en la historia reciente argentina. Nuevos abordajes a 40 años del golpe*, edited by Gabriela Águila, Pablo Scatizza and Santiago Garaño, 47–71. La Plata: Facultad de Humanidades y Ciencias de la Educación de La Plata Ed.

Quieto, Lucila. 2011. *Arqueología de la ausencia*. Buenos Aires: Editores Casa Nova.

Quieto, Lucila. 2013. "Filiación." Photographic exhibition. Buenos Aires, Centro Cultural Haroldo Conti, March 23. Exhibition catalogue available at https://issuu.com/ccmharoldoconti/docs/lucila_quieto_issuu

Rancière, Jacques. 2010. *El Espectador emancipado*. Buenos Aires: Manantial.

Ránciere, Jacques. 2013. *The Politics of Aesthetics*. Translated and edited by Gabriel Rockhill. London: Bloomsbury Publishing.

Res. 1984. "¿Dónde están?" Photographic series. Available at www.boladenieve.org.ar/artista/979/res

Res. 2011. Personal communication with Natalia Fortuny. Buenos Aires.

Research Dept. of Provincial Memory Archive. 2012. "Instantes de verdad. Fotografias del Registro Extremistas del D2." In *Diario de la Memoria*, March 28, 35–36.

Ribalta, Jorge. 2004. *Efecto real. Debates posmodernos sobre fotografía*. Barcelona: Gustavo Gili.

Ribalta, Jorge. 2018. *El Espacio público de la fotografía*. Barcelona: Arcadia.

Richard, Nelly, ed. 2000. *Políticas y estéticas de la memoria*. Santiago de Chile: Cuarto Propio.

Richard, Nelly. 2007. *Fracturas de la memoria. Arte y pensamiento crítico*. Buenos Aires: Siglo XXI.

Ríos, Gloria. 2003. Personal communication with Ludmila da Silva Catela. Tumbaya, Jujuy.

Robben, Antonius, C.G. 2007. *Political Violence and Trauma in Argentina*. Philadelphia: University of Pennsylvania Press.

Robles, Miguel. 2010. *La Búsqueda. Una entrevista con Charlie Moore*. Córdoba: Ediciones del Pasaje.

Rosenwein, Barbara. 2011. *História das emoções: Problemas e métodos*. Sao Paulo: Letra e Voz.

Santos, Felisa. 2014. "Prólogo." In *La Pervivencia De Las Imágenes*, by Aby Warburg, 9–18. Buenos Aires: Miluno.

Schäfer, David. 2017. *El registro bruto. Prácticas fotográficas en un centro clandestino de detención*. Córdoba: Imprenta de la Facultad de Filosofía y Humanidades de la U.N.C.

Schmucler, Héctor. 1996. "Ni siquiera un rostro donde la muerte hubiera podido estampar su sello (reflexiones sobre los desaparecidos y la memoria)." *Pensamiento de los Confines* 3, September, 137–144.

Schoellkopf, Sarah A. 2017. "The Disappearing of the Disappeared in the Plaza De Mayo: Who Will Hold the Space of the Madres Once They Are Gone?" In *Mothers in Public and Political Life*, edited by Simone Bohn and Pinar Melis Yelsali Parmaksiz, 269–286. Bradford: Demeter Press.

Sebald, Winfried Georg. 2002. *Austerlitz*. Translated by Anthea Bell. London: Penguin.

Sekula, Allan. 1982. "On the Invention of Photographic Meaning." In *Thinking Photography*, edited by Victor Burgin, 84–109. London: Macmillan Press.

Simmel, Georg. 2014. *Filosofía del paisaje*. Madrid: Casimiro Libros.

Sontag, Susan. 1978. *On Photography*. London: Allen Lane.

Szalkowicz, Gerardo. 2019. *Norita. La Madre de todas las batallas*. Buenos Aires: Sudestada.

Tagg, John. 1988. *The Burden of Representation: Essays on Photographies and Histories*. Basingstoke and New York: Palgrave Macmillan.

Taussig, Michael. 2002. *Chamanismo, colonialismo y el hombre salvaje: un estudio del terror y la curación*. Bogotá: Norma Editorial.

Tello, Andrés. 2016. "Foucault y la escisión del archivo." *Revista de Humanidades* 34, July–December, 37–61.

Tello, Mariana. 2014. "Una vara con qué medirnos. Una lectura antropológica sobre los sentidos de la transgresión y la traición en las memorias sobre la militancia en los '70." *Revista Contenciosa* 3(2). Available at https://doi.org/10.14409/contenciosa.v0i3.5076

Tello, Mariana. 2015. "Yo acuso: un análisis antropológico sobre lo jurídico en los primeros testimonios acerca de La Perla." *Revista interdisciplinaria de estudios sobre memoria Clepsidra* 4, 90–115.

Tello, Mariana. 2017. " 'Disculpe Señor Juez… ¿Me permite decir unas palabras?' Identidades, performances jurídicas y drama social en los testimonios de sobrevivientes en la Mega Causa La Perla, Córdoba (Argentina)." *Papeles del CEIC* 1. Available at www.redalyc.org/articulo.oa?id=76549920005

Tello Weiss, Mariana. 2008. "La sociedad del secreto. Violencia, política y militancia clandestina en las memorias sobre la lucha armada." *Revista Lucha Armada en Argentina* 10.

Tello Weiss, Mariana and González Tizón. 2021. *Informe sobre las tareas realizadas por el Archivo Nacional de la Memoria en torno al álbum de Inteligencia hallado en la AFI.* Buenos Aires: Archivo Nacional de la Memoria.

Thayer, Willy. 2003. "Del aceite al collage." In *Cambio de aceite. Pintura chilena contemporánea*, edited by Francisco Brugnoli and María Irene Alcalde, 95–101. Santiago de Chile: Ocho Libros Editores.

Toconás, Rosalía. 2004. Personal communication with Ludmila da Silva Catela. Tumbaya, Jujuy.

Todorov, Tzvetan. 2000. *Los Abusos de la memoria.* Barcelona: Paidós.

Triquell, Agustina. 2012. *Fotografías e historias. La construcción narrativa de la memoria y las identidades en el álbum fotográfico familiar.* Montevideo: CdF Ediciones.

Triquell, Agustina. 2013. "Otras siluetas: Conmemoraciones virtuales de la última dictadura." *Estudios de Comunicación y Política - Nueva Época* 32, 9–21.

Turner, Victor. 1990. *La selva de los símbolos.* Madrid: Editores Siglo XXI.

Ulanovsky, Carlos. 1997. *Paren las rotativas. Diarios, revistas y periodistas (1970–2000).* Buenos Aires: Emecé.

Ulanovsky, Inés. 2006. *Fotos tuyas.* Buenos Aires: Ministerio de Cultura Buenos Aires.

Ulanovsky, Inés. 2011. "ESMA." Photographic series. Available at https://vimeo.com/49512838

Ulanovsky, Inés. 2020. *Las Fotos.* Buenos Aires: Paisanita Editora.

van Alphen, Ernst. 2014. "Time Saturation: The Photography of Awoiska van der Molen." *Theories and Practices of Visual Culture* 8, 1–12.

van Alphen, Ernst. 2015. "Whose Museums? Affective Encounters and the Museum's Public." *In La invención de lo nuestro: Arte, patrimonio y cultura visual en América*

Latina, edited by Beatriz Sarlo and Andrea Giunta, 201–216. Buenos Aires: Siglo Veintiuno Editores.

Warnke, Martin. 1994. *Political Landscape: Art History of Nature.* London: Reaktion Books.

Zout, Helen. 2009. *Desapariciones.* Buenos Aires: Dilan Editores.

Zout, Helen. 2011. Personal communication with Natalia Fortuny. Buenos Aires.

Zubillaga, Paula. 2019. "Orígenes y consolidación de la Asociación Madres de Plaza de Mayo de Mar del Plata. Estrategias locales y construcción política-identitaria (1976–1989)." MA diss. Universidad Nacional de La Plata.

Filmography

Arraya, Liliana and Eugenia Monti, dirs. 2007. *Señor Presidente.* Argentina: CyC Producciones. Stream.

Carri, Albertina, dir. 2003. *Los Rubios.* Argentina: Tacuara Pictures. DVD.

Cieplak, Piotr, dir. 2023. *(Dis)Appear.* United Kingdom: Piotr Cieplak. Stream.

Mitre, Santiago, dir. 2022. *Argentina 1985.* Amazon Studios. Stream.

Index

Entries in *italics* denote figures; references to notes are provided as the page number followed by 'n' and the note number, e.g. 48n2.